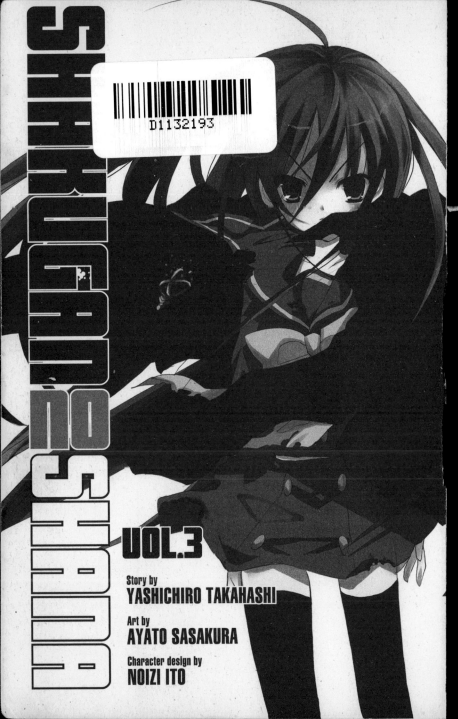

SHAKUGAN NO SHANA

VOL.3

Story by
YASHICHIRO TAKAHASHI

Art by
AYATO SASAKURA

Character design by
NOIZI ITO

FROM THE AUTHOR AND CHARACTER DESIGNER

シャナ3巻
発売!!
おめでとう
ございマス♡
from のいぢ!!

congrats on the
publication of
Shana Volume 3!
- Noizi

Hello. I'm Takahashi, the author of this story.

Thank you very much for buying Volume 3 of the *Shakugan no Shana* manga. This is the manga version of the last part of the Volume 1 novel—which I realize was not the easiest thing to read.

If you've read this manga this far, you've already seen how amazing Ayato Sasakura's artwork is. Seeing the images I'd imagined for the climax of the first novel come to life was truly an experience beyond words, and all I can say is that I'm very grateful. Thank you so much.

Readers, I hope you will enjoy the conclusion to this important first episode of *Shakugan no Shana*.

I thank the heavens for bringing this person into my life when they did.

Yashichiro Takahashi, March 2007

Contents

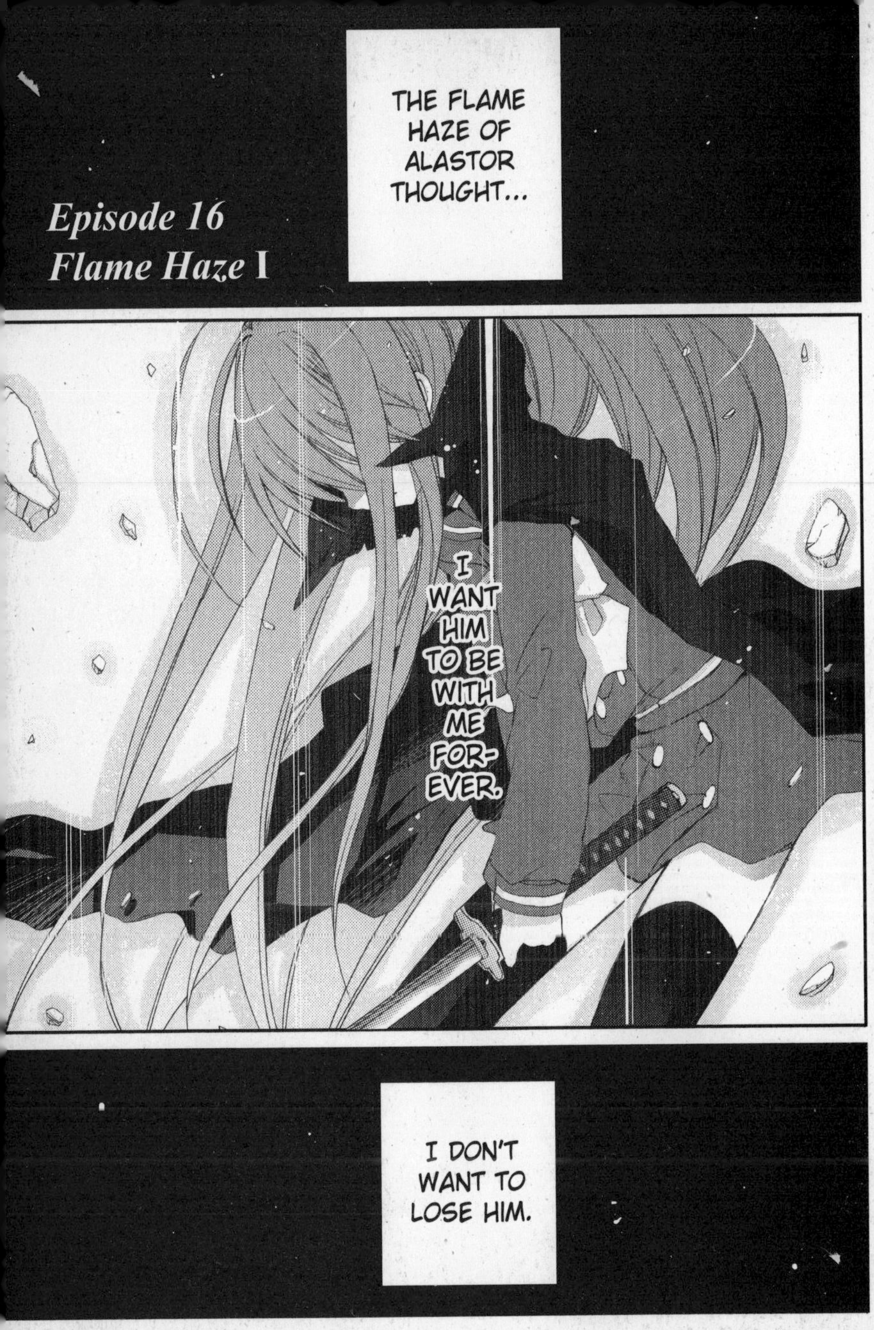
THE FLAME HAZE OF ALASTOR THOUGHT...
Episode 16
Flame Haze I
I WANT HIM TO BE WITH ME FOREVER.
I DON'T WANT TO LOSE HIM.

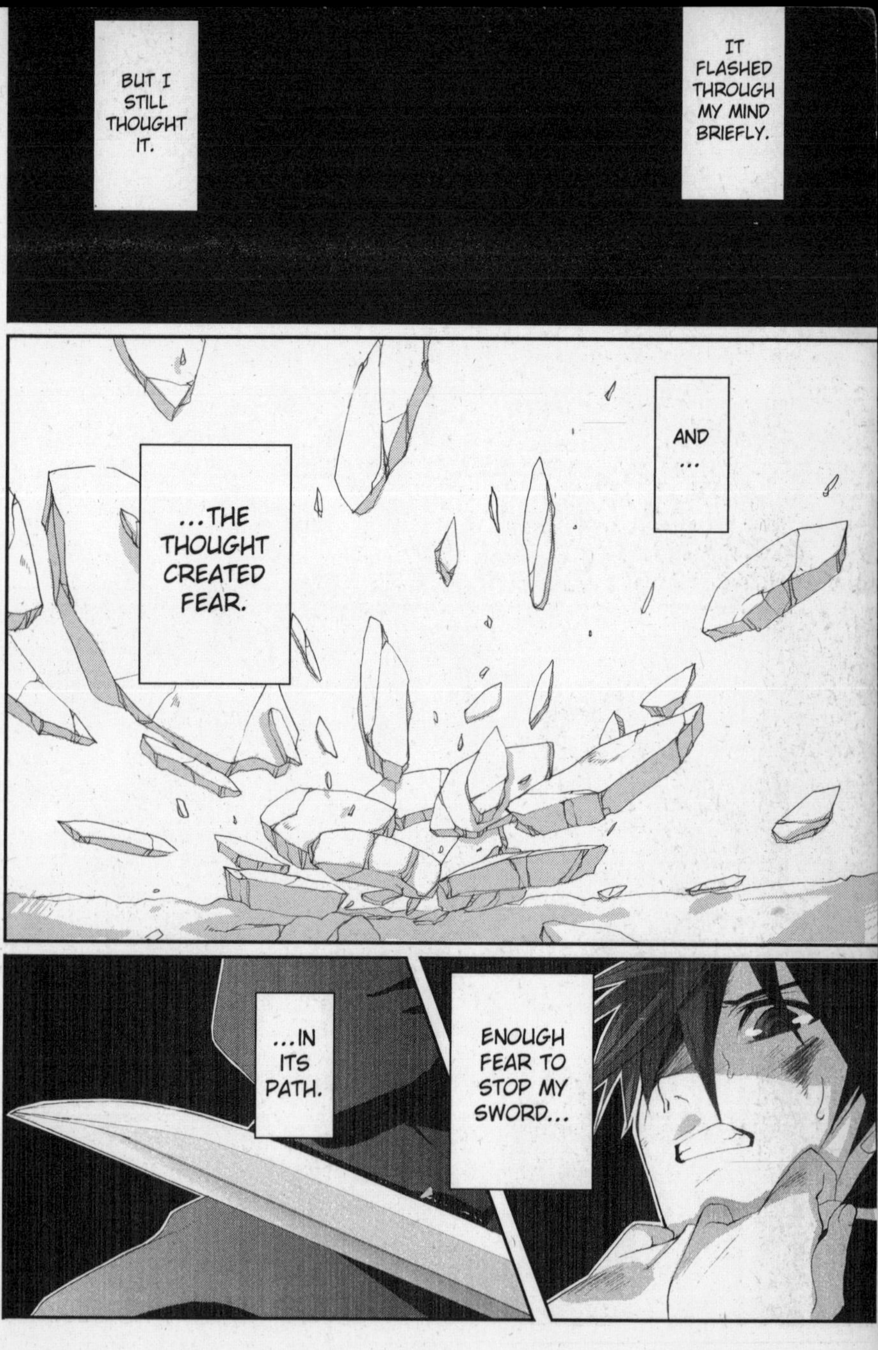
IT FLASHED THROUGH MY MIND BRIEFLY.
BUT I STILL THOUGHT IT.
AND ...
...THE THOUGHT CREATED FEAR.
ENOUGH FEAR TO STOP MY SWORD...
...IN ITS PATH.

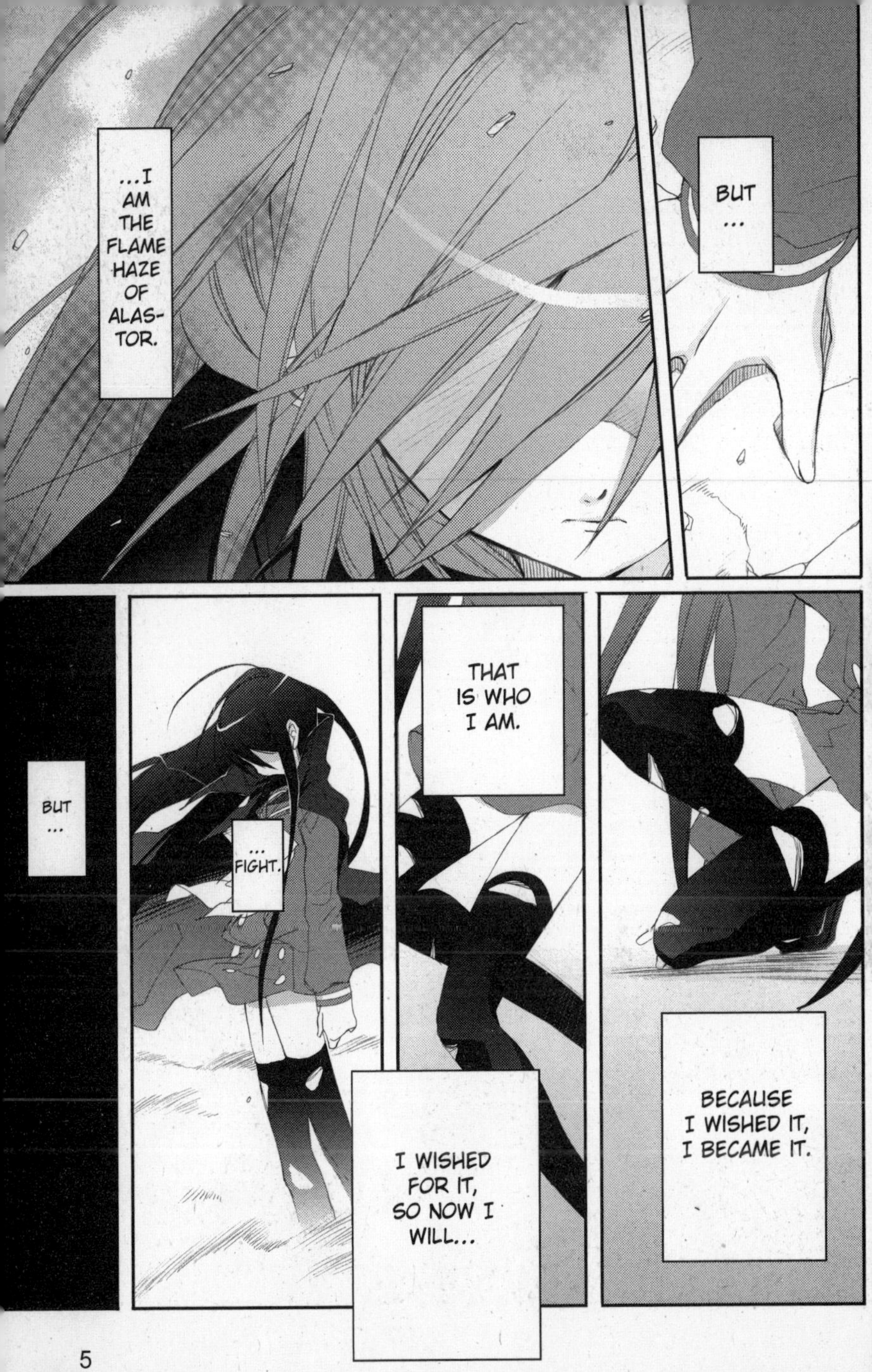
BUT ...
...I AM THE FLAME HAZE OF ALAS-TOR.
BECAUSE I WISHED IT, I BECAME IT.
THAT IS WHO I AM.
I WISHED FOR IT, SO NOW I WILL...
...FIGHT.
BUT ...

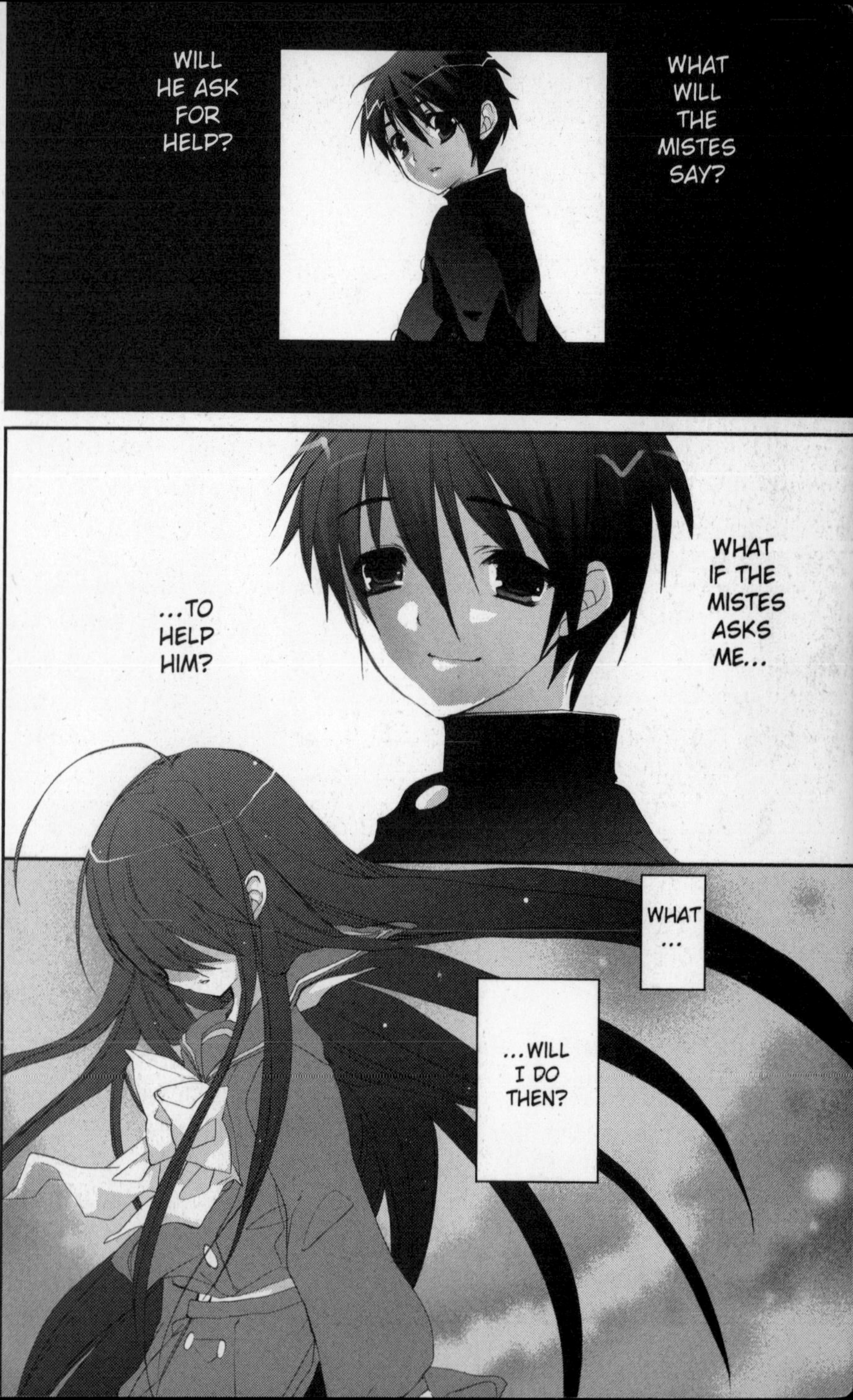
WHAT WILL THE MISTES SAY?
WILL HE ASK FOR HELP?
WHAT IF THE MISTES ASKS ME...
...TO HELP HIM?
WHAT ...
...WILL I DO THEN?

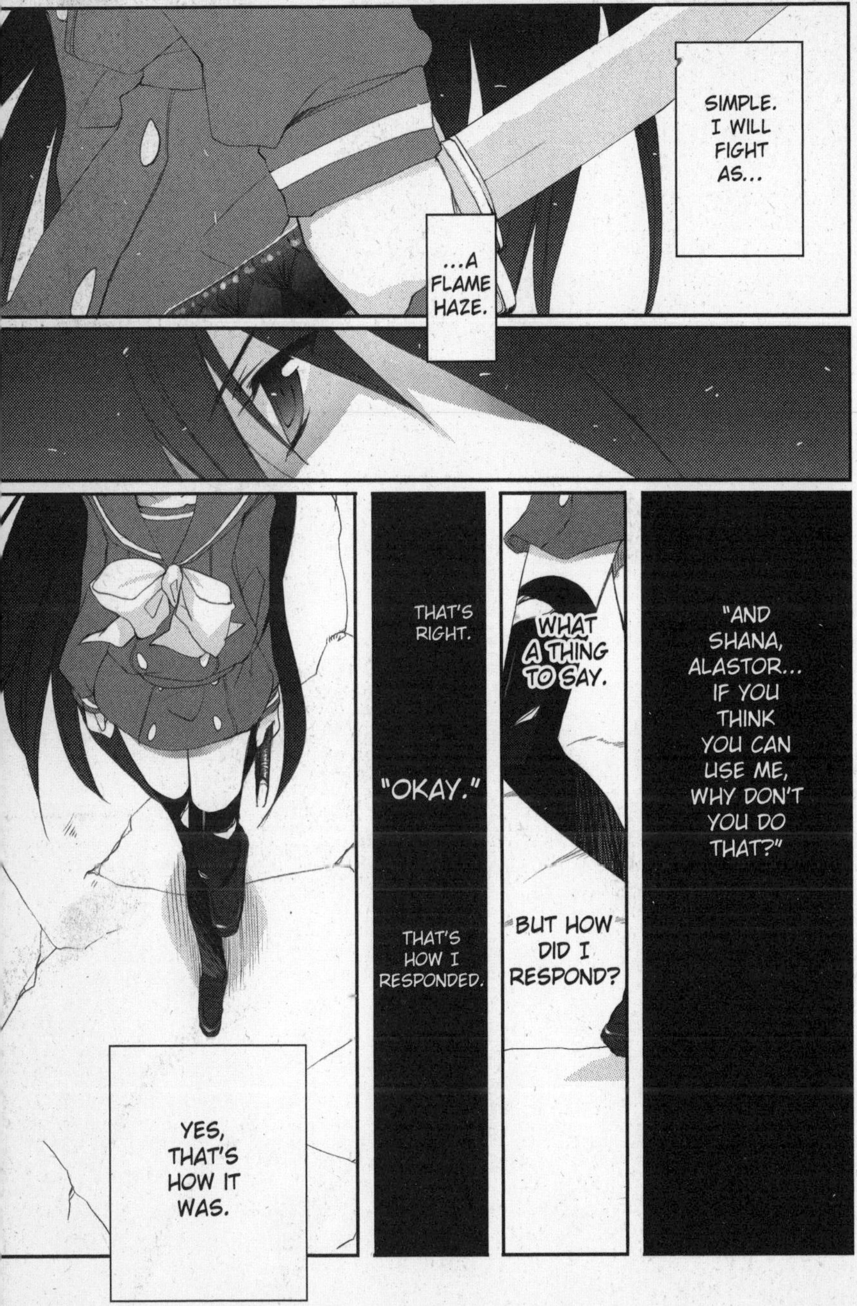
SIMPLE. I WILL FIGHT AS...
...A FLAME HAZE.
"AND SHANA, ALASTOR... IF YOU THINK YOU CAN USE ME, WHY DON'T YOU DO THAT?"
WHAT A THING TO SAY.
BUT HOW DID I RESPOND?
THAT'S RIGHT.
"OKAY."
THAT'S HOW I RESPONDED.
YES, THAT'S HOW IT WAS.

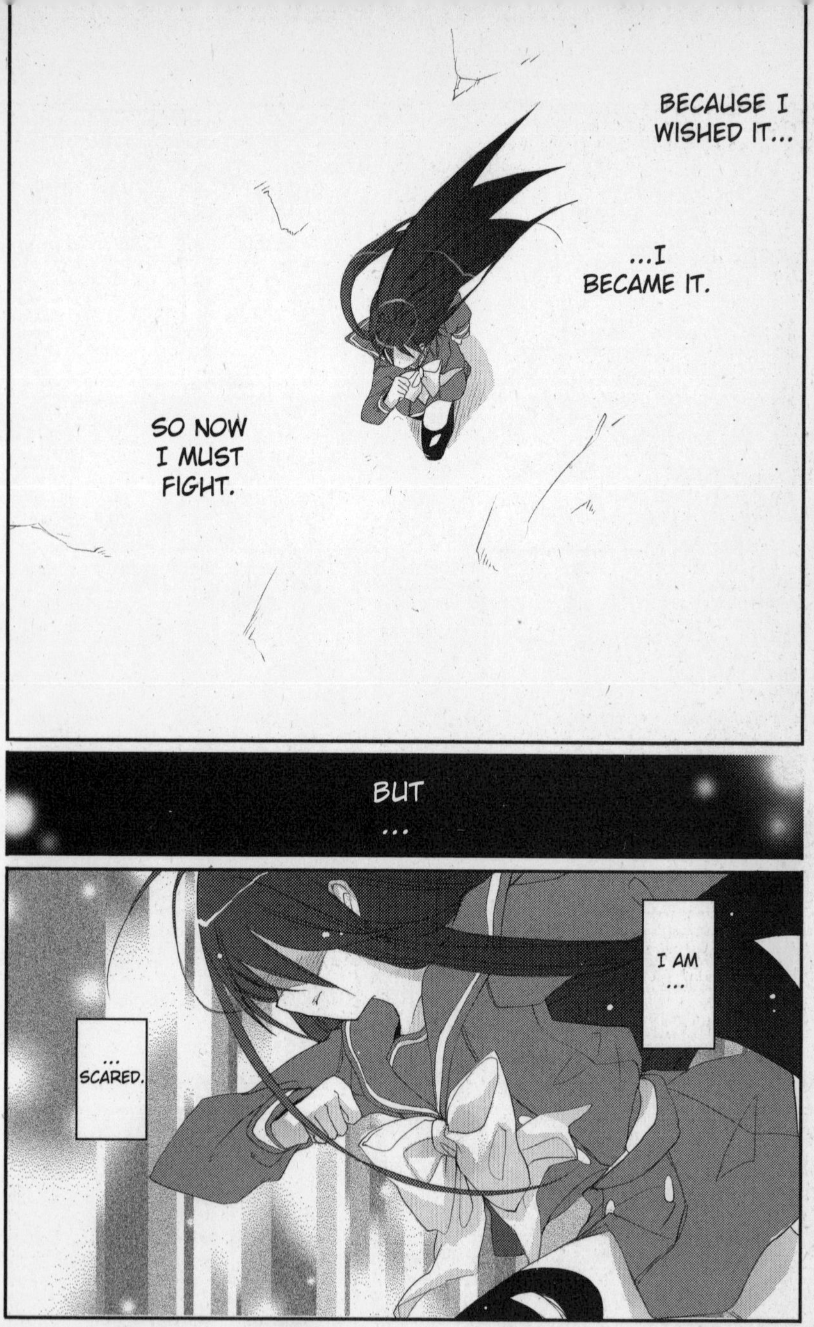
BECAUSE I WISHED IT...
...I BECAME IT.
SO NOW I MUST FIGHT.
BUT ...
I AM ...
... SCARED.

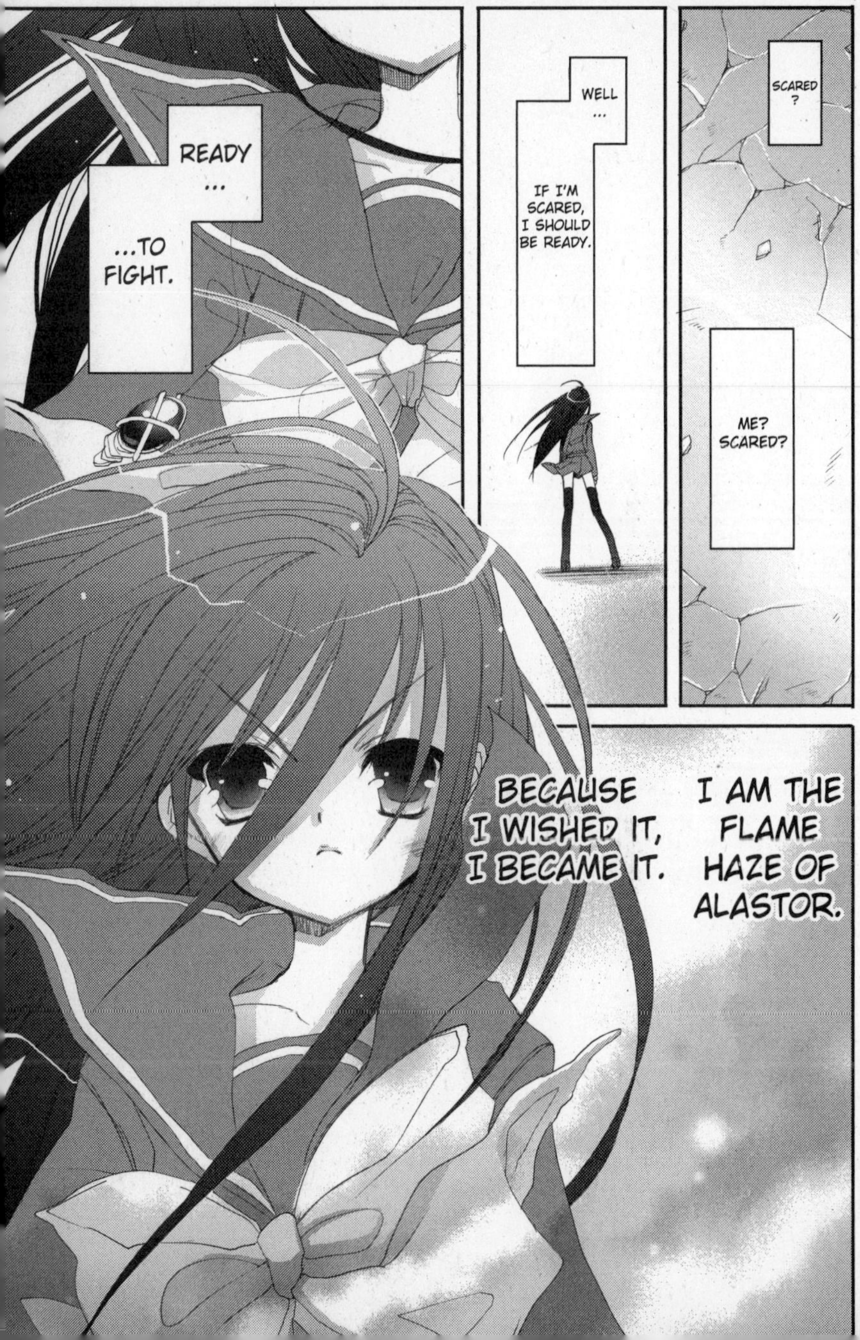
SCARED?
ME? SCARED?
WELL...
IF I'M SCARED, I SHOULD BE READY.
READY...
...TO FIGHT.
I AM THE FLAME HAZE OF ALASTOR.
BECAUSE I WISHED IT, I BECAME IT.

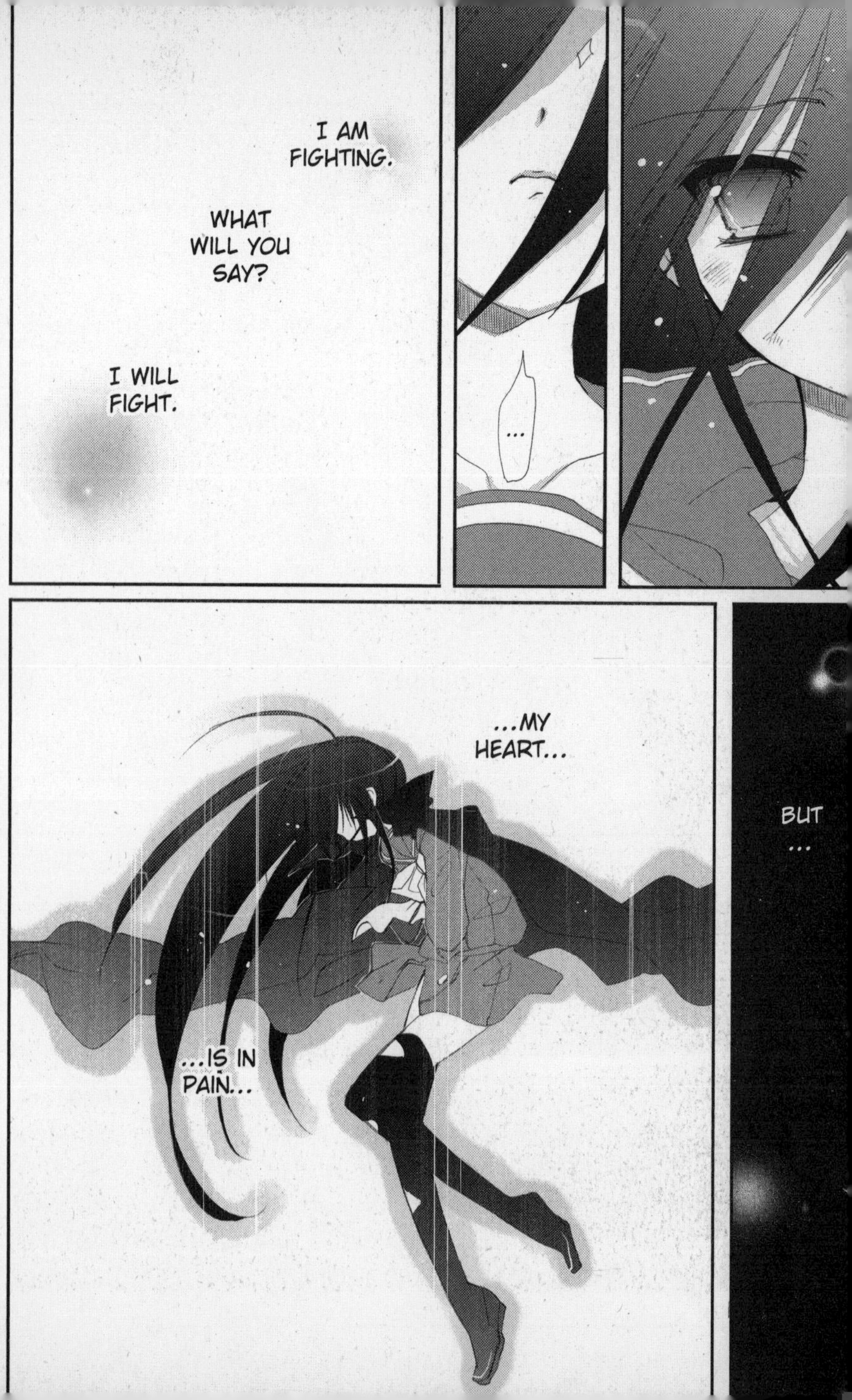
...
I AM FIGHTING.
WHAT WILL YOU SAY?
I WILL FIGHT.
BUT ...
...MY HEART...
...IS IN PAIN...

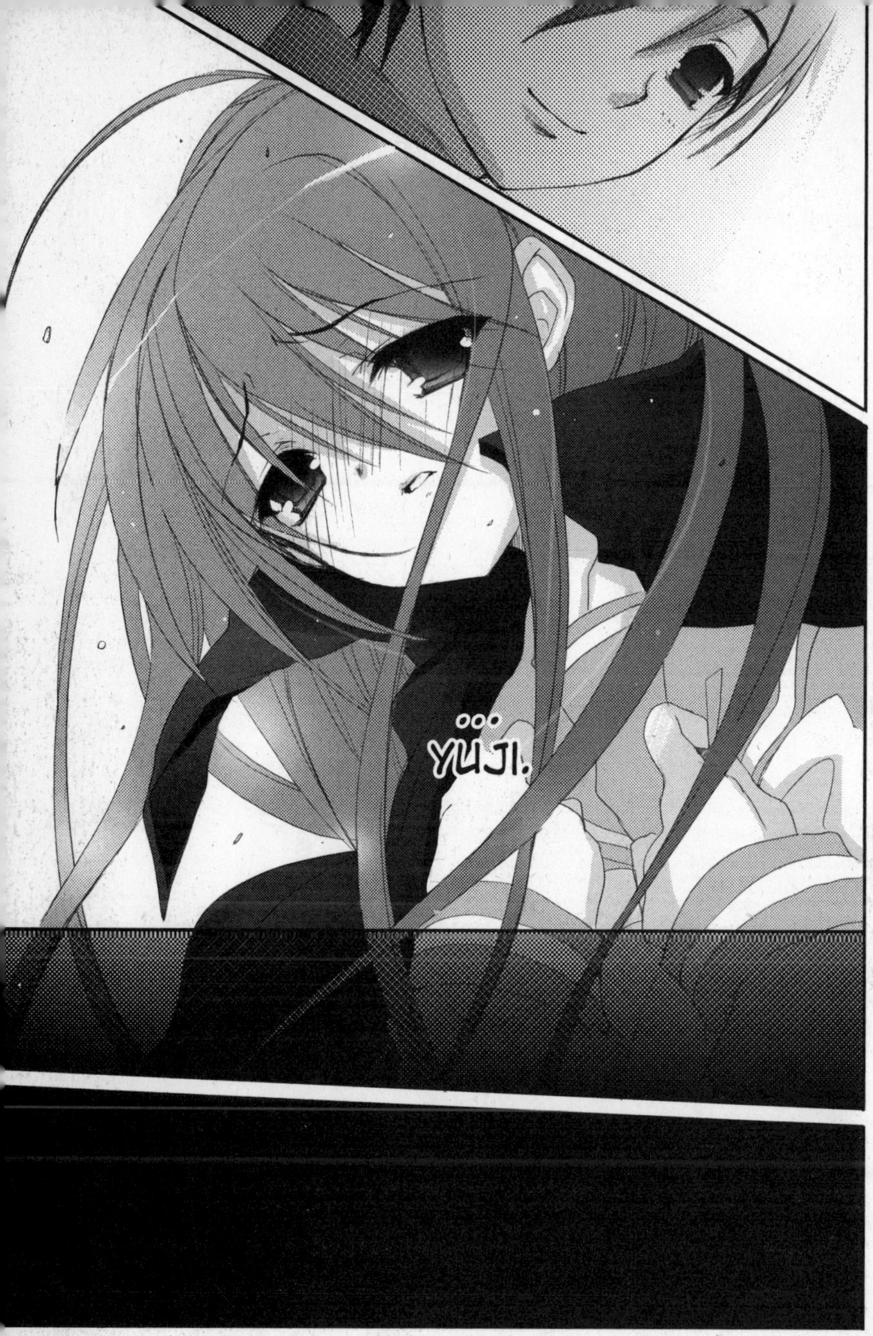
...
YUJI.

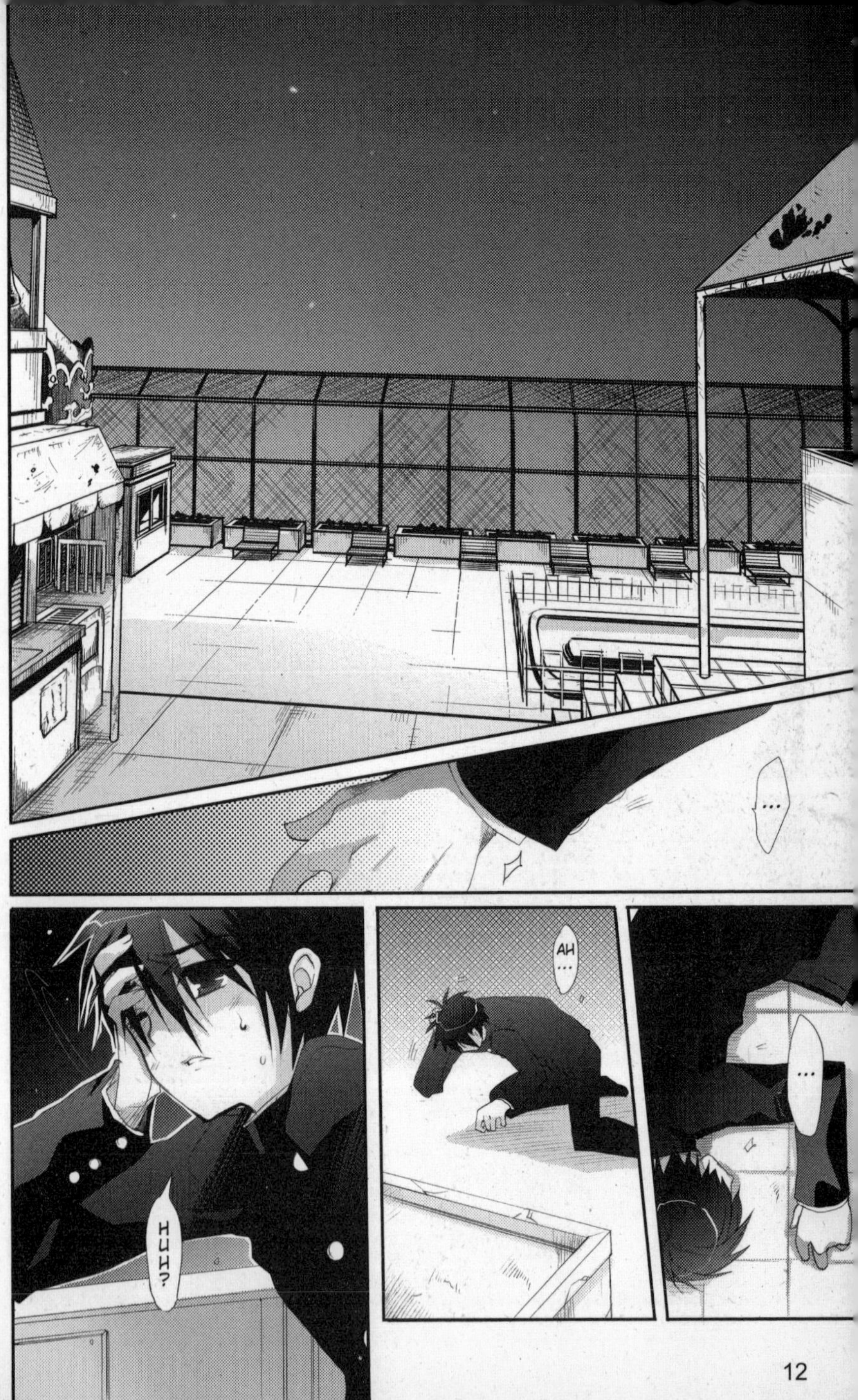
...
...
AH ...
HUH?

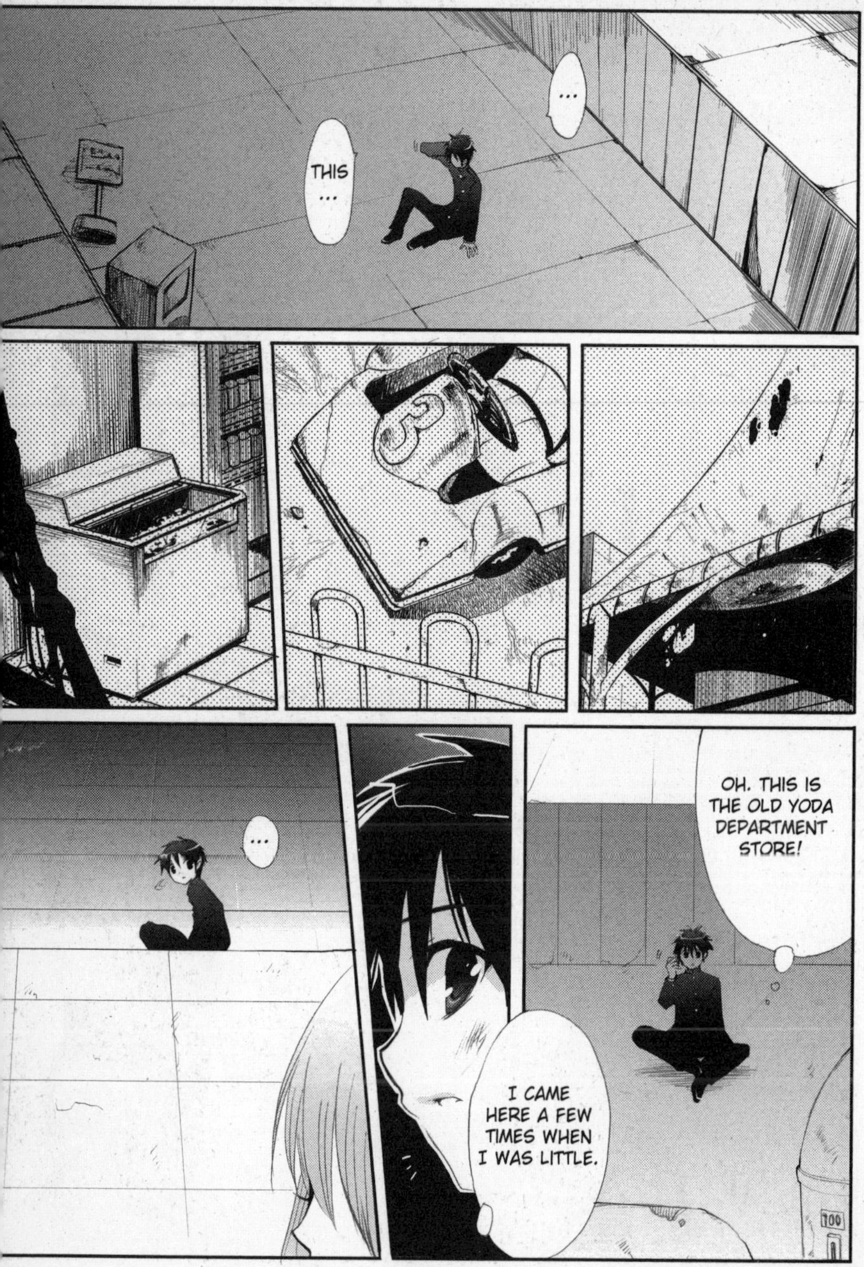
...
THIS ...
OH. THIS IS THE OLD YODA DEPARTMENT STORE!
I CAME HERE A FEW TIMES WHEN I WAS LITTLE.
...

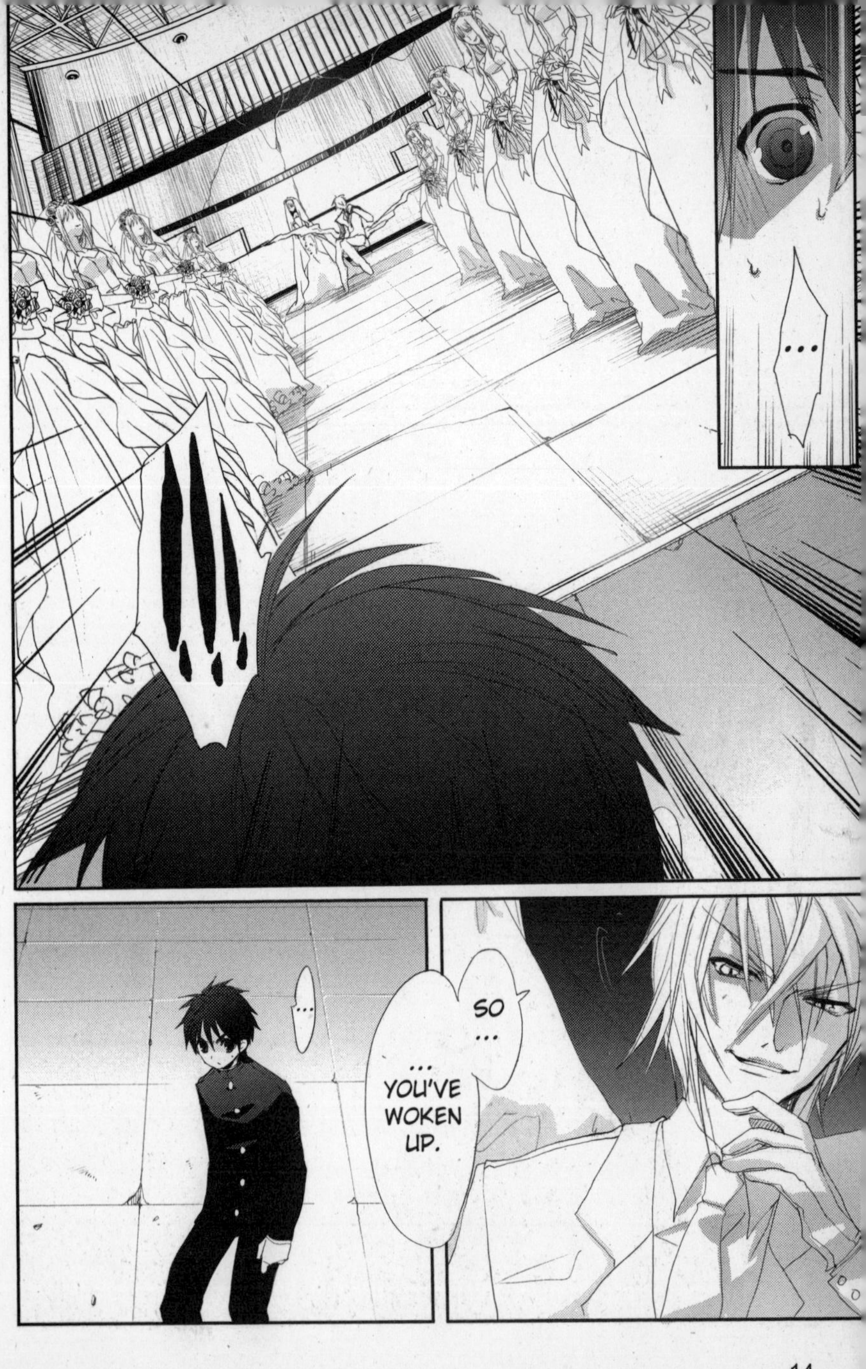
...
SO ...
... YOU'VE WOKEN UP.
...

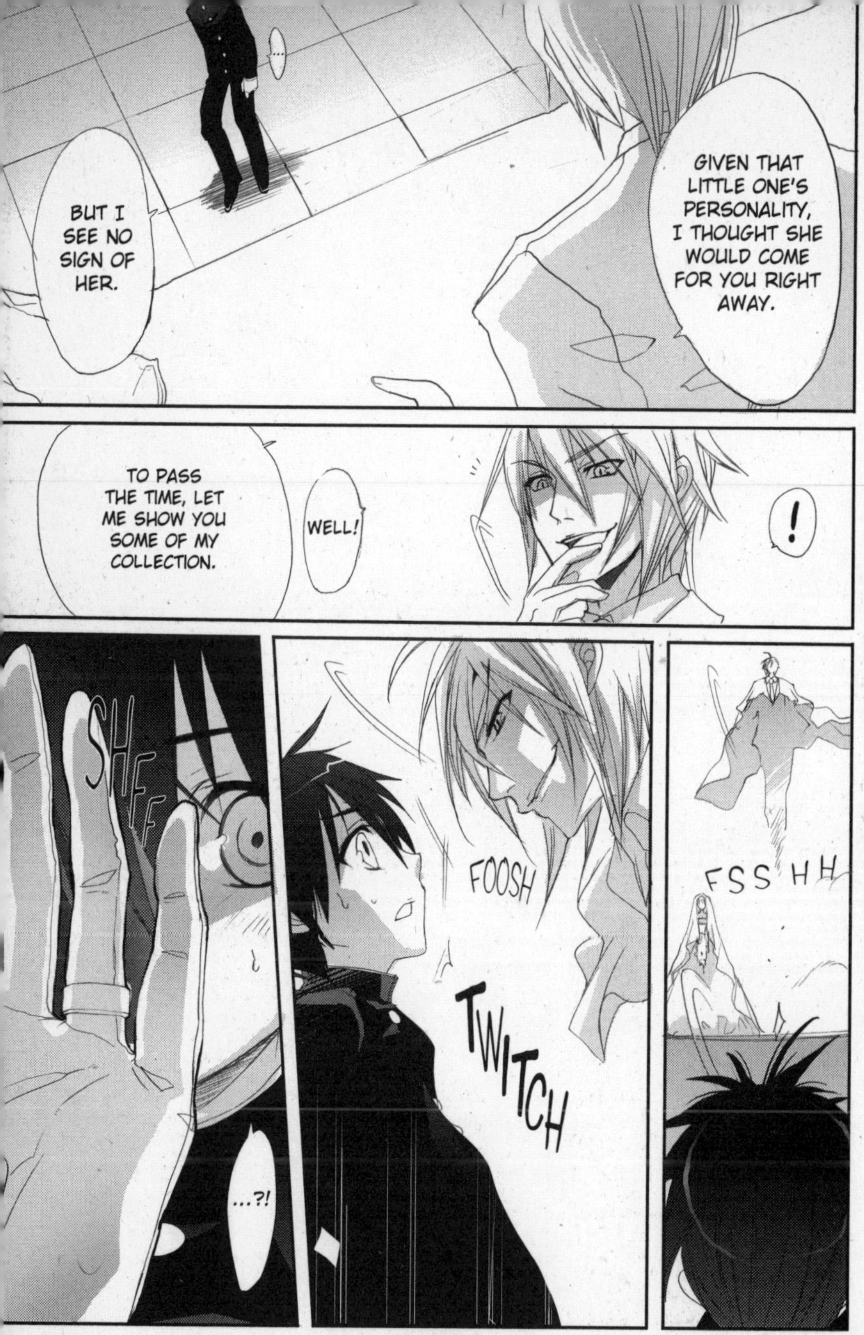
GIVEN THAT LITTLE ONE'S PERSONALITY, I THOUGHT SHE WOULD COME FOR YOU RIGHT AWAY.
...
BUT I SEE NO SIGN OF HER.
!
WELL!
TO PASS THE TIME, LET ME SHOW YOU SOME OF MY COLLECTION.
FSS HH
FOOSH
TWITCH
SHFF
...?!

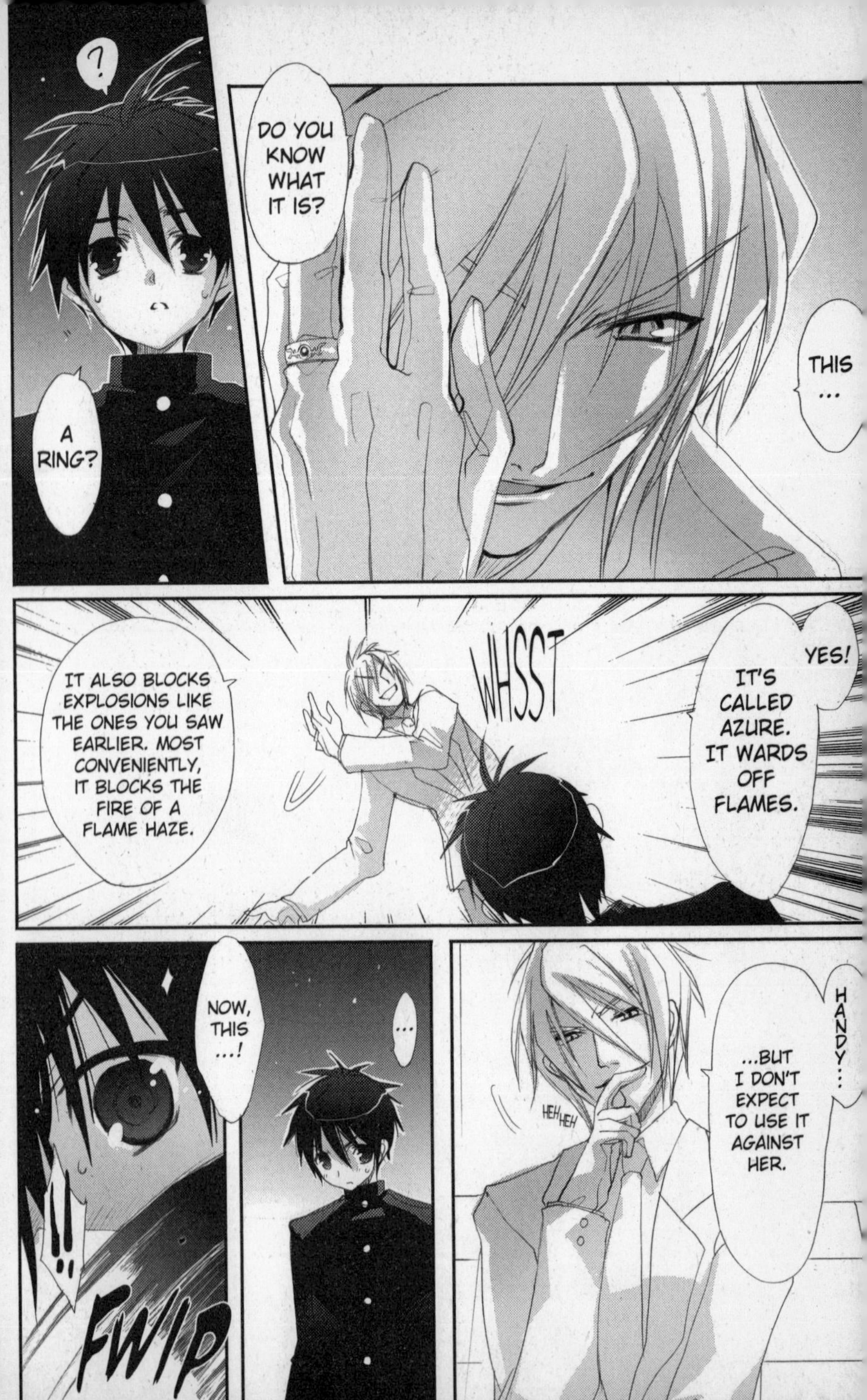
THIS ...
DO YOU KNOW WHAT IT IS?
?
A RING?
YES!
IT'S CALLED AZURE. IT WARDS OFF FLAMES.
WHSST
IT ALSO BLOCKS EXPLOSIONS LIKE THE ONES YOU SAW EARLIER. MOST CONVENIENTLY, IT BLOCKS THE FIRE OF A FLAME HAZE.
HANDY...
...BUT I DON'T EXPECT TO USE IT AGAINST HER.
HEH HEH
...
NOW, THIS ...!
!!
FWIP

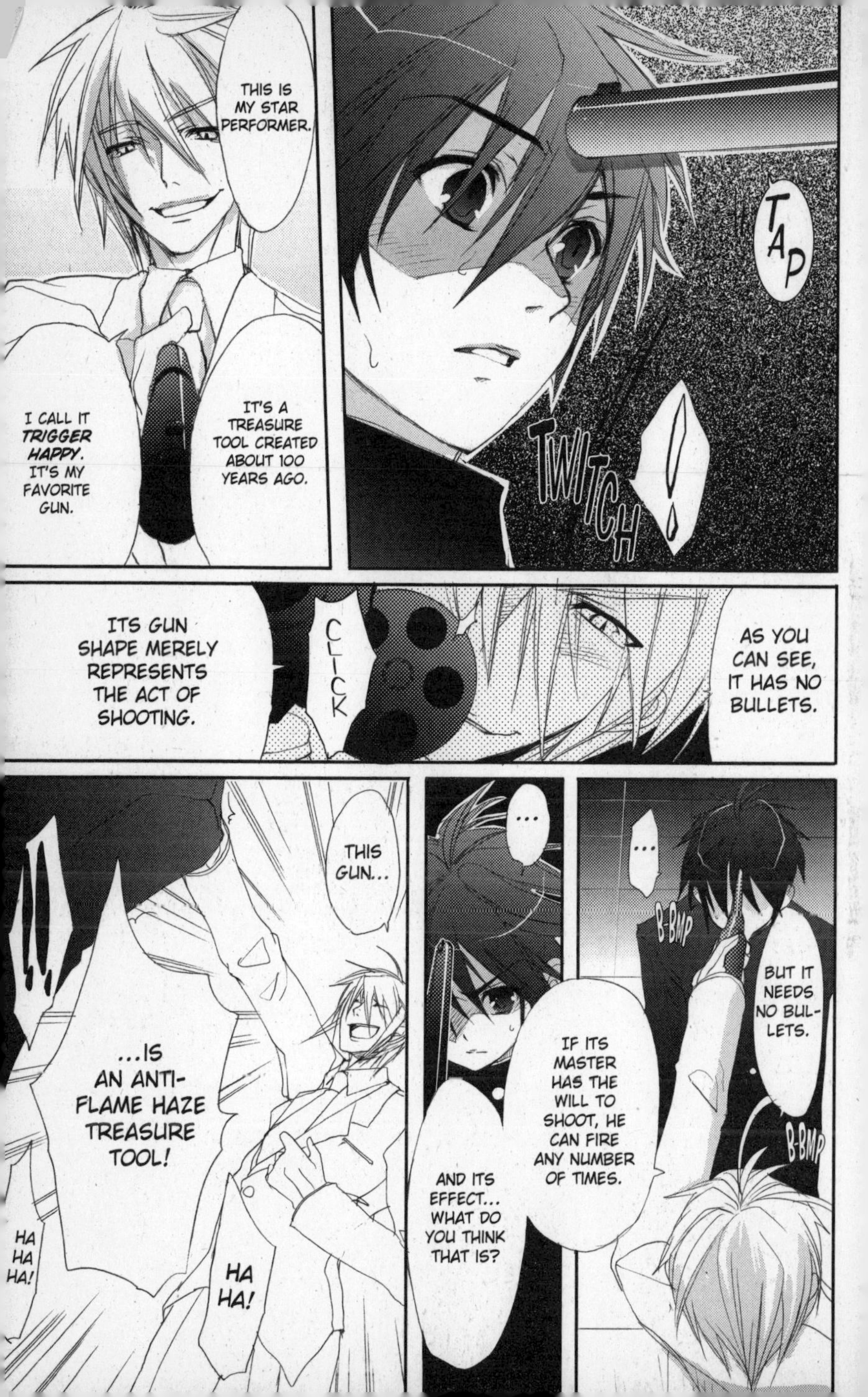
TAP
TWITCH
!
THIS IS MY STAR PERFORMER.
IT'S A TREASURE TOOL CREATED ABOUT 100 YEARS AGO.
I CALL IT *TRIGGER HAPPY*. IT'S MY FAVORITE GUN.
AS YOU CAN SEE, IT HAS NO BULLETS.
CLICK
ITS GUN SHAPE MERELY REPRESENTS THE ACT OF SHOOTING.
...
B-BMP
BUT IT NEEDS NO BUL-LETS.
B-BMP
...
IF ITS MASTER HAS THE WILL TO SHOOT, HE CAN FIRE ANY NUMBER OF TIMES.
AND ITS EFFECT... WHAT DO YOU THINK THAT IS?
THIS GUN...
!!
...IS AN ANTI-FLAME HAZE TREASURE TOOL!
HA HA!
HA HA HA!

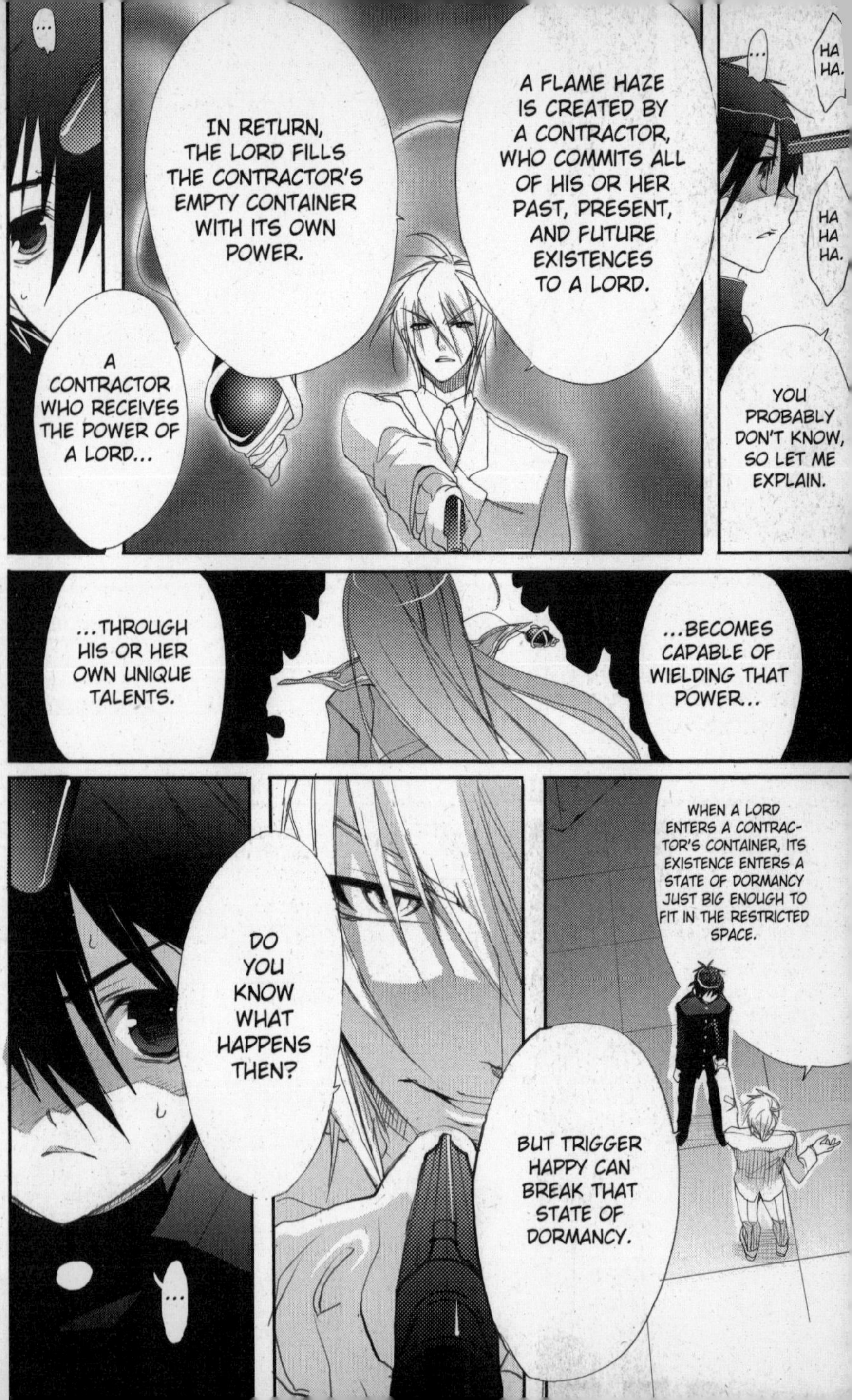
HA HA.
...
HA HA HA.
YOU PROBABLY DON'T KNOW, SO LET ME EXPLAIN.
A FLAME HAZE IS CREATED BY A CONTRACTOR, WHO COMMITS ALL OF HIS OR HER PAST, PRESENT, AND FUTURE EXISTENCES TO A LORD.
IN RETURN, THE LORD FILLS THE CONTRACTOR'S EMPTY CONTAINER WITH ITS OWN POWER.
...
A CONTRACTOR WHO RECEIVES THE POWER OF A LORD...
...BECOMES CAPABLE OF WIELDING THAT POWER...
...THROUGH HIS OR HER OWN UNIQUE TALENTS.
WHEN A LORD ENTERS A CONTRACTOR'S CONTAINER, ITS EXISTENCE ENTERS A STATE OF DORMANCY JUST BIG ENOUGH TO FIT IN THE RESTRICTED SPACE.
BUT TRIGGER HAPPY CAN BREAK THAT STATE OF DORMANCY.
DO YOU KNOW WHAT HAPPENS THEN?
...

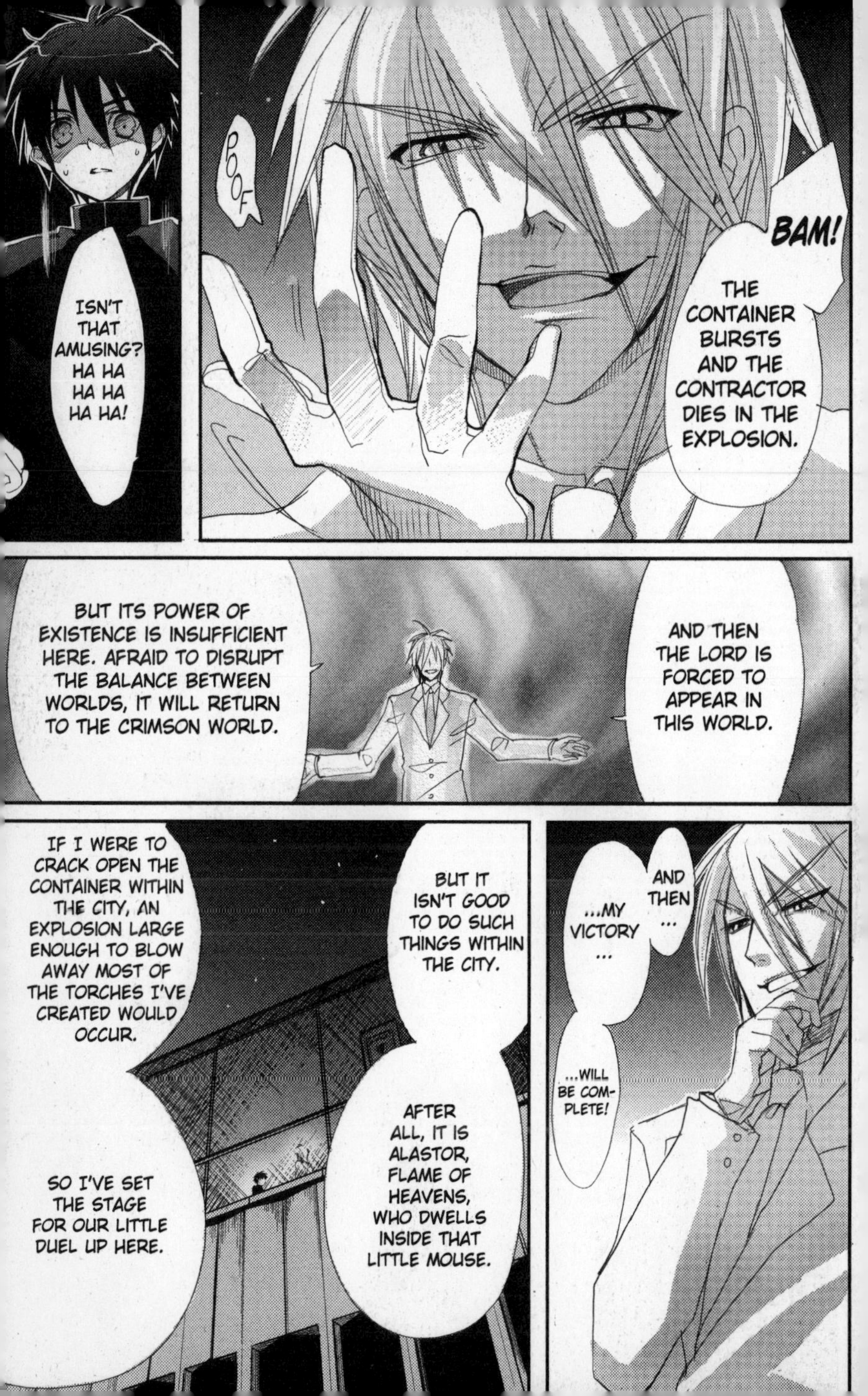
BAM!
THE CONTAINER BURSTS AND THE CONTRACTOR DIES IN THE EXPLOSION.
POOF
ISN'T THAT AMUSING? HA HA HA HA HA HA!
AND THEN THE LORD IS FORCED TO APPEAR IN THIS WORLD.
BUT ITS POWER OF EXISTENCE IS INSUFFICIENT HERE. AFRAID TO DISRUPT THE BALANCE BETWEEN WORLDS, IT WILL RETURN TO THE CRIMSON WORLD.
AND THEN...
...MY VICTORY...
...WILL BE COMPLETE!
BUT IT ISN'T GOOD TO DO SUCH THINGS WITHIN THE CITY.
IF I WERE TO CRACK OPEN THE CONTAINER WITHIN THE CITY, AN EXPLOSION LARGE ENOUGH TO BLOW AWAY MOST OF THE TORCHES I'VE CREATED WOULD OCCUR.
AFTER ALL, IT IS ALASTOR, FLAME OF HEAVENS, WHO DWELLS INSIDE THAT LITTLE MOUSE.
SO I'VE SET THE STAGE FOR OUR LITTLE DUEL UP HERE.

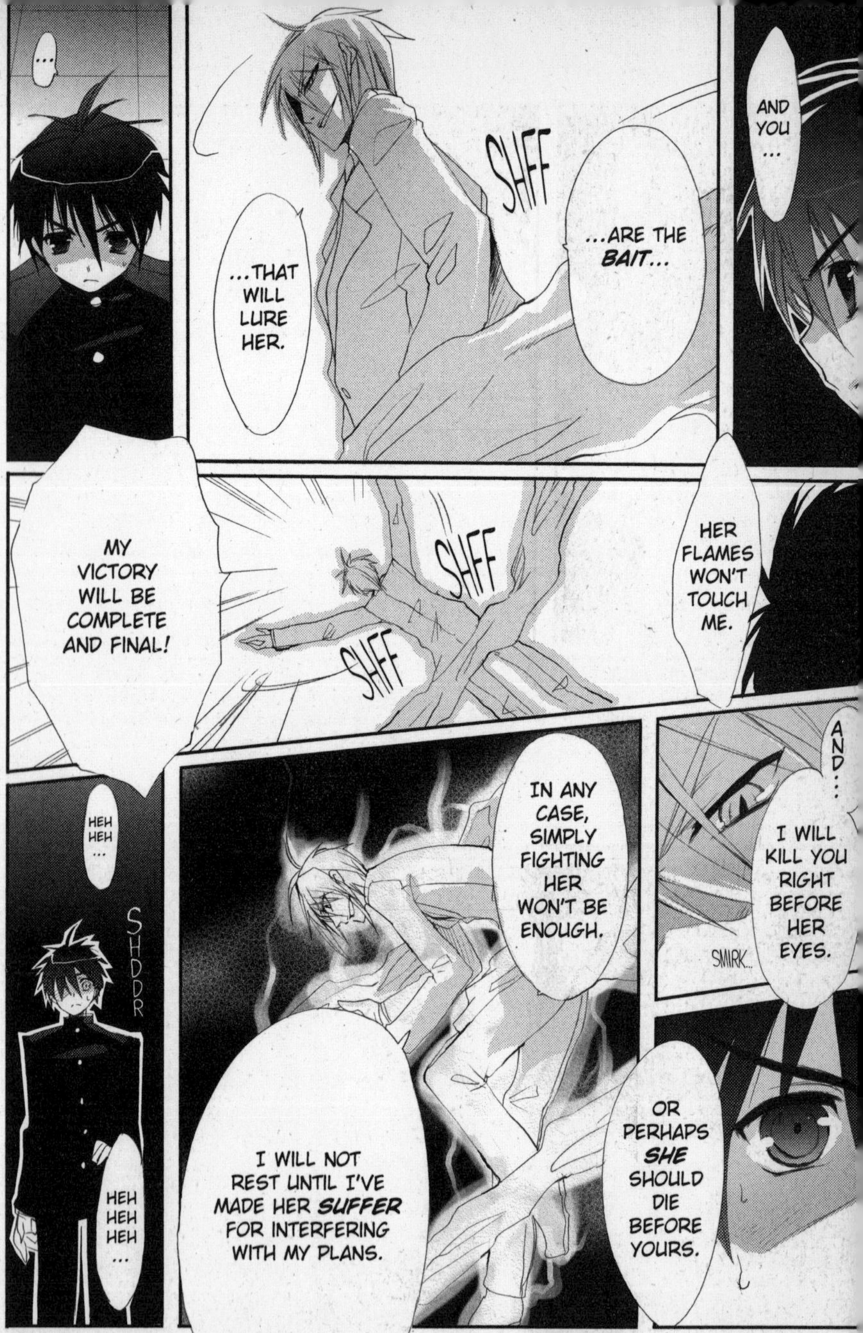
AND YOU ...
...ARE THE *BAIT*...
SHFF
...THAT WILL LURE HER.
...
HER FLAMES WON'T TOUCH ME.
SHFF
SHFF
MY VICTORY WILL BE COMPLETE AND FINAL!
AND...
I WILL KILL YOU RIGHT BEFORE HER EYES.
SMIRK...
OR PERHAPS *SHE* SHOULD DIE BEFORE YOURS.
IN ANY CASE, SIMPLY FIGHTING HER WON'T BE ENOUGH.
I WILL NOT REST UNTIL I'VE MADE HER *SUFFER* FOR INTERFERING WITH MY PLANS.
HEH HEH ...
SHDDR
HEH HEH HEH ...

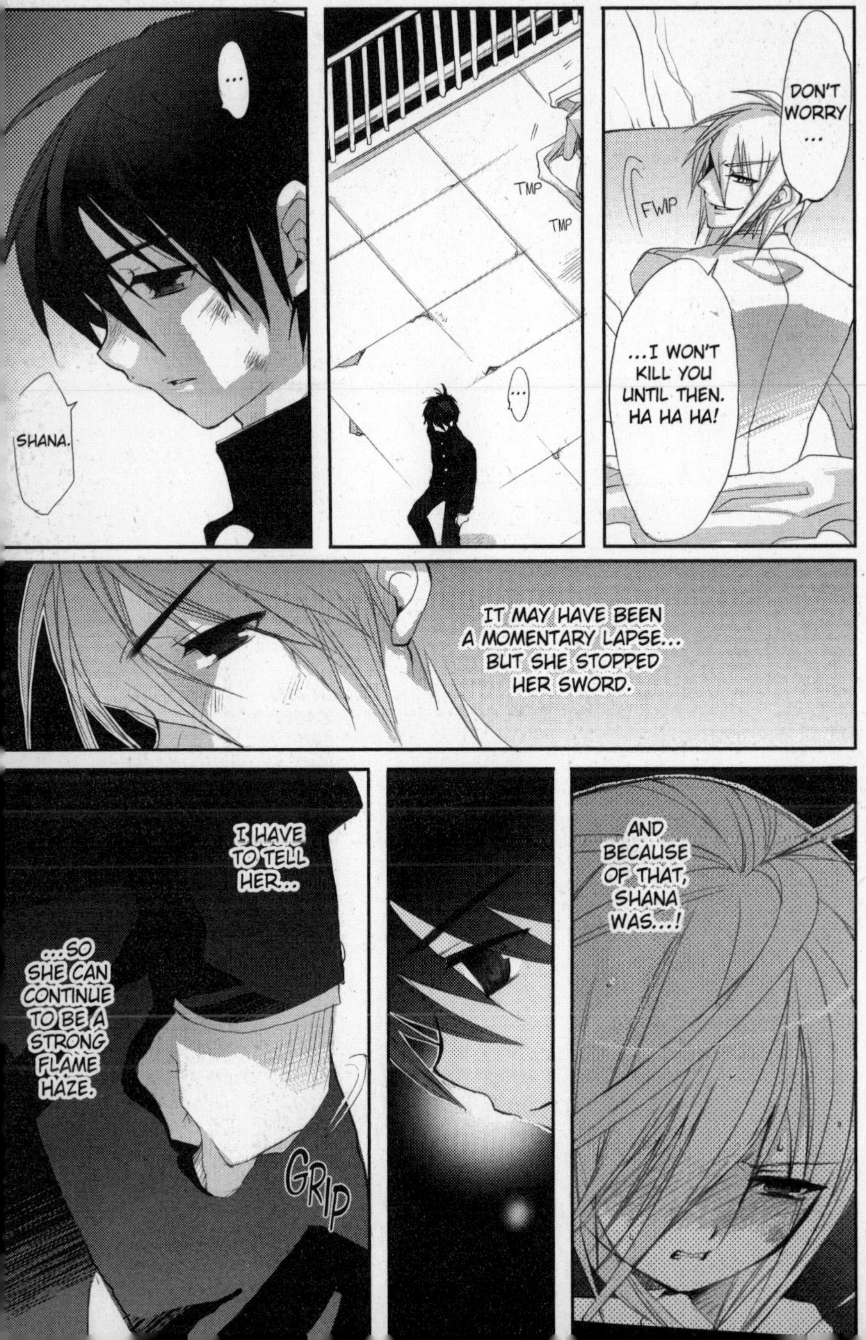
DON'T WORRY ...
FWIP
...I WON'T KILL YOU UNTIL THEN. HA HA HA!
TMP
TMP
...
...
SHANA.
IT MAY HAVE BEEN A MOMENTARY LAPSE... BUT SHE STOPPED HER SWORD.
AND BECAUSE OF THAT, SHANA WAS...!
I HAVE TO TELL HER...
...SO SHE CAN CONTINUE TO BE A STRONG FLAME HAZE.
GRIP

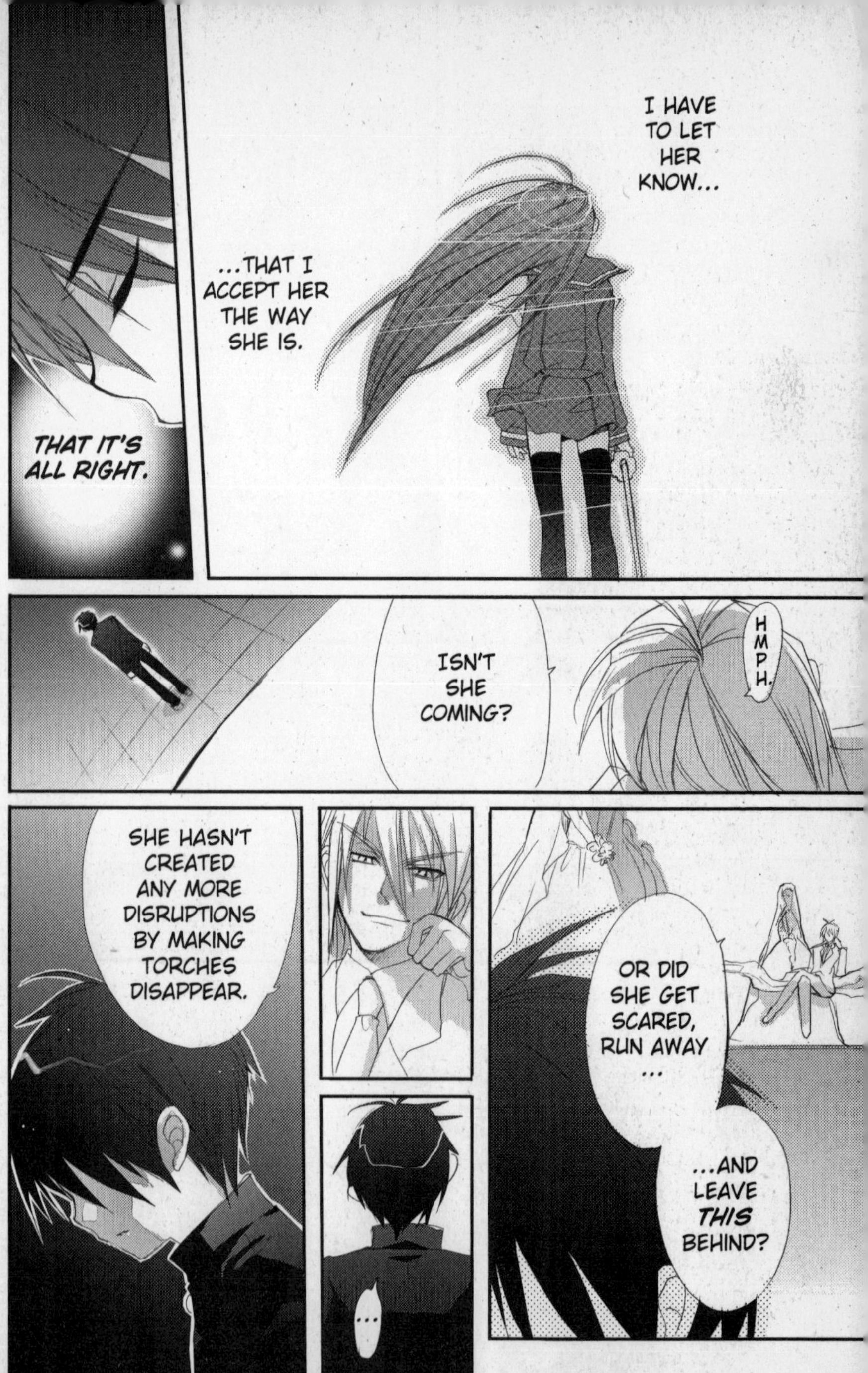
I HAVE TO LET HER KNOW...
...THAT I ACCEPT HER THE WAY SHE IS.
THAT IT'S ALL RIGHT.
HMPH.
ISN'T SHE COMING?
OR DID SHE GET SCARED, RUN AWAY...
...AND LEAVE *THIS* BEHIND?
...
SHE HASN'T CREATED ANY MORE DISRUPTIONS BY MAKING TORCHES DISAPPEAR.

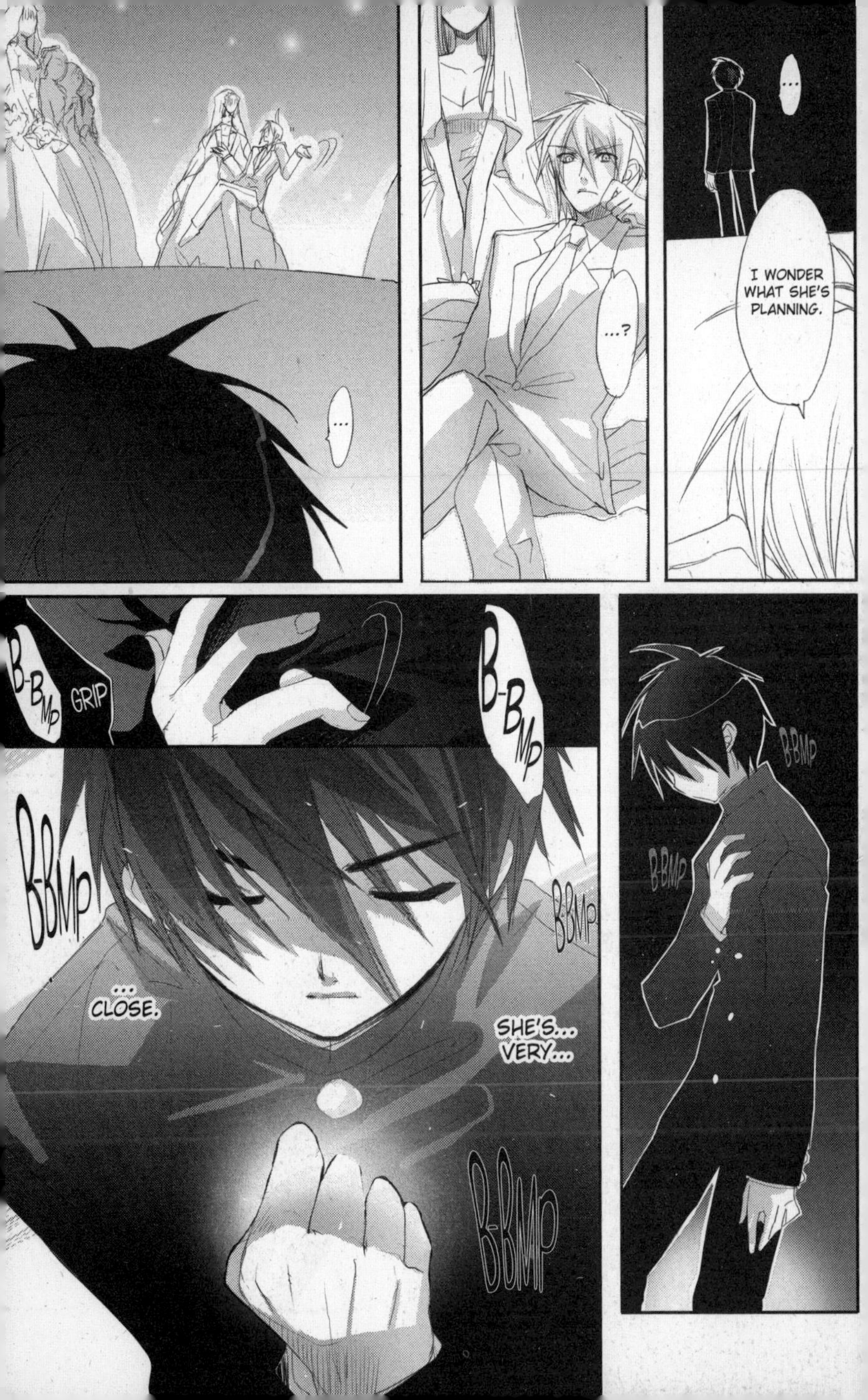
...
I WONDER WHAT SHE'S PLANNING.
...?
...
B-BMP
B-BMP
B-BMP
GRIP
B-BMP
B-BMP
SHE'S... VERY...
B-BMP
... CLOSE.
B-BMP

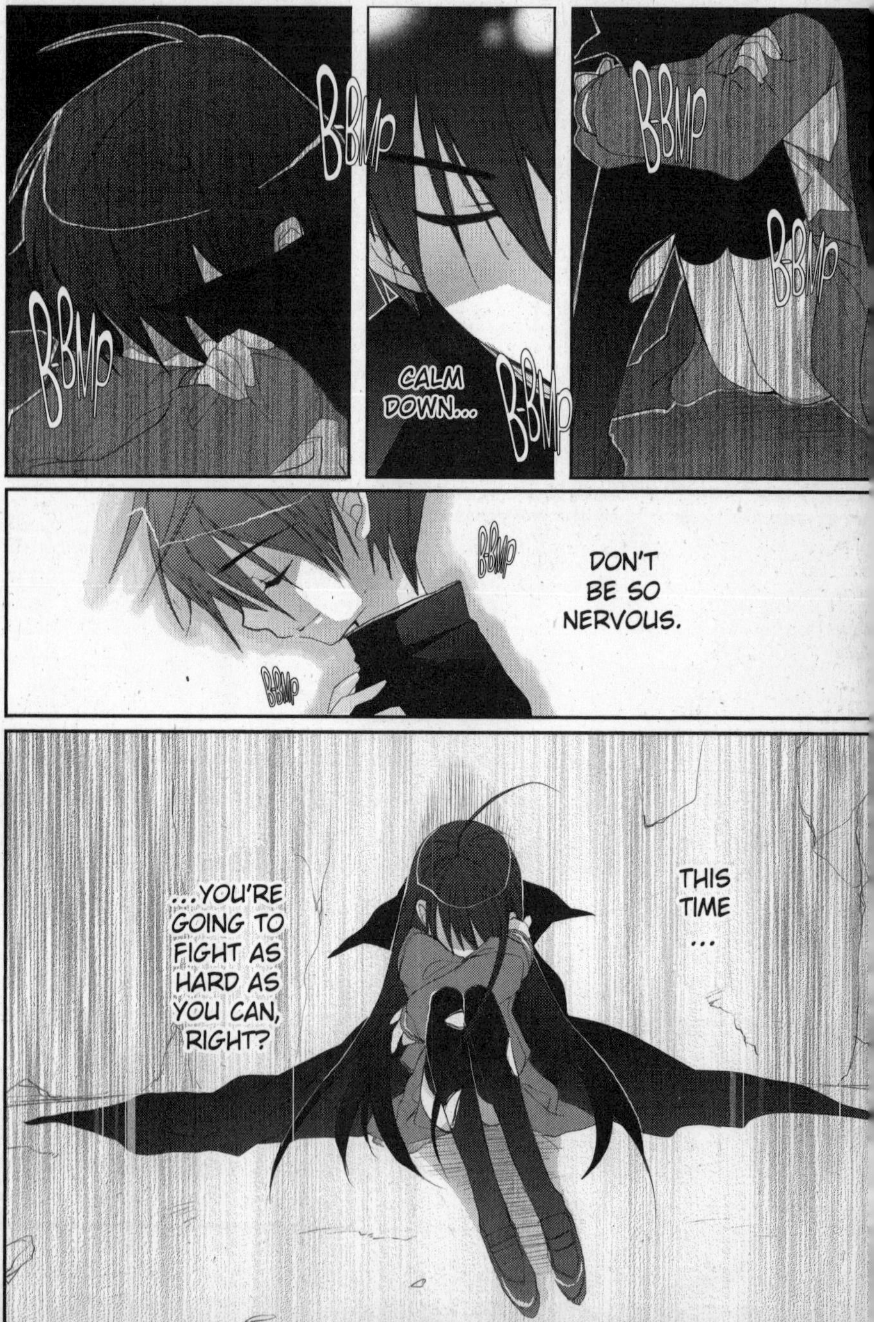

B-BMP
B-BMP
B-BMP
B-BMP
CALM DOWN...
B-BMP
B-BMP
DON'T BE SO NERVOUS.
B-BMP
B-BMP
THIS TIME ...
...YOU'RE GOING TO FIGHT AS HARD AS YOU CAN, RIGHT?

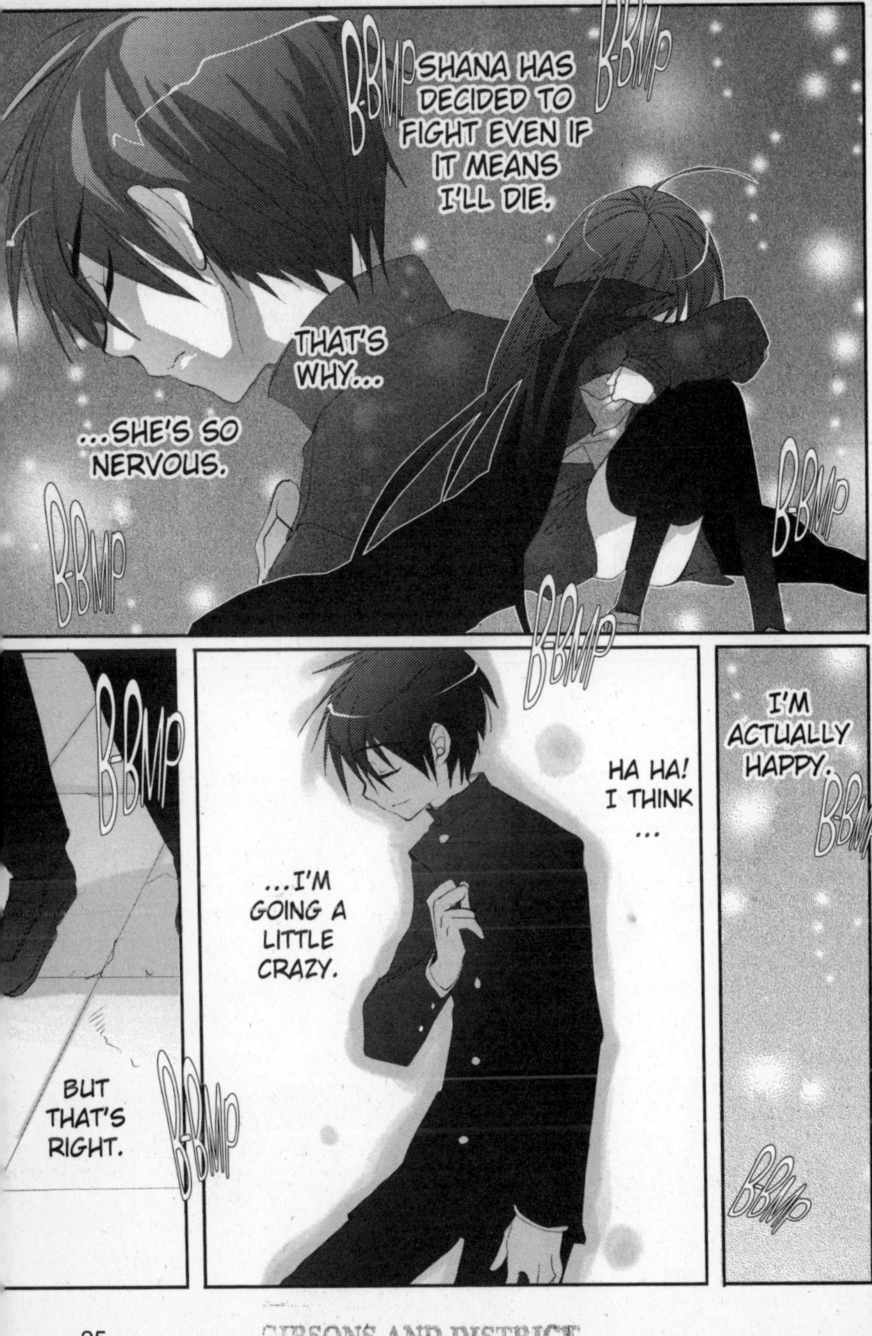
B-BMP
SHANA HAS DECIDED TO FIGHT EVEN IF IT MEANS I'LL DIE.
B-BMP
THAT'S WHY...
...SHE'S SO NERVOUS.
B-BMP
B-BMP
B-BMP
I'M ACTUALLY HAPPY.
B-BMP
B-BMP
B-BMP
HA HA! I THINK ...
...I'M GOING A LITTLE CRAZY.
B-BMP
BUT THAT'S RIGHT.
B-BMP

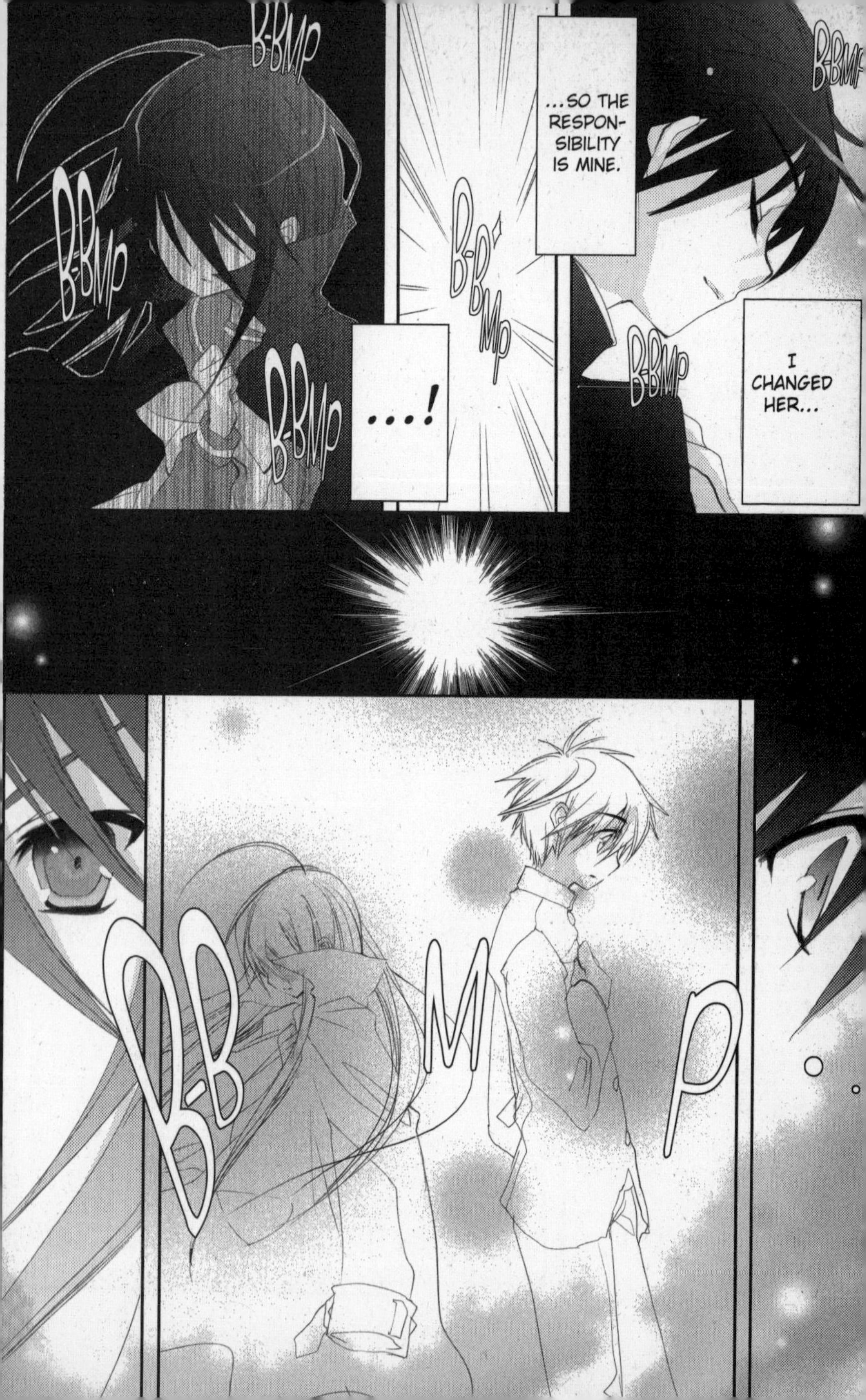
B-BMP
I CHANGED HER...
B-BMP
...SO THE RESPONSIBILITY IS MINE.
B-B-BMP
...!
B-BMP
B-BMP
B-BMP
B-BMP

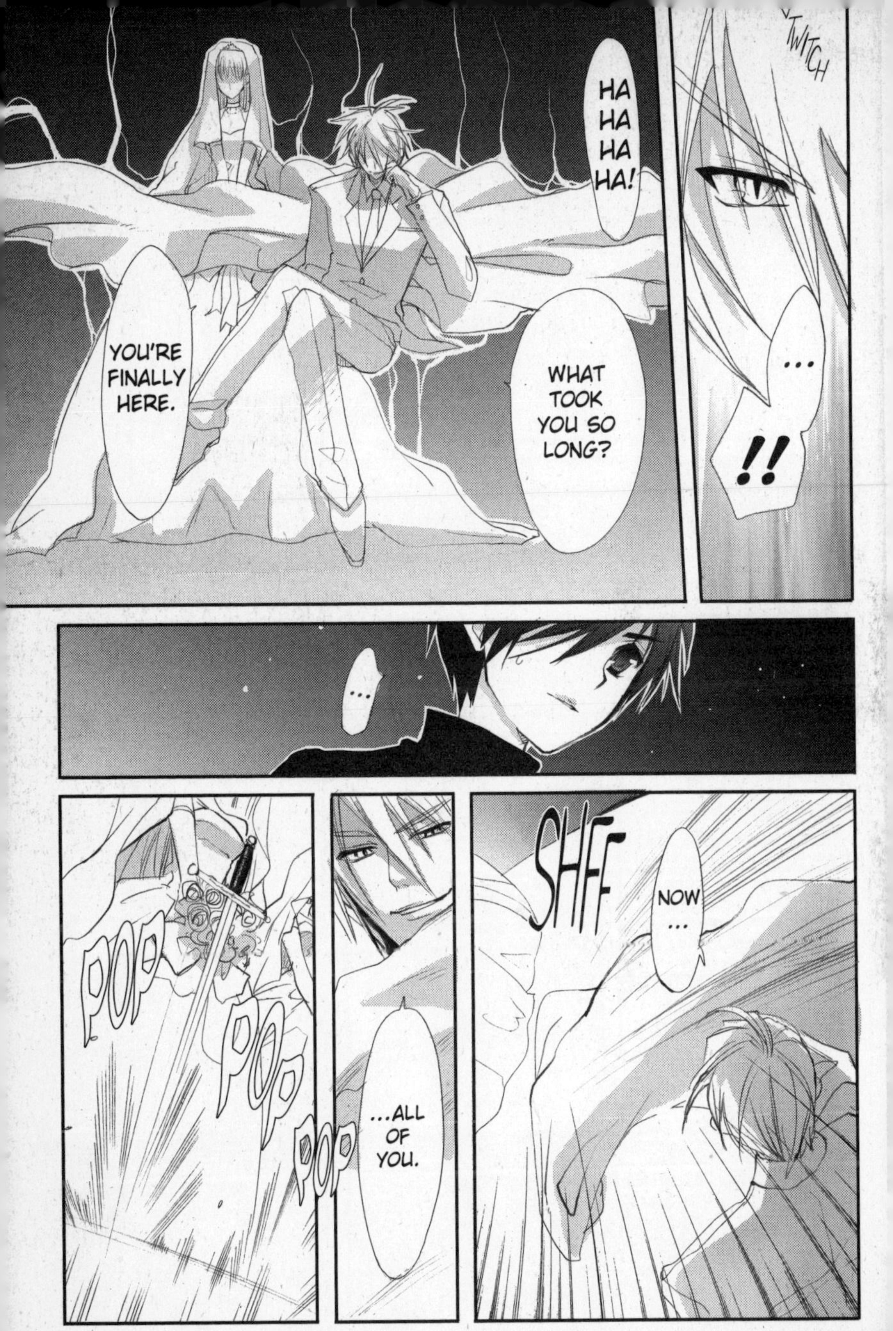
TWITCH
...
!!
HA HA HA HA!
WHAT TOOK YOU SO LONG?
YOU'RE FINALLY HERE.
...
SHFF
NOW...
...ALL OF YOU.
POP POP POP

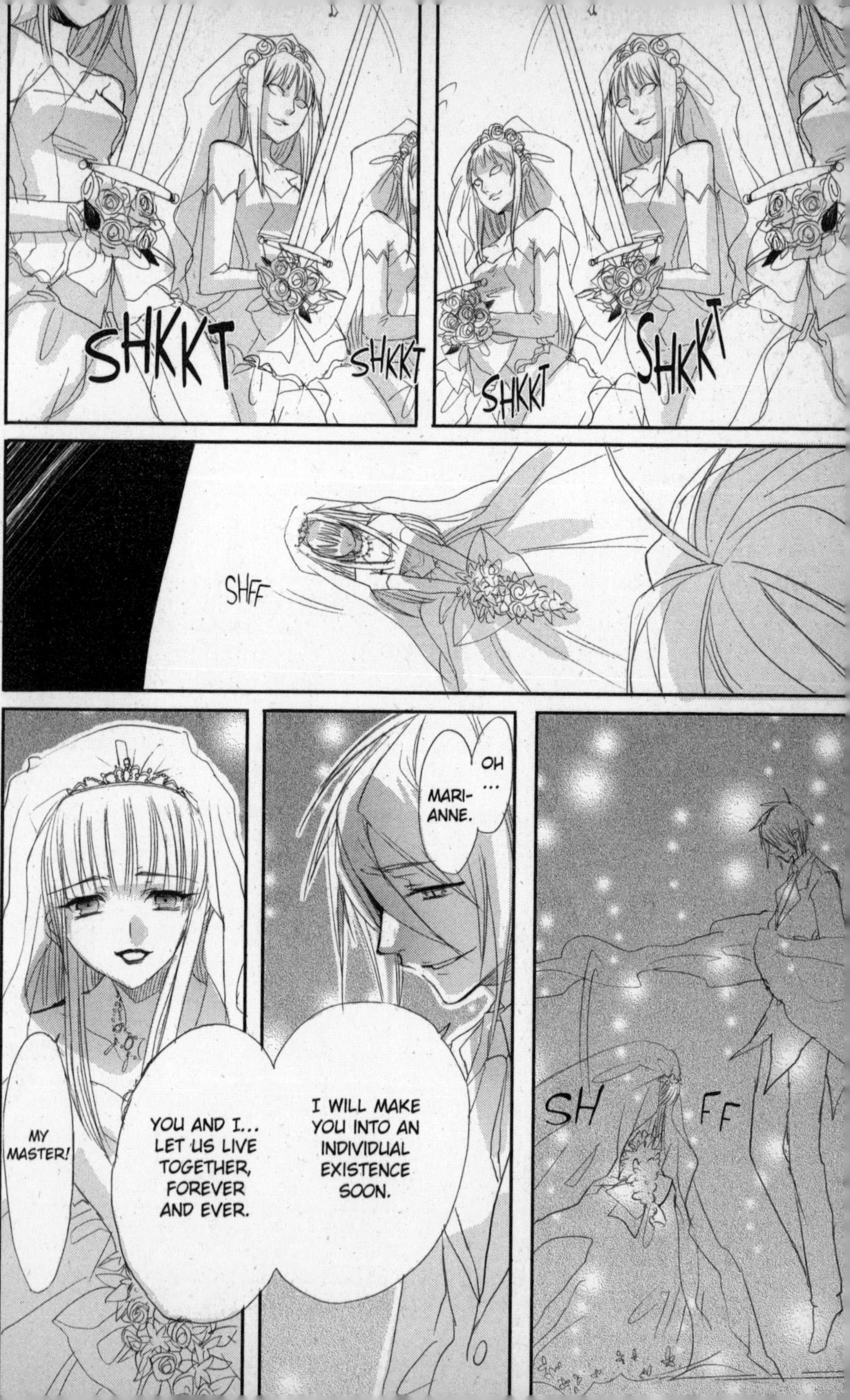
SHKKT
SHKKT
SHKKT
SHKKT
SHFF
SH FF
OH... MARI-ANNE.
I WILL MAKE YOU INTO AN INDIVIDUAL EXISTENCE SOON.
YOU AND I... LET US LIVE TOGETHER, FOREVER AND EVER.
MY MASTER!

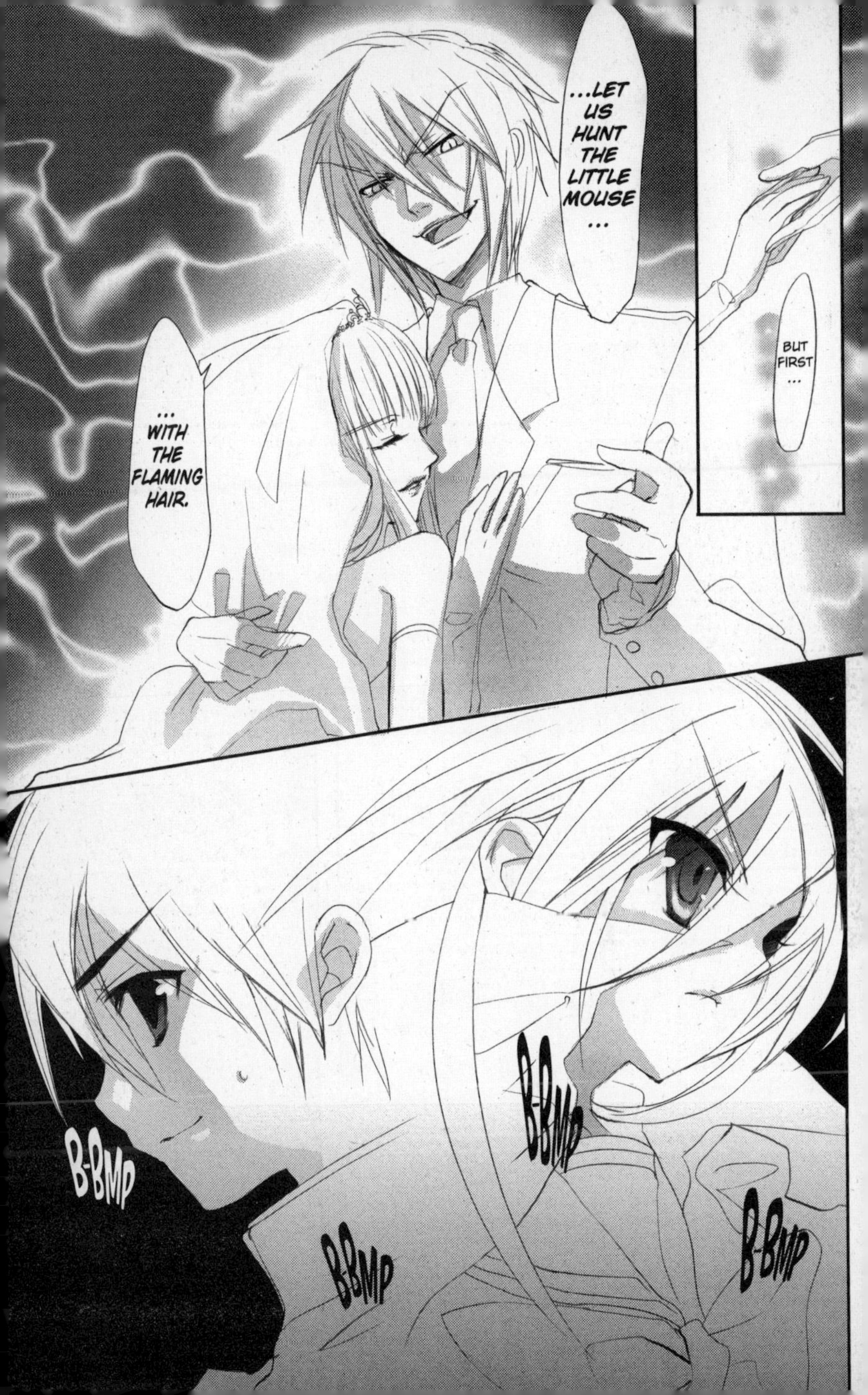

BUT FIRST...
...LET US HUNT THE LITTLE MOUSE...
...WITH THE FLAMING HAIR.
B-BMP
B-BMP
B-BMP
B-BMP

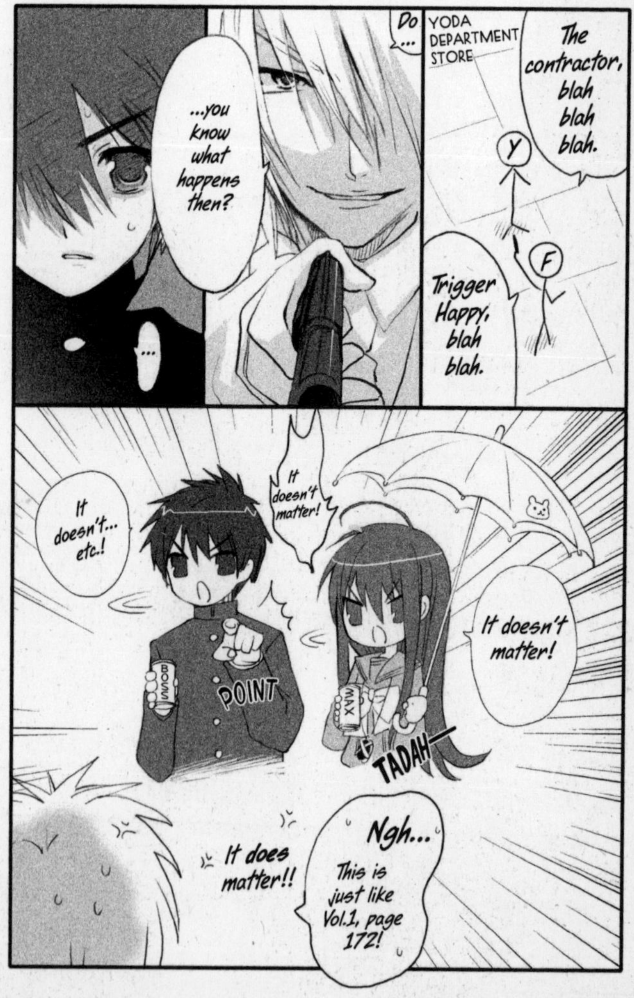
YODA DEPARTMENT STORE
The contractor, blah blah blah.
Y
F
Trigger Happy, blah blah.
Do...
...you know what happens then?
...
It doesn't matter!
It doesn't matter!
It doesn't... etc.!
BOSS
POINT
MAX
TADAH
Ngh... This is just like Vol.1, page 172!
It does matter!!

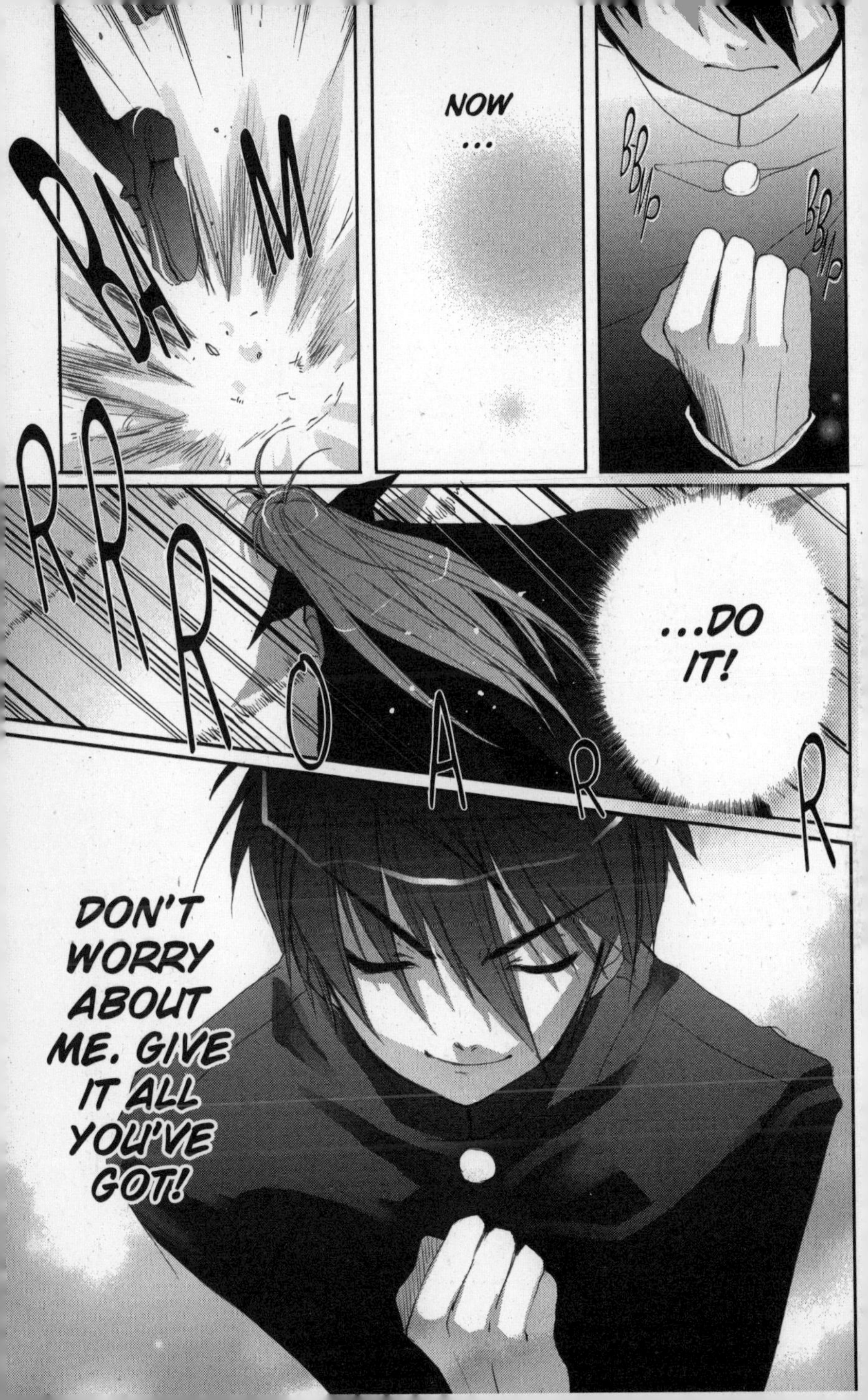
BBMP
BBMP
NOW ...
BAM
...DO IT!
RRROAR
RRROAR
DON'T WORRY ABOUT ME. GIVE IT ALL YOU'VE GOT!

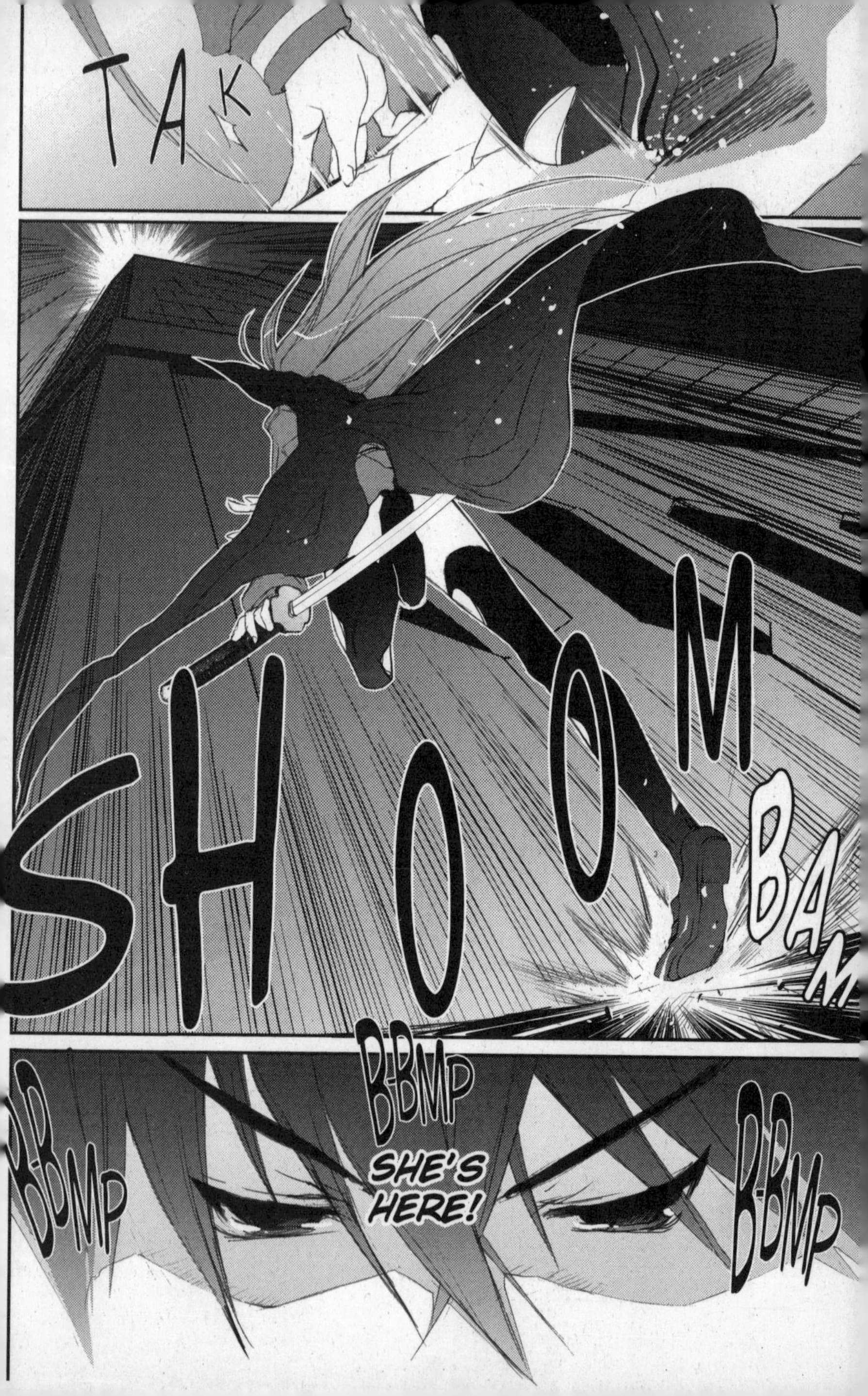
TAK
SHOOM
BAM
B-BMP
SHE'S HERE!
B-BMP
B-BMP

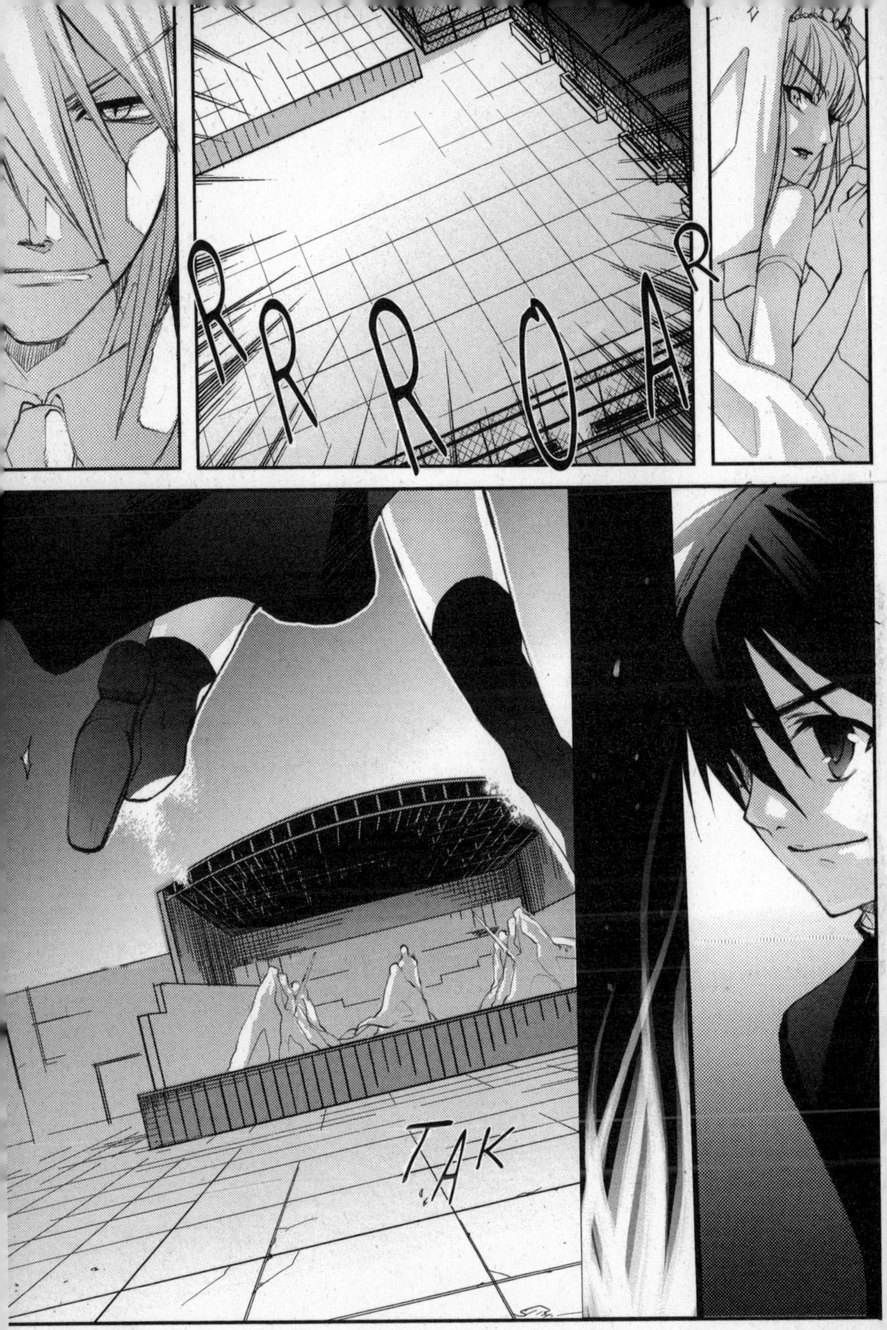
RRROAR
TAK

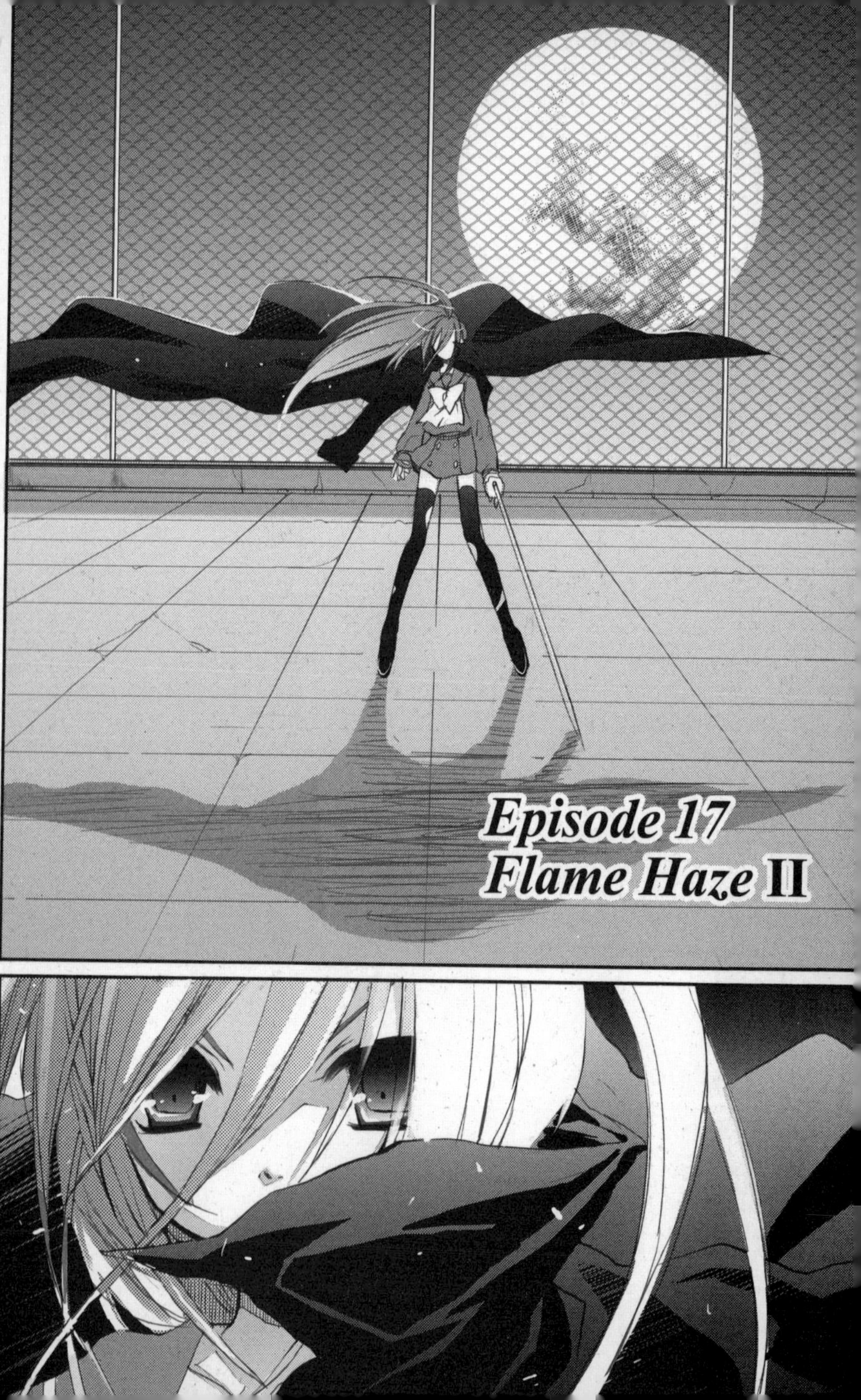
Episode 17
Flame Haze II

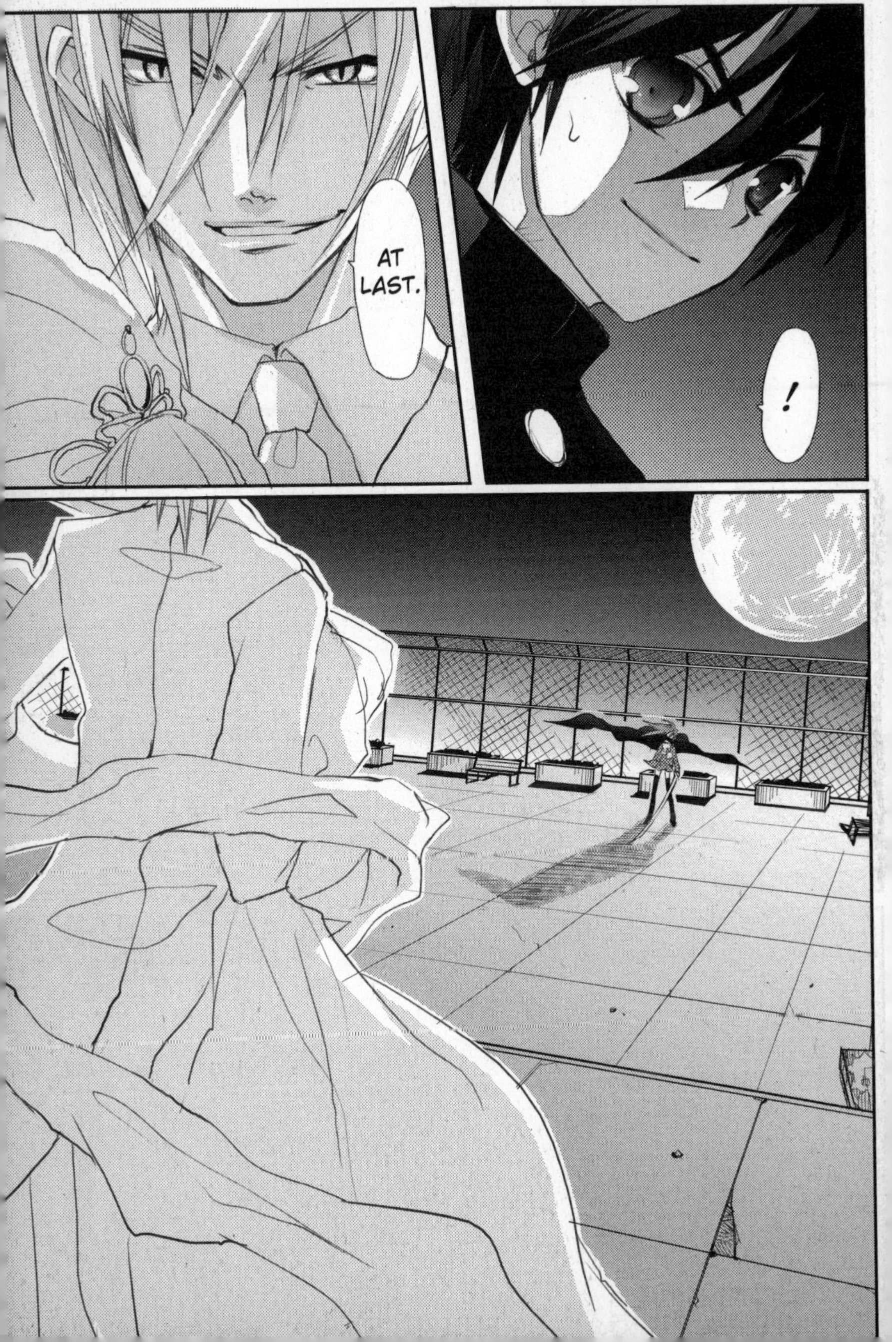
!
AT LAST.

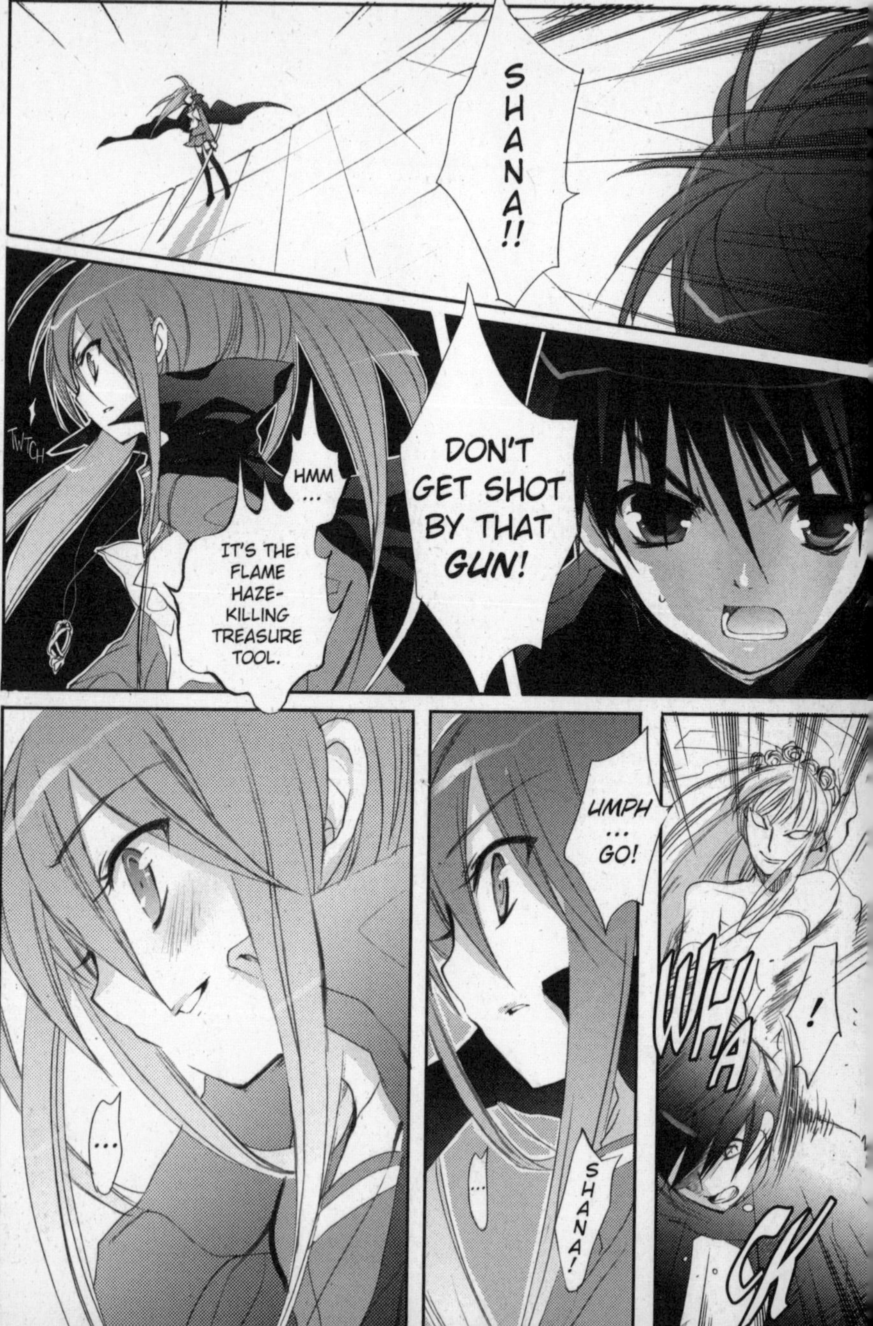
SHANA!!
DON'T GET SHOT BY THAT GUN!
HMM...
IT'S THE FLAME HAZE-KILLING TREASURE TOOL.
TWITCH
UMPH... GO!
WHA!
CH
SHANA!
...
...

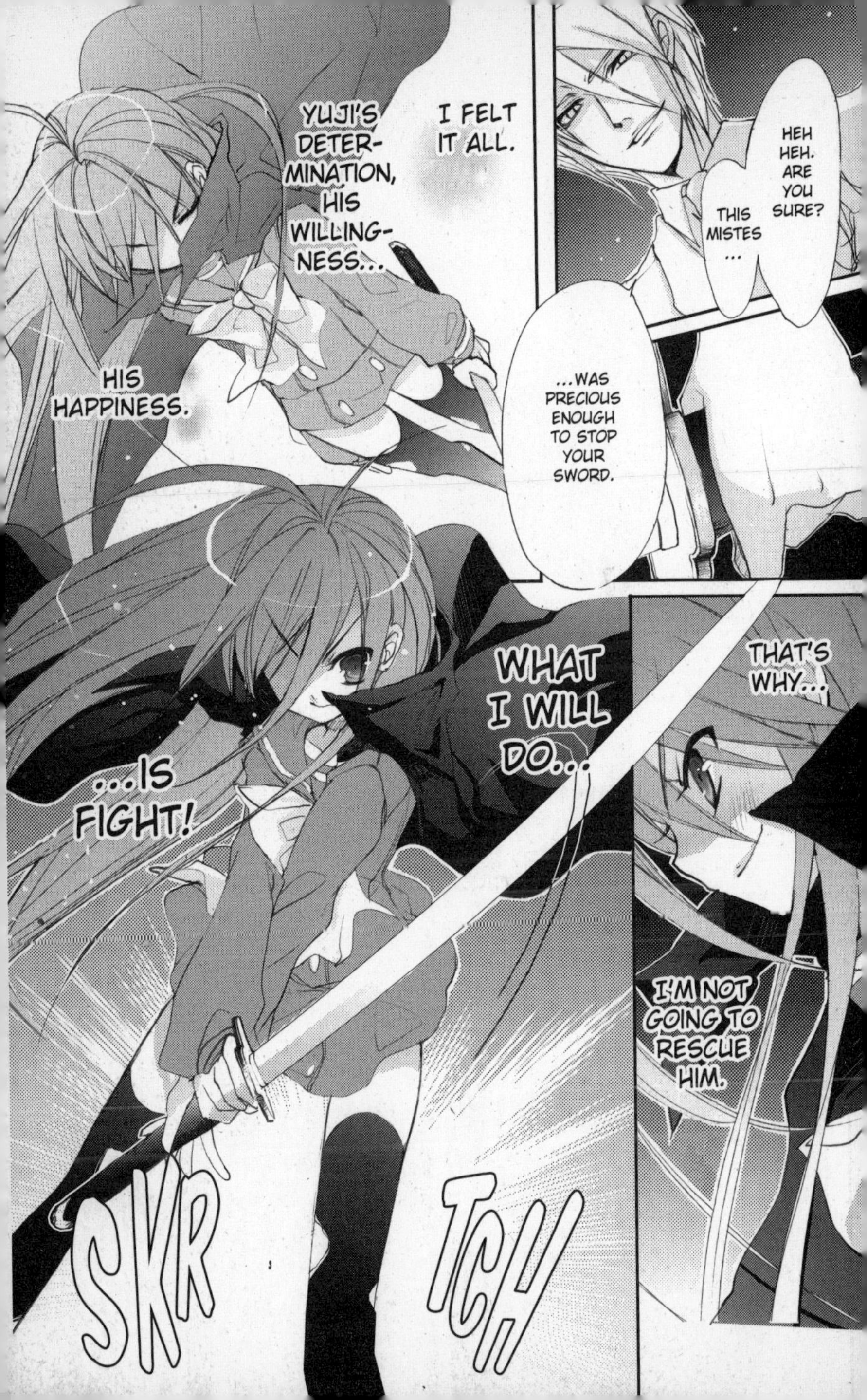
HEH HEH. ARE YOU SURE?
THIS MISTES ...
...WAS PRECIOUS ENOUGH TO STOP YOUR SWORD.
I FELT IT ALL.
YUJI'S DETERMINATION, HIS WILLINGNESS...
HIS HAPPINESS.
THAT'S WHY...
I'M NOT GOING TO RESCUE HIM.
WHAT I WILL DO...
...IS FIGHT!
SKR TCH

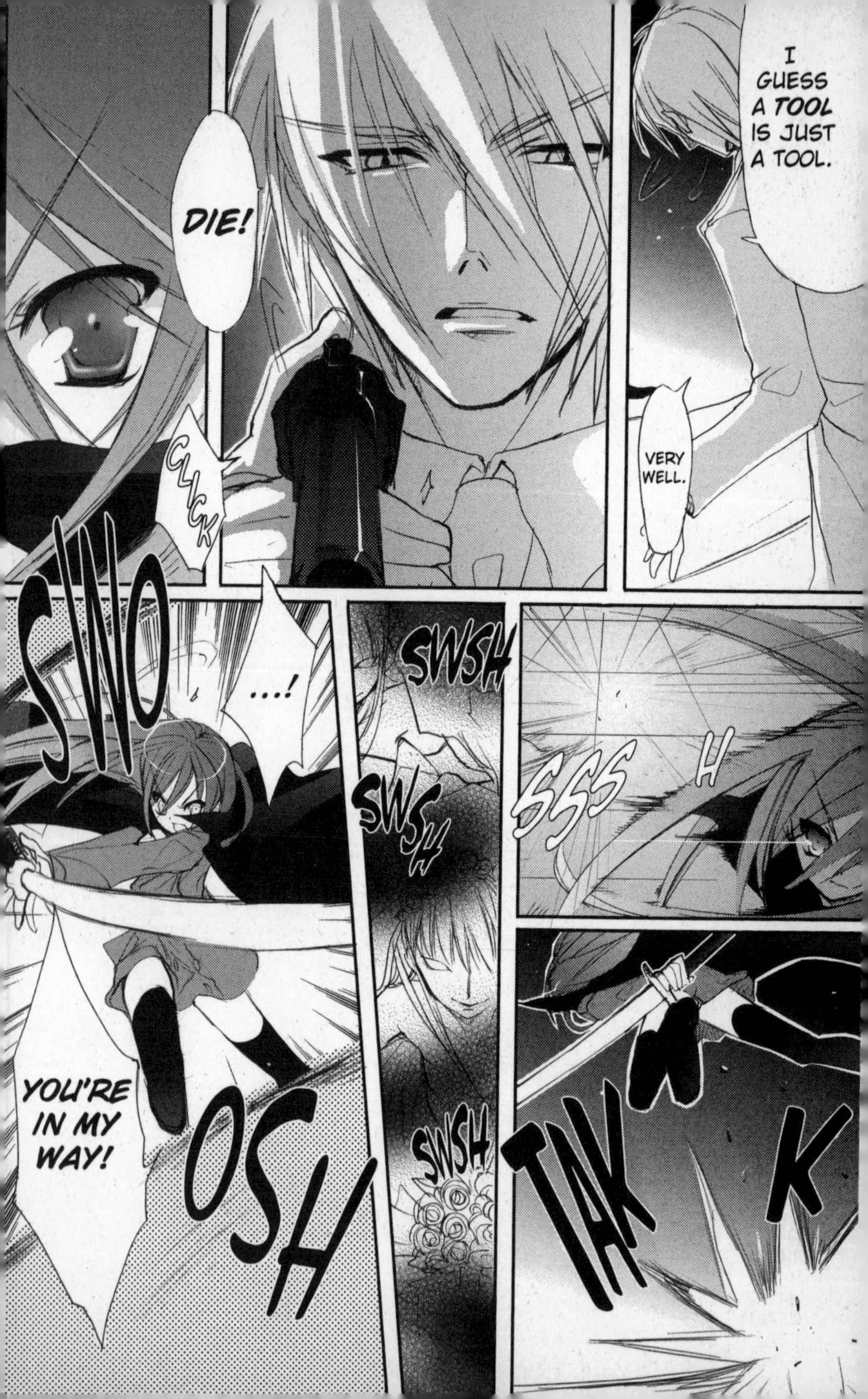
I GUESS A *TOOL* IS JUST A TOOL.
VERY WELL.
DIE!
CLICK
SSSSH
TAKK
SWSH
SWSH
SWSH
SWOOSH
...!
YOU'RE IN MY WAY!

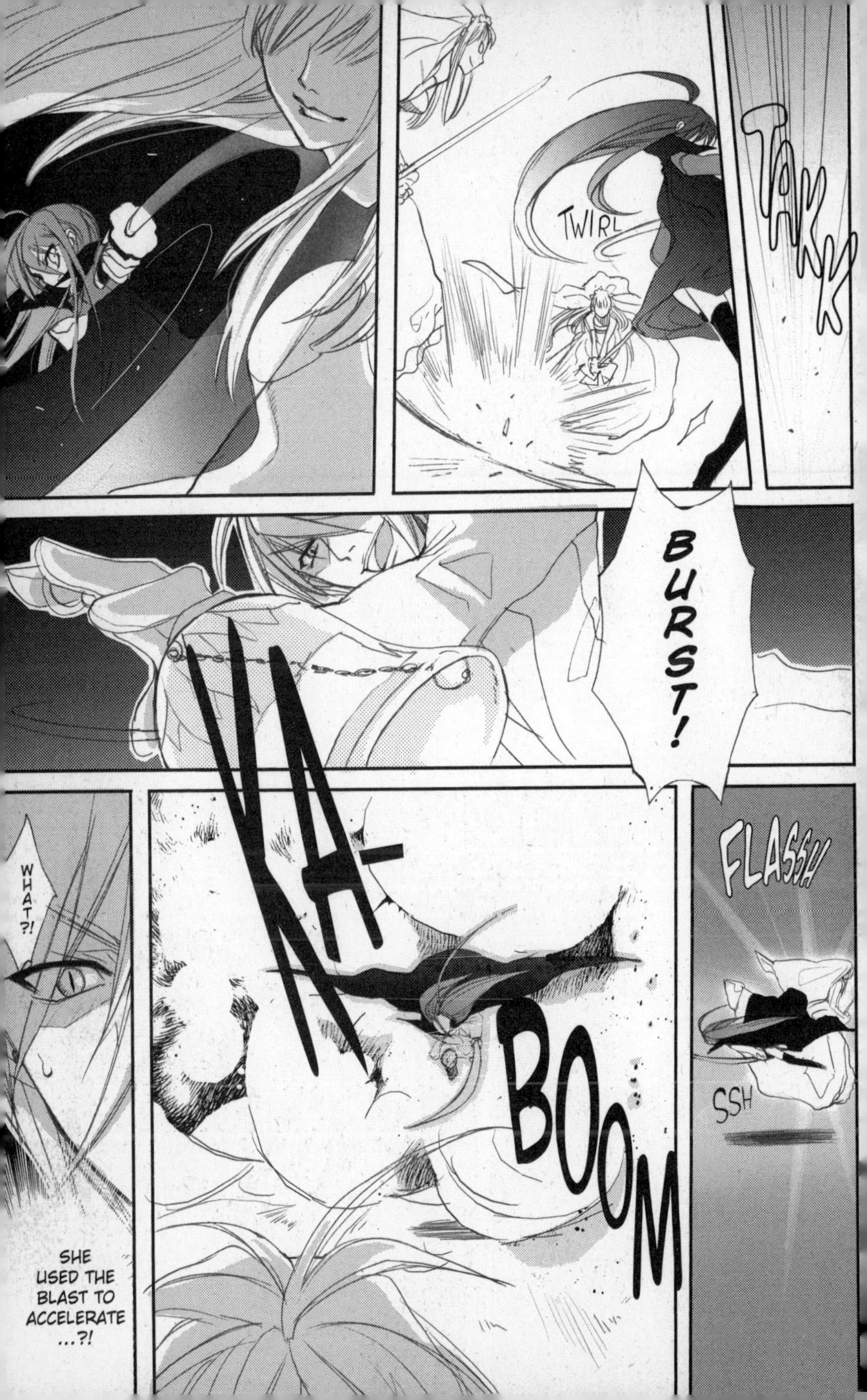

TAKK
TWIRL
BURST!
FLASSH
SSH
KA-BOOM
WHAT?!
SHE USED THE BLAST TO ACCELERATE ...?!

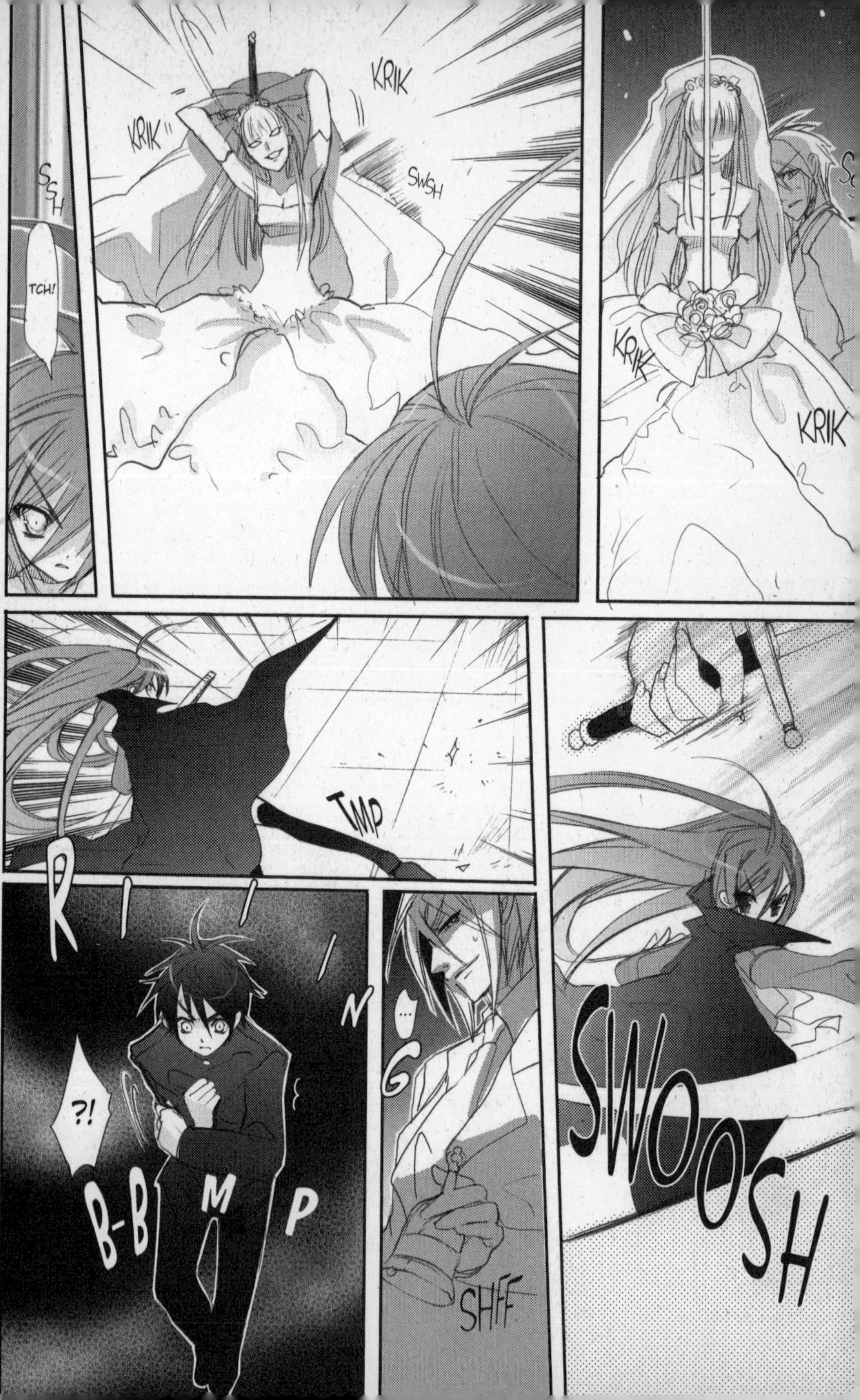

KRIK
KRIK
KRIK
KRIK
SWSH
SSH
TCH!
SWOOSH
TMP
RIIING
...
SHFF
?!
B-BMP

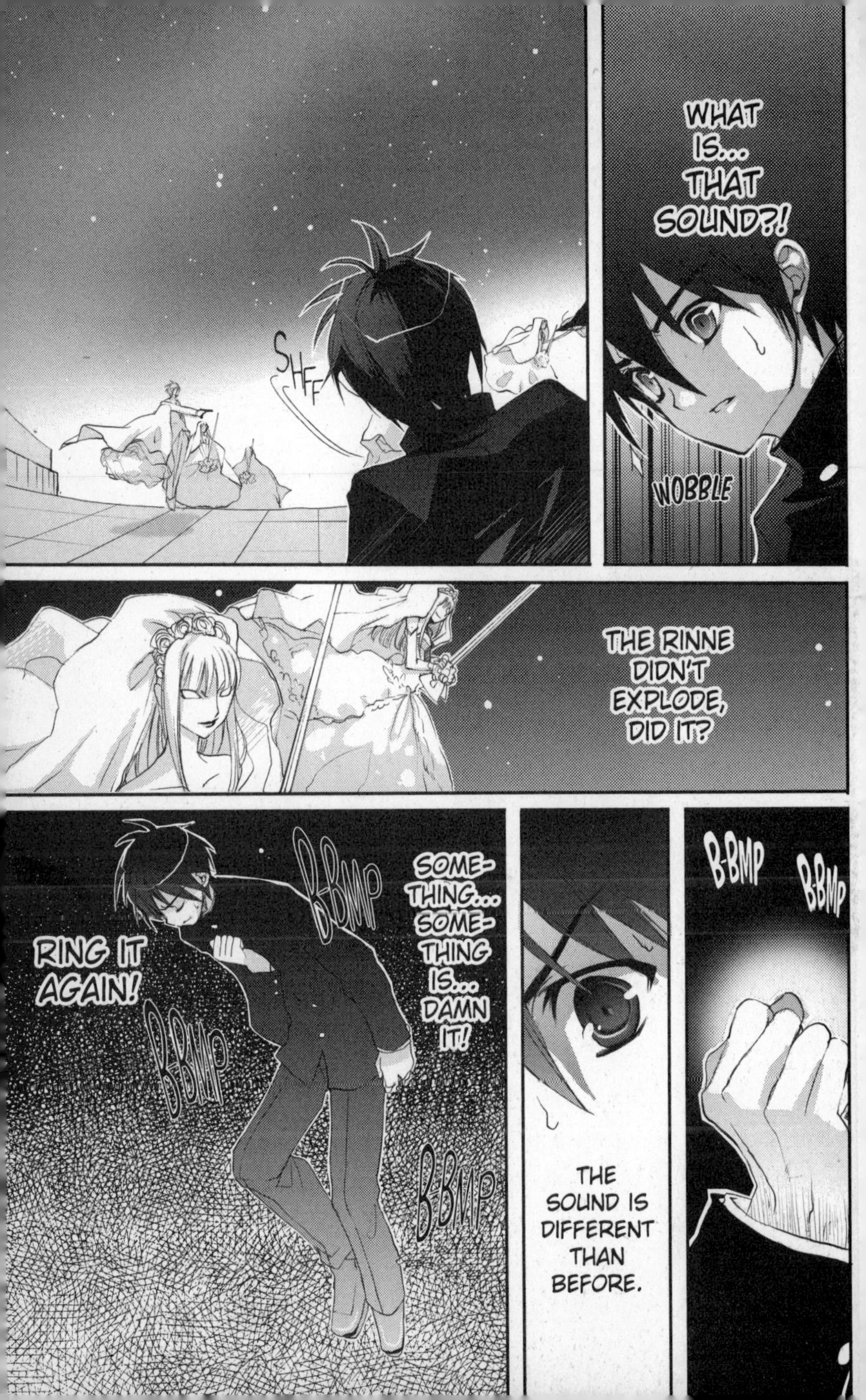
WHAT IS... THAT SOUND?!
WOBBLE
SHFF
THE RINNE DIDN'T EXPLODE, DID IT?
B-BMP
B-BMP
THE SOUND IS DIFFERENT THAN BEFORE.
B-BMP
SOME-THING... SOME-THING IS... DAMN IT!
RING IT AGAIN!
B-BMP
B-BMP

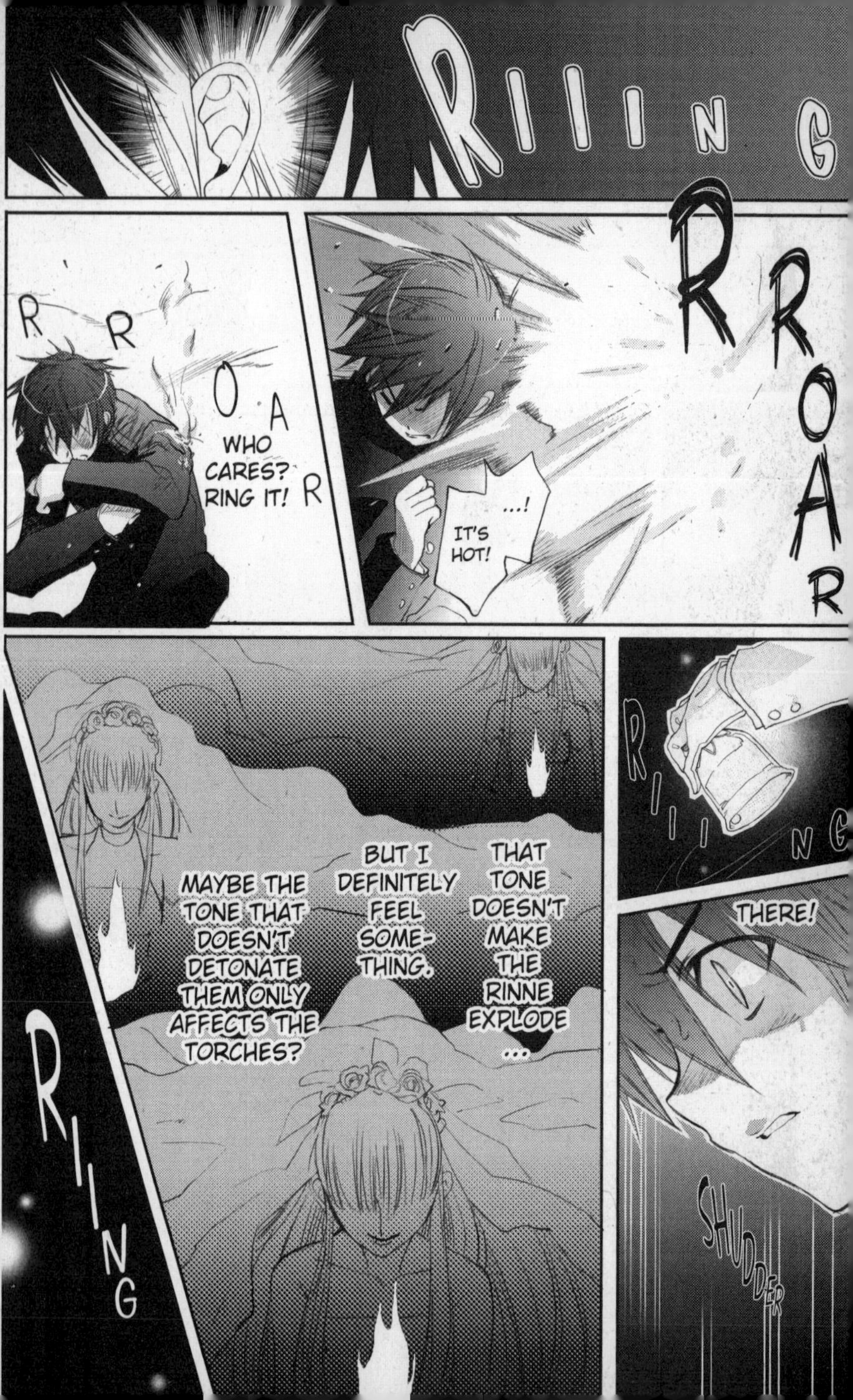
RIIING
RRROAR
...!
IT'S HOT!
RROAR
WHO CARES? RING IT!
RIIING
THERE!
SHUDDER
THAT TONE DOESN'T MAKE THE RINNE EXPLODE...
BUT I DEFINITELY FEEL SOMETHING.
MAYBE THE TONE THAT DOESN'T DETONATE THEM ONLY AFFECTS THE TORCHES?
RIIING

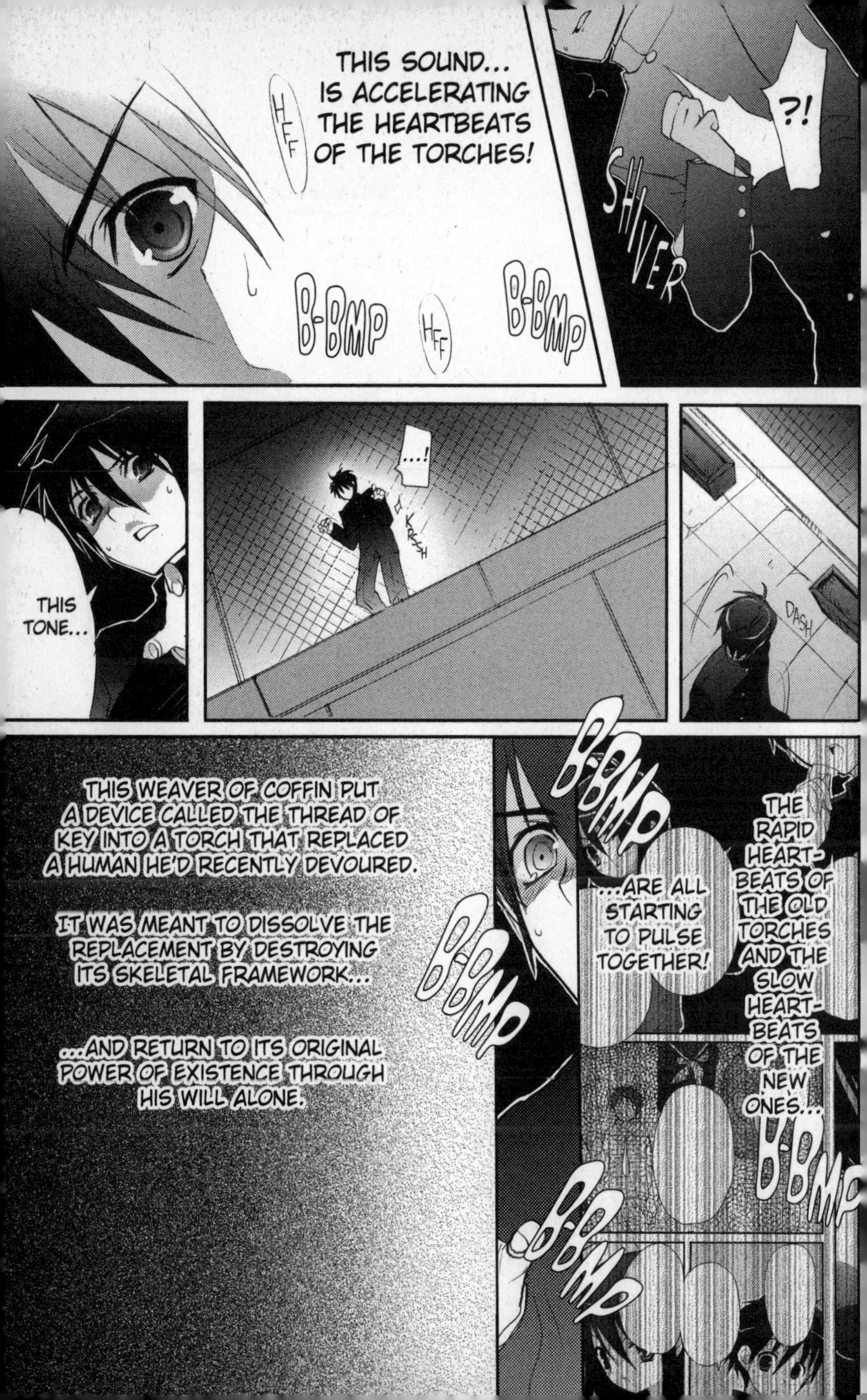
?!
SHIVER
THIS SOUND... IS ACCELERATING THE HEARTBEATS OF THE TORCHES!
HFF
B-BMP
HFF
B-BMP
DASH
...!
KRSSH
THIS TONE...
B-BMP
THE RAPID HEARTBEATS OF THE OLD TORCHES AND THE SLOW HEARTBEATS OF THE NEW ONES...
...ARE ALL STARTING TO PULSE TOGETHER!
B-BMP
B-BMP
B-BMP
THIS WEAVER OF COFFIN PUT A DEVICE CALLED THE THREAD OF KEY INTO A TORCH THAT REPLACED A HUMAN HE'D RECENTLY DEVOURED.
IT WAS MEANT TO DISSOLVE THE REPLACEMENT BY DESTROYING ITS SKELETAL FRAMEWORK...
...AND RETURN TO ITS ORIGINAL POWER OF EXISTENCE THROUGH HIS WILL ALONE.

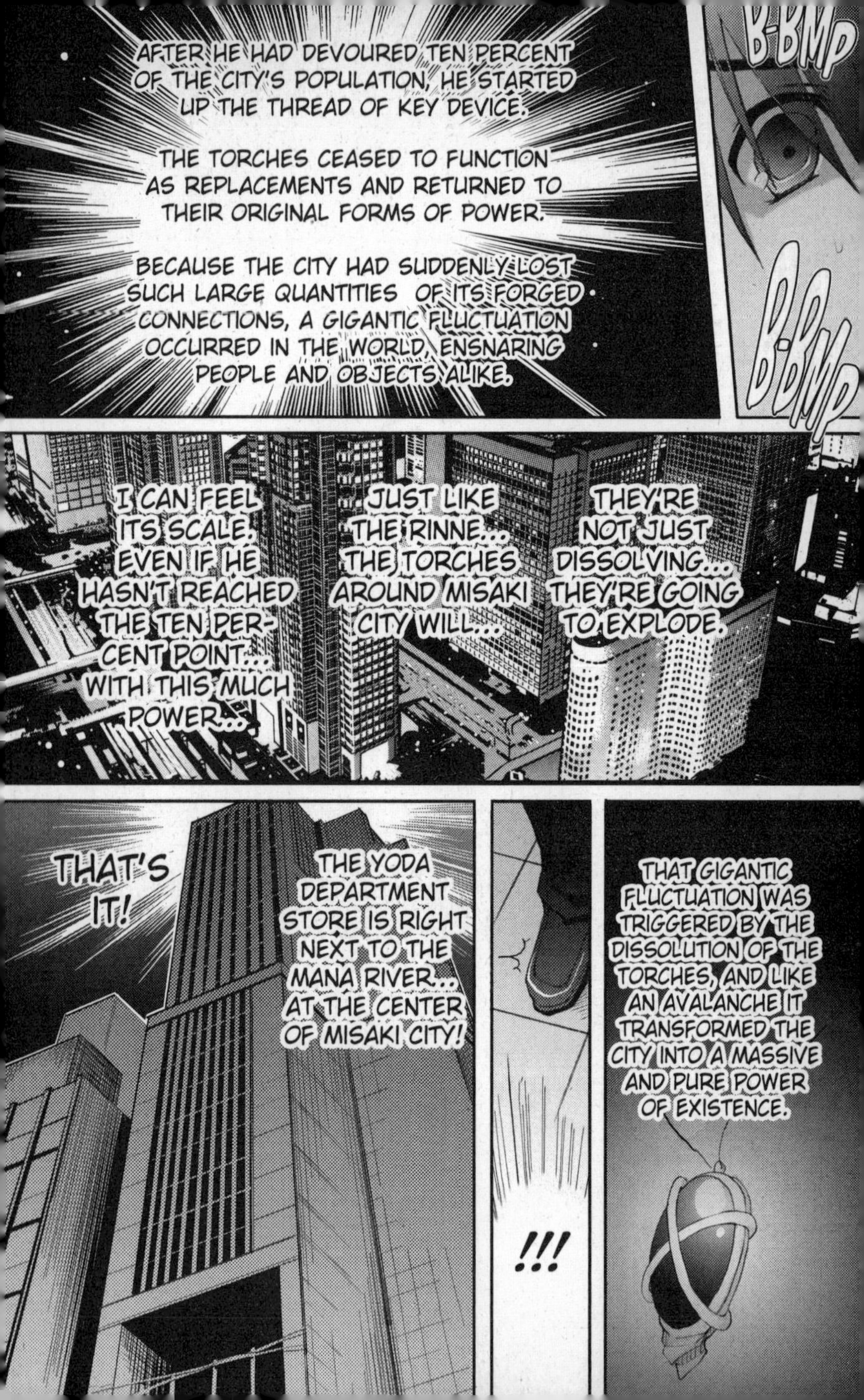
B-BMP
B-BMP
AFTER HE HAD DEVOURED TEN PERCENT OF THE CITY'S POPULATION, HE STARTED UP THE THREAD OF KEY DEVICE.
THE TORCHES CEASED TO FUNCTION AS REPLACEMENTS AND RETURNED TO THEIR ORIGINAL FORMS OF POWER.
BECAUSE THE CITY HAD SUDDENLY LOST SUCH LARGE QUANTITIES OF ITS FORGED CONNECTIONS, A GIGANTIC FLUCTUATION OCCURRED IN THE WORLD, ENSNARING PEOPLE AND OBJECTS ALIKE.
THEY'RE NOT JUST DISSOLVING... THEY'RE GOING TO EXPLODE.
JUST LIKE THE RINNE... THE TORCHES AROUND MISAKI CITY WILL...
I CAN FEEL ITS SCALE. EVEN IF HE HASN'T REACHED THE TEN PER-CENT POINT... WITH THIS MUCH POWER...
THAT GIGANTIC FLUCTUATION WAS TRIGGERED BY THE DISSOLUTION OF THE TORCHES, AND LIKE AN AVALANCHE IT TRANSFORMED THE CITY INTO A MASSIVE AND PURE POWER OF EXISTENCE.
!!!
THE YODA DEPARTMENT STORE IS RIGHT NEXT TO THE MANA RIVER... AT THE CENTER OF MISAKI CITY!
THAT'S IT!

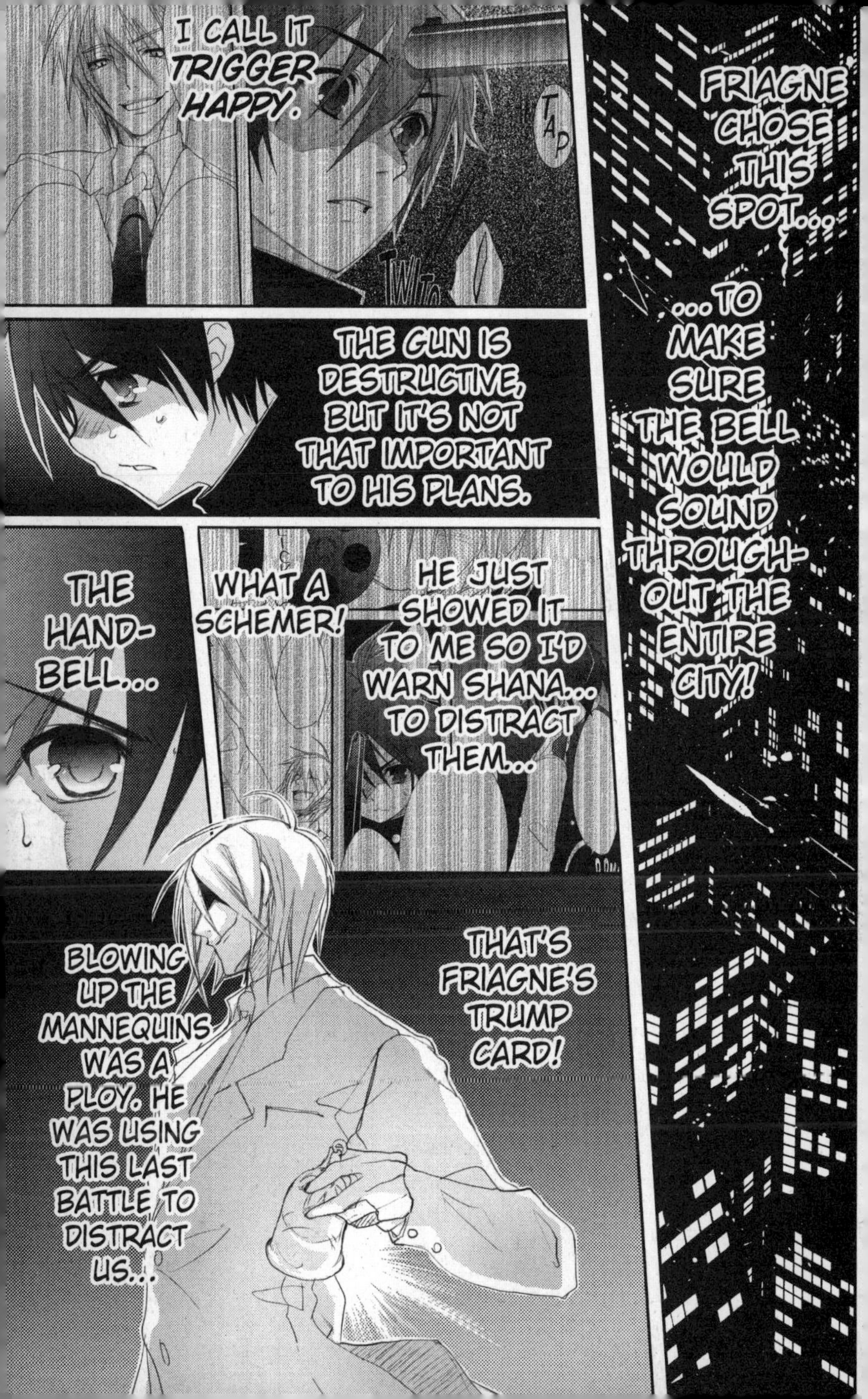
FRIAGNE CHOSE THIS SPOT...
...TO MAKE SURE THE BELL WOULD SOUND THROUGH-OUT THE ENTIRE CITY!
I CALL IT TRIGGER HAPPY.
TAP
THE GUN IS DESTRUCTIVE, BUT IT'S NOT THAT IMPORTANT TO HIS PLANS.
HE JUST SHOWED IT TO ME SO I'D WARN SHANA... TO DISTRACT THEM...
WHAT A SCHEMER!
THE HAND-BELL...
THAT'S FRIAGNE'S TRUMP CARD!
BLOWING UP THE MANNEQUINS WAS A PLOY. HE WAS USING THIS LAST BATTLE TO DISTRACT US...

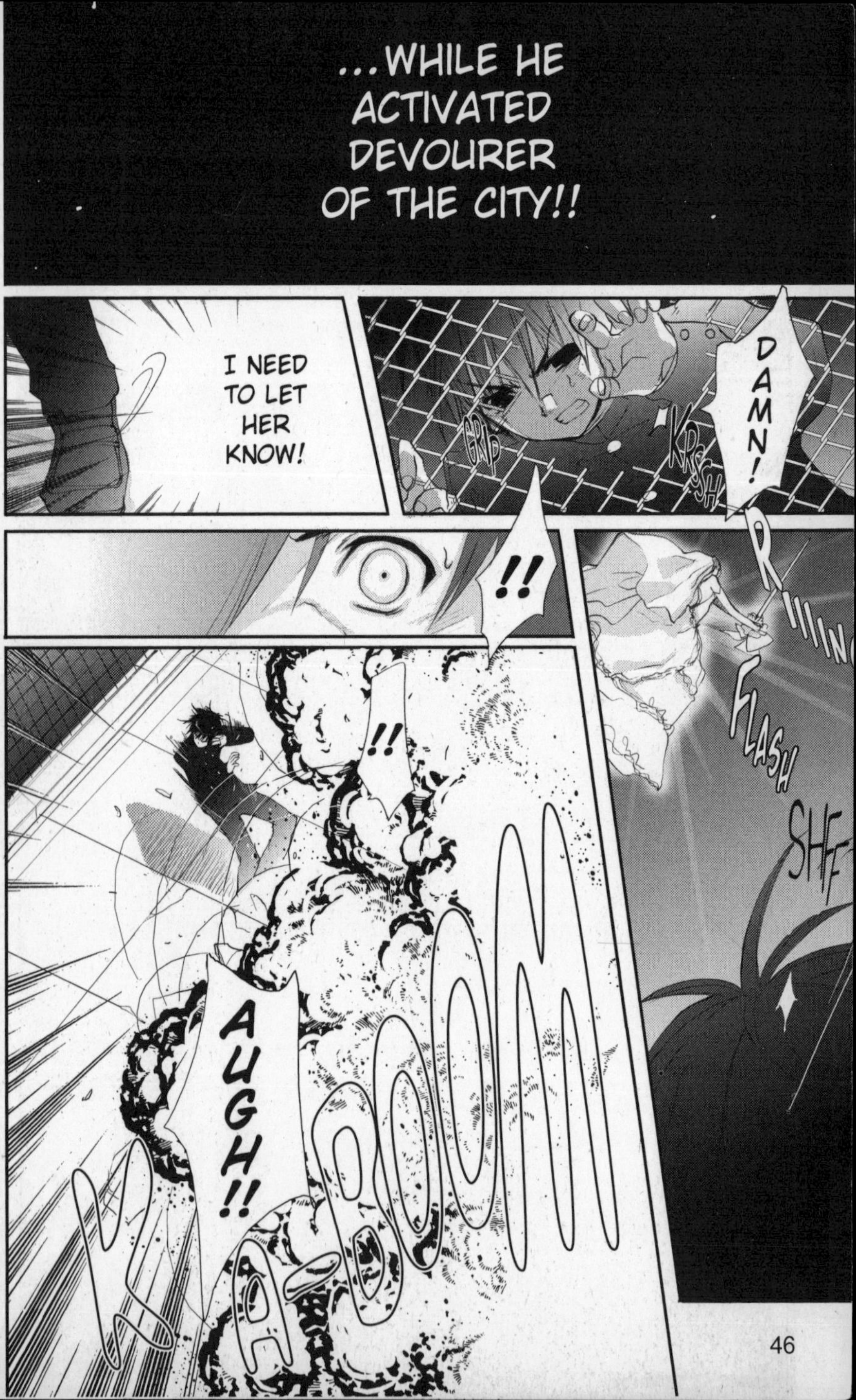
...WHILE HE ACTIVATED DEVOURER OF THE CITY!!
GRIP
KRSSH
DAMN!
I NEED TO LET HER KNOW!
RIIIING
FLASH
SHFF
!!
!!
AUGH!!

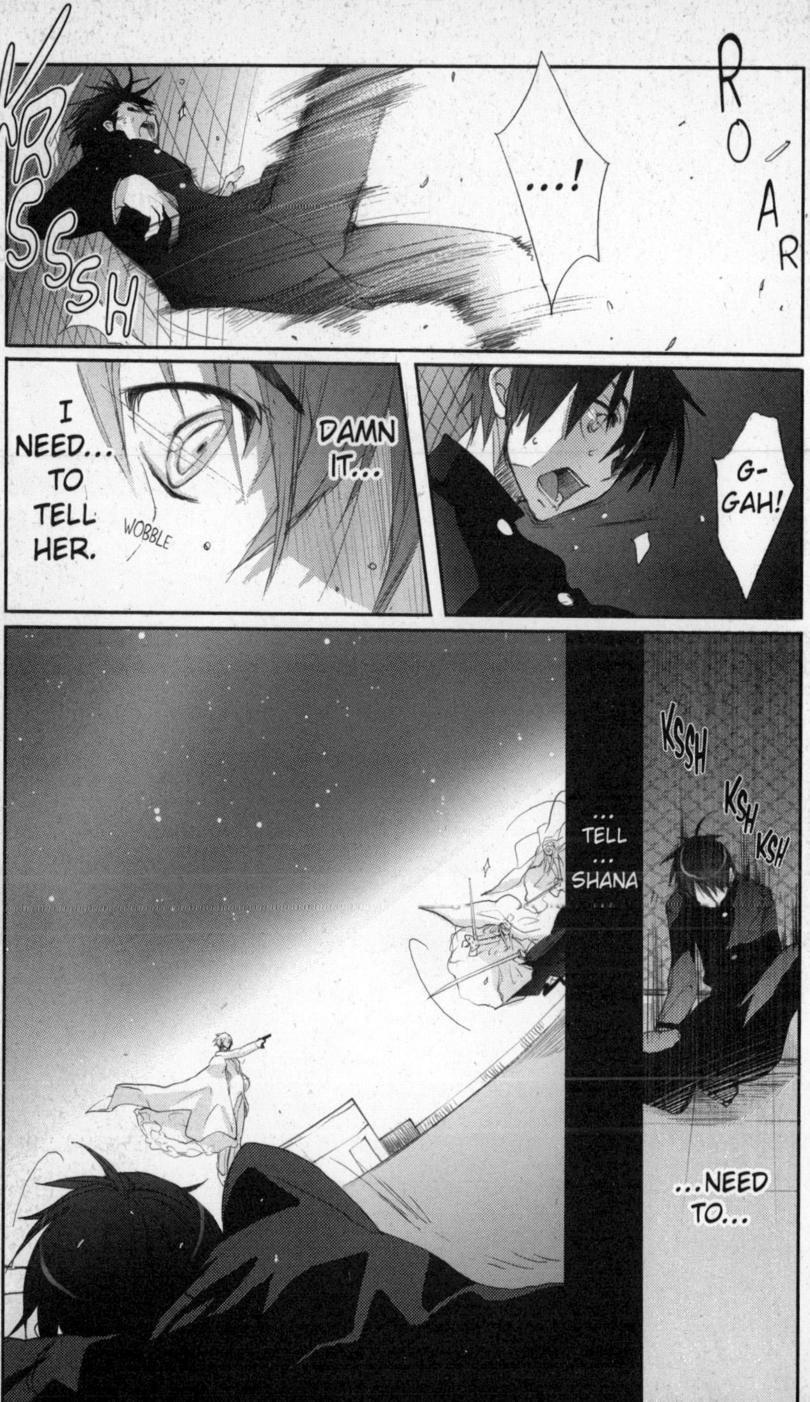
ROAR
...!
KRSSSSH
G-GAH!
DAMN IT...
I NEED... TO TELL HER.
WOBBLE
KSSH
KSH
KSH
...NEED TO...
... TELL ... SHANA ...

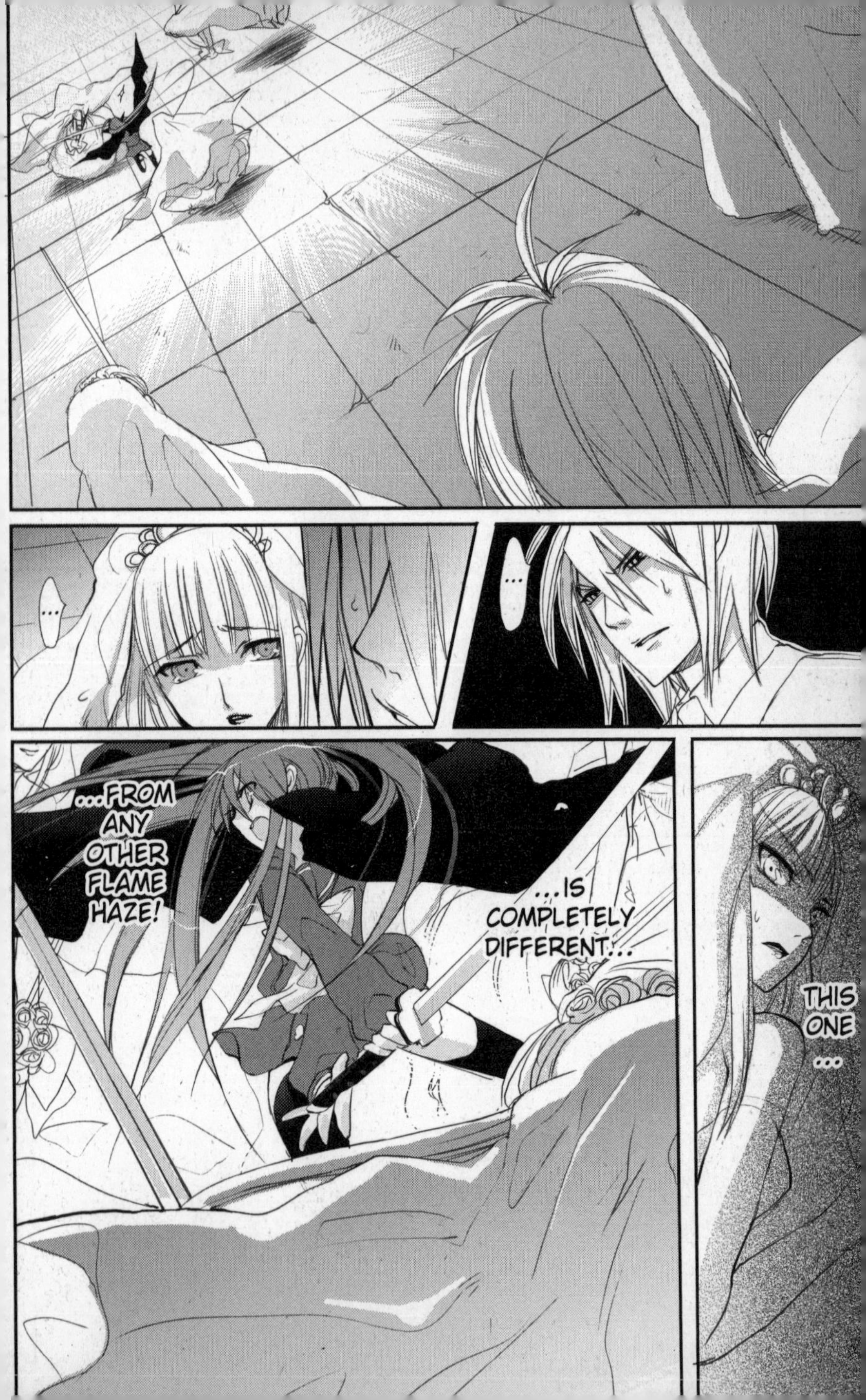
...
...
THIS ONE ...
...IS COMPLETELY DIFFERENT...
...FROM ANY OTHER FLAME HAZE!

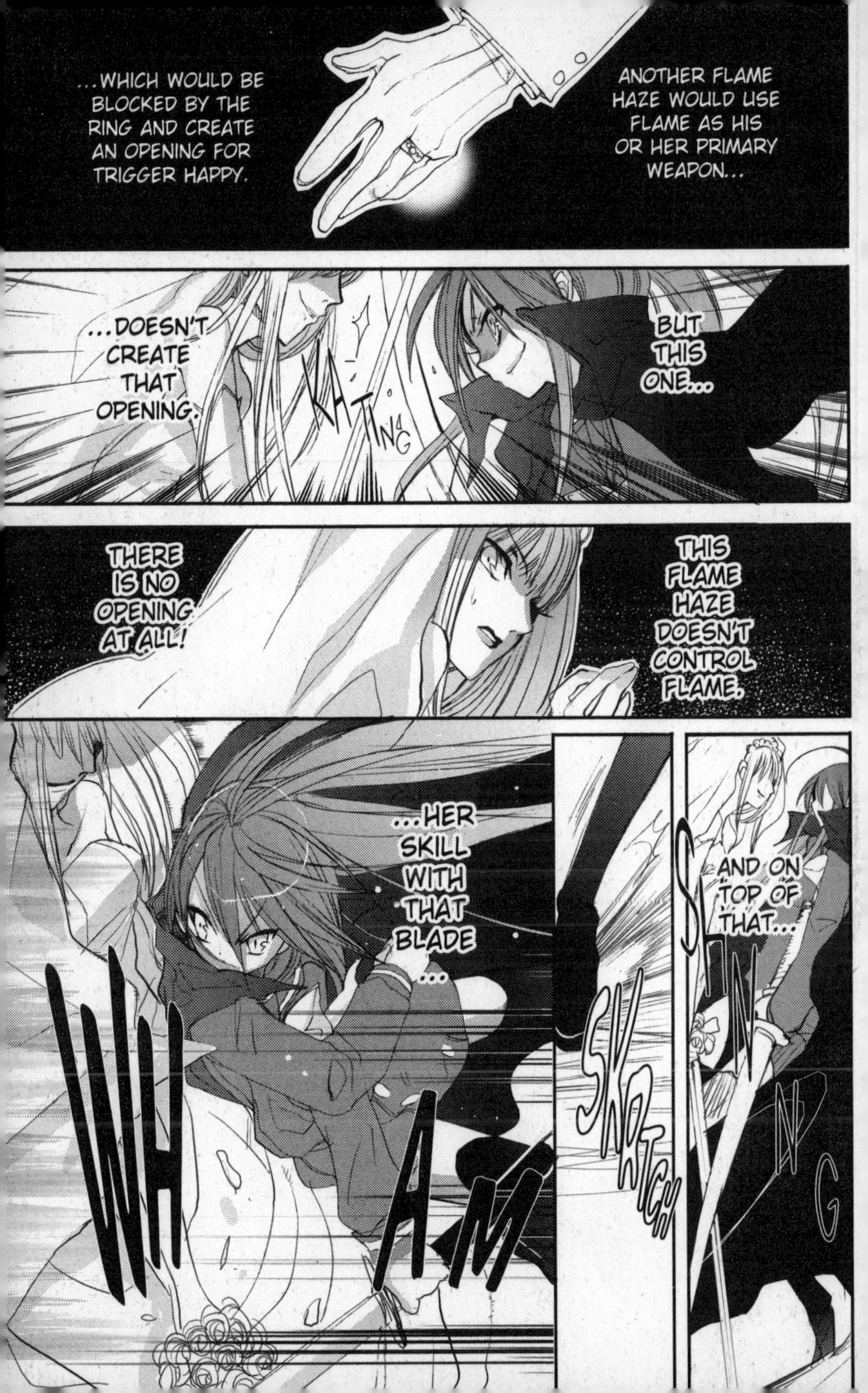
ANOTHER FLAME HAZE WOULD USE FLAME AS HIS OR HER PRIMARY WEAPON...
...WHICH WOULD BE BLOCKED BY THE RING AND CREATE AN OPENING FOR TRIGGER HAPPY.
BUT THIS ONE...
KATING
...DOESN'T CREATE THAT OPENING.
THIS FLAME HAZE DOESN'T CONTROL FLAME.
THERE IS NO OPENING AT ALL!
AND ON TOP OF THAT...
SHING
SNATCH
...HER SKILL WITH THAT BLADE...
WHAM

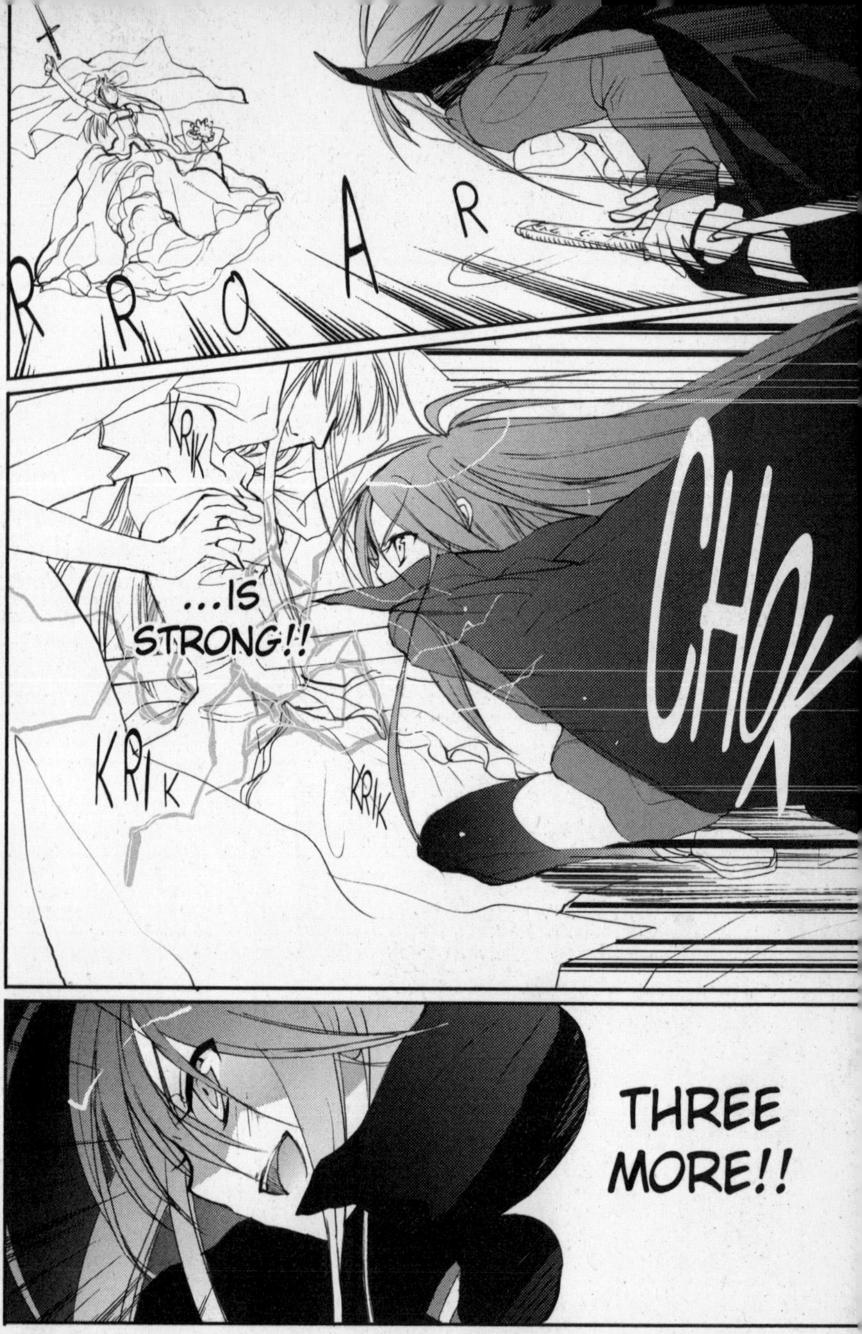
RROAR
CHOK
KRIK
...IS STRONG!!
KRIK
KRIK
THREE MORE!!

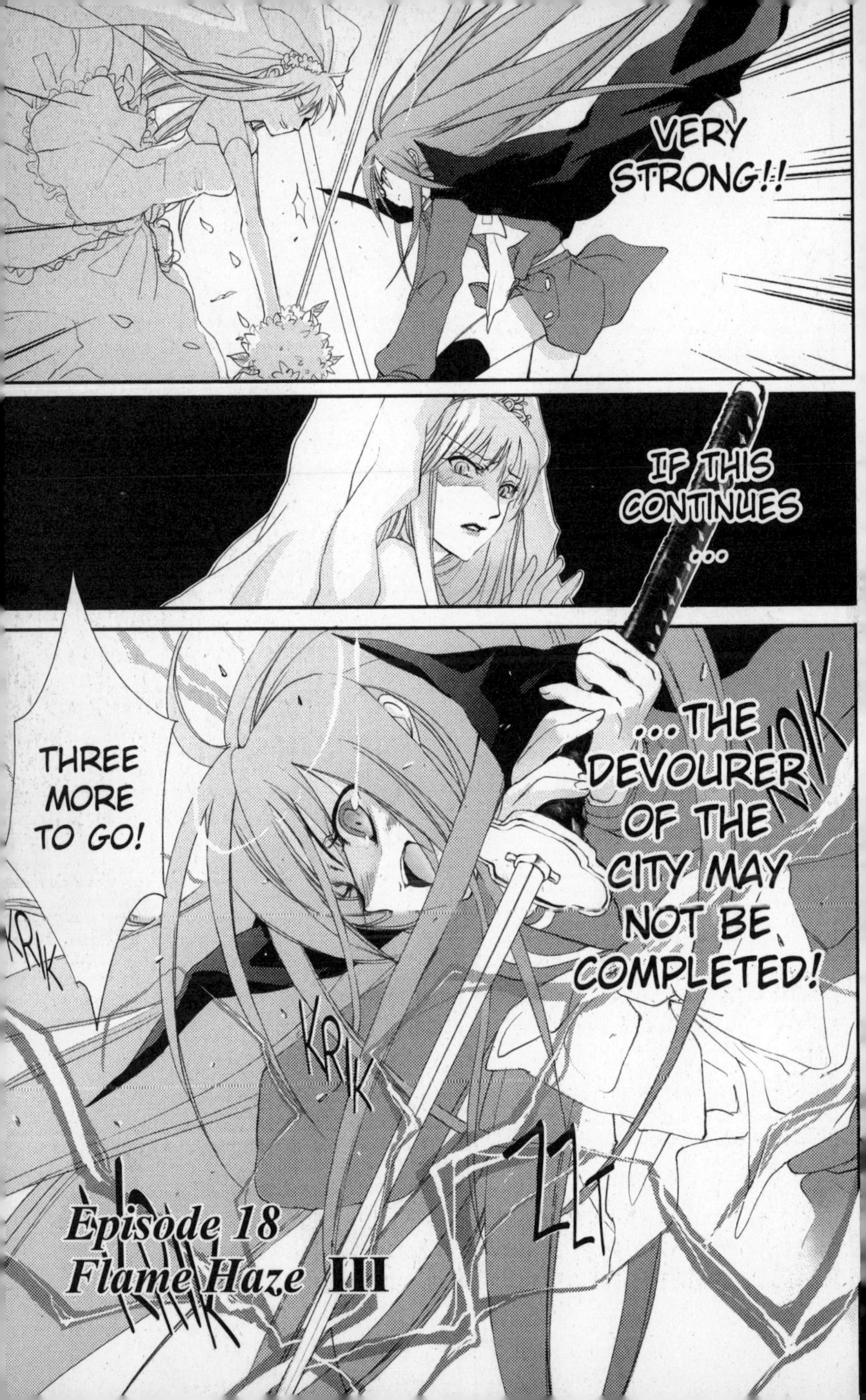
VERY STRONG!!
IF THIS CONTINUES ...
KRIK
...THE DEVOURER OF THE CITY MAY NOT BE COMPLETED!
THREE MORE TO GO!
KRIK
KRIK
ZZT
Episode 18
Flame Haze III

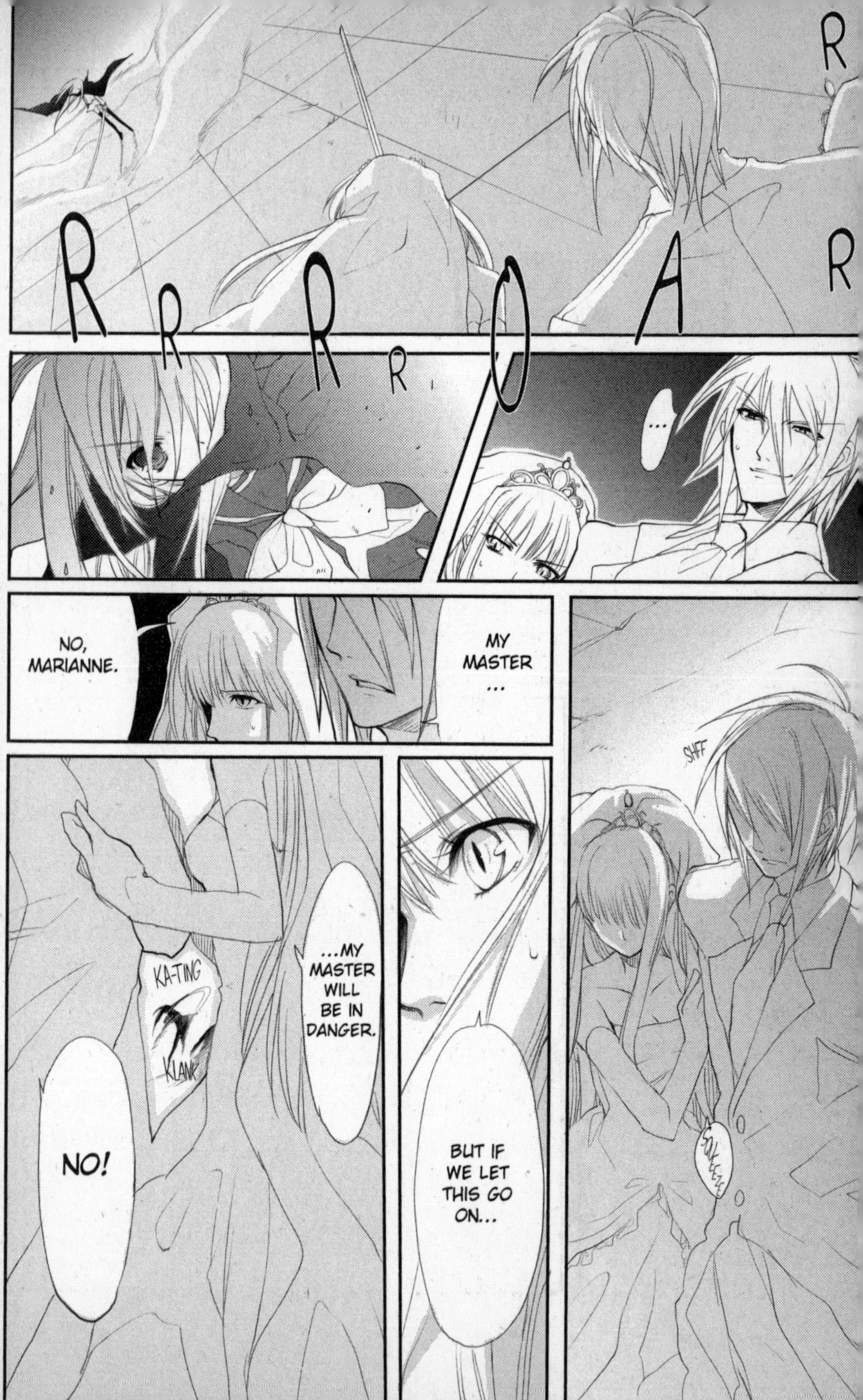
RRRROARR
...
SHFF
MY MASTER...
NO, MARIANNE.
BUT IF WE LET THIS GO ON...
...MY MASTER WILL BE IN DANGER.
KA-TING
KLANK
NO!

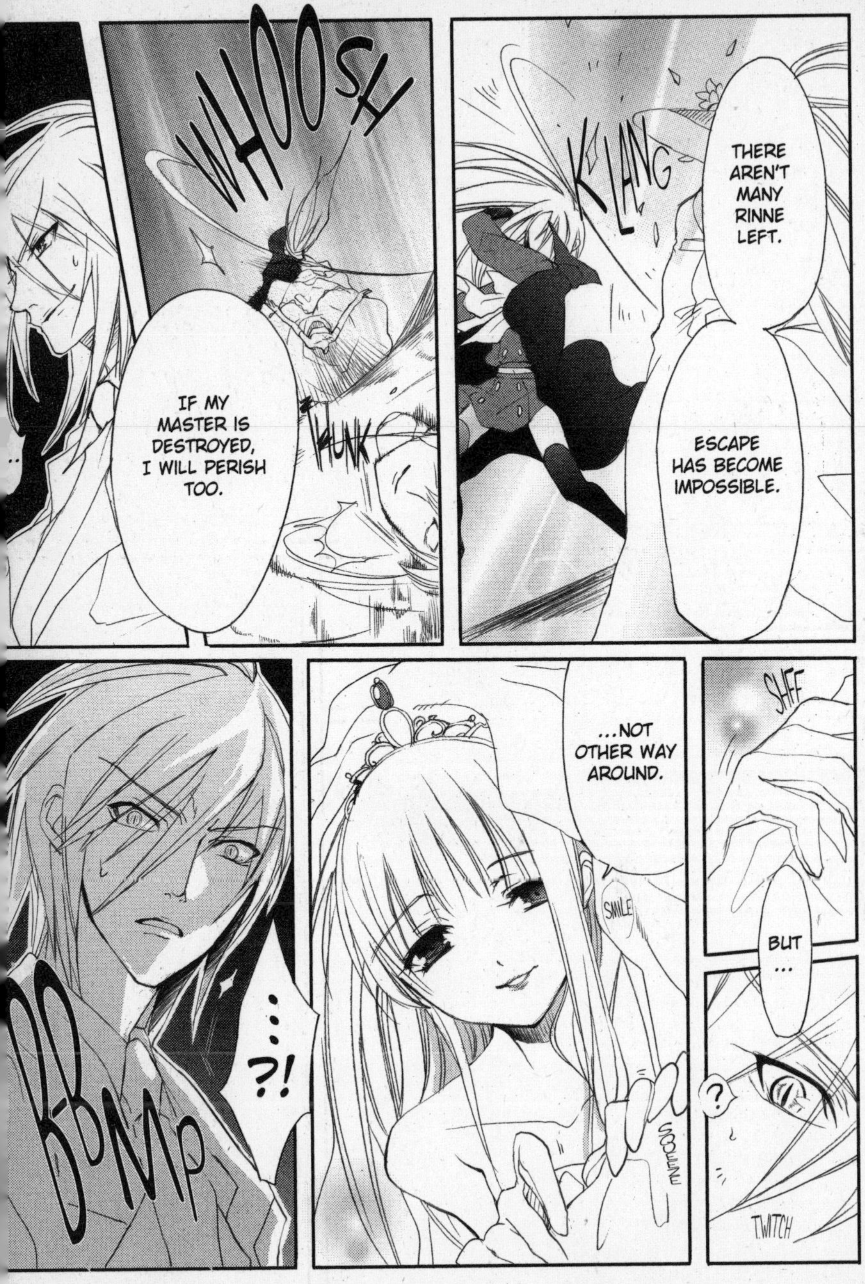
THERE AREN'T MANY RINNE LEFT.
K'LANG
ESCAPE HAS BECOME IMPOSSIBLE.
WHOOSH
IF MY MASTER IS DESTROYED, I WILL PERISH TOO.
THUNK
...
SHFF
BUT ...
?
TWITCH
...NOT OTHER WAY AROUND.
SMILE
SQUEEZE
...
?!

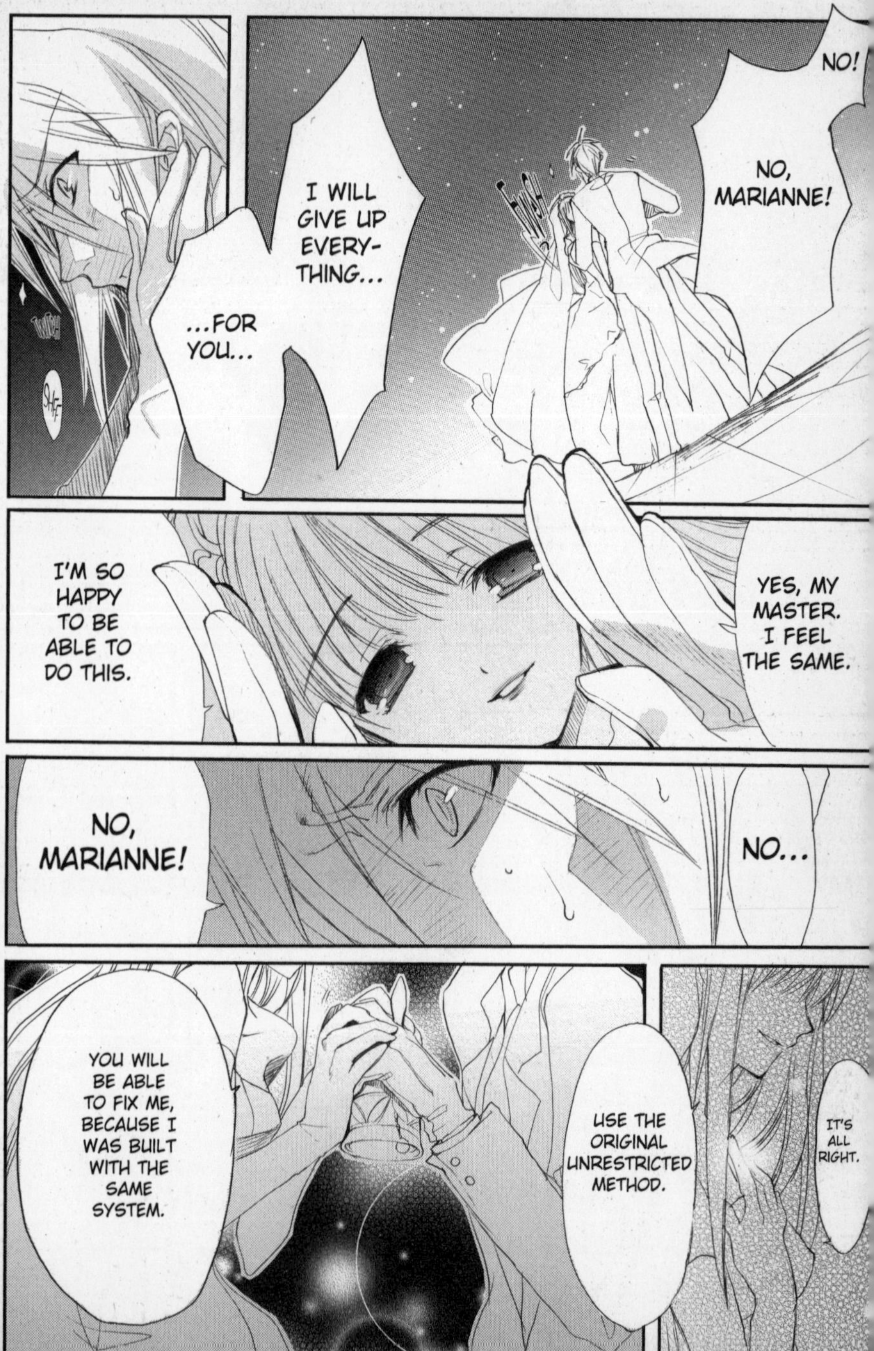
NO!
NO, MARIANNE!
I WILL GIVE UP EVERY-THING...
...FOR YOU...
TWITCH
SHFF
YES, MY MASTER. I FEEL THE SAME.
I'M SO HAPPY TO BE ABLE TO DO THIS.
NO...
NO, MARIANNE!
IT'S ALL RIGHT.
USE THE ORIGINAL UNRESTRICTED METHOD.
YOU WILL BE ABLE TO FIX ME, BECAUSE I WAS BUILT WITH THE SAME SYSTEM.

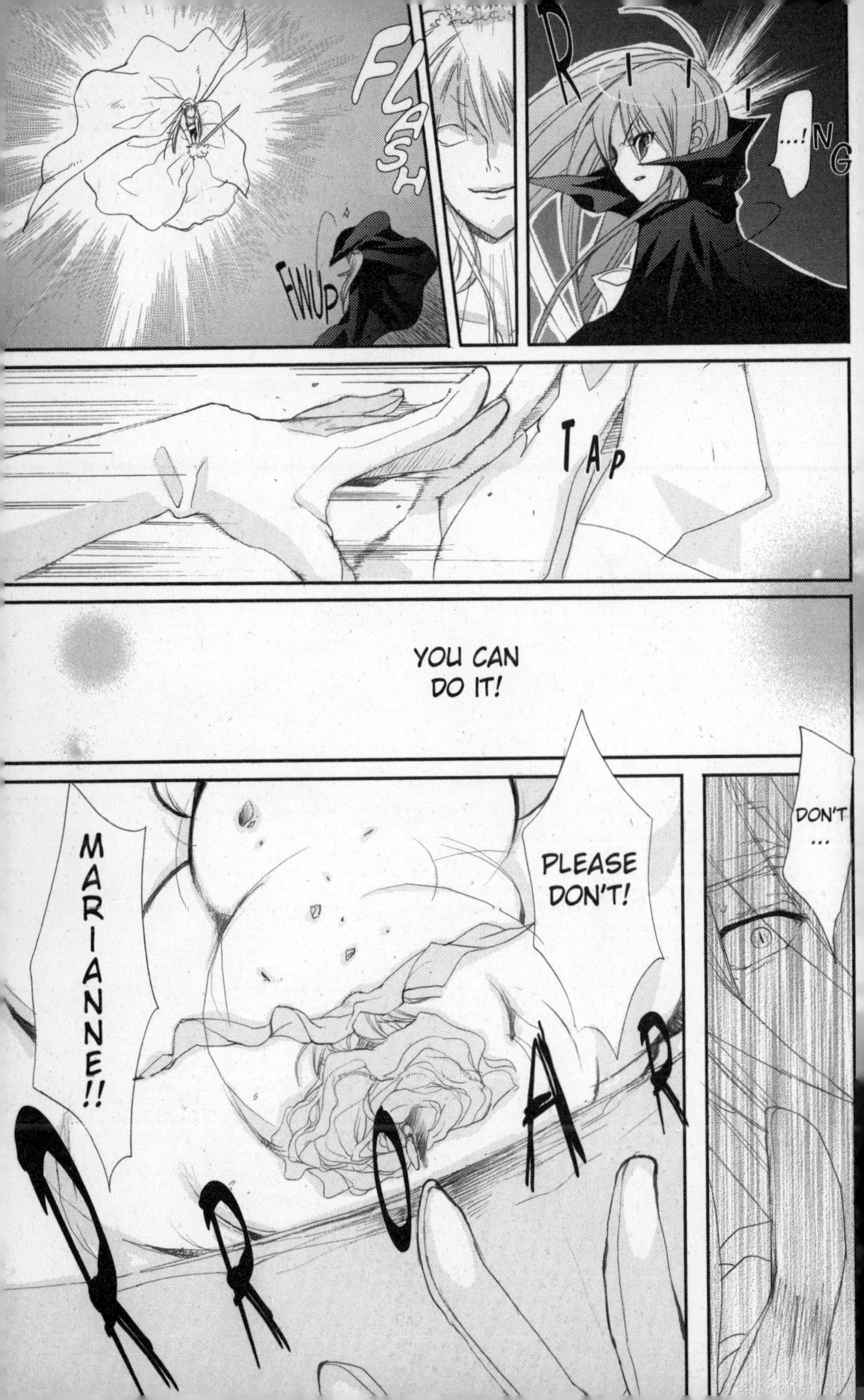
RIIING
...!
FLASH
FWUP
TAP
YOU CAN DO IT!
DON'T ...
PLEASE DON'T!
MARIANNE!!

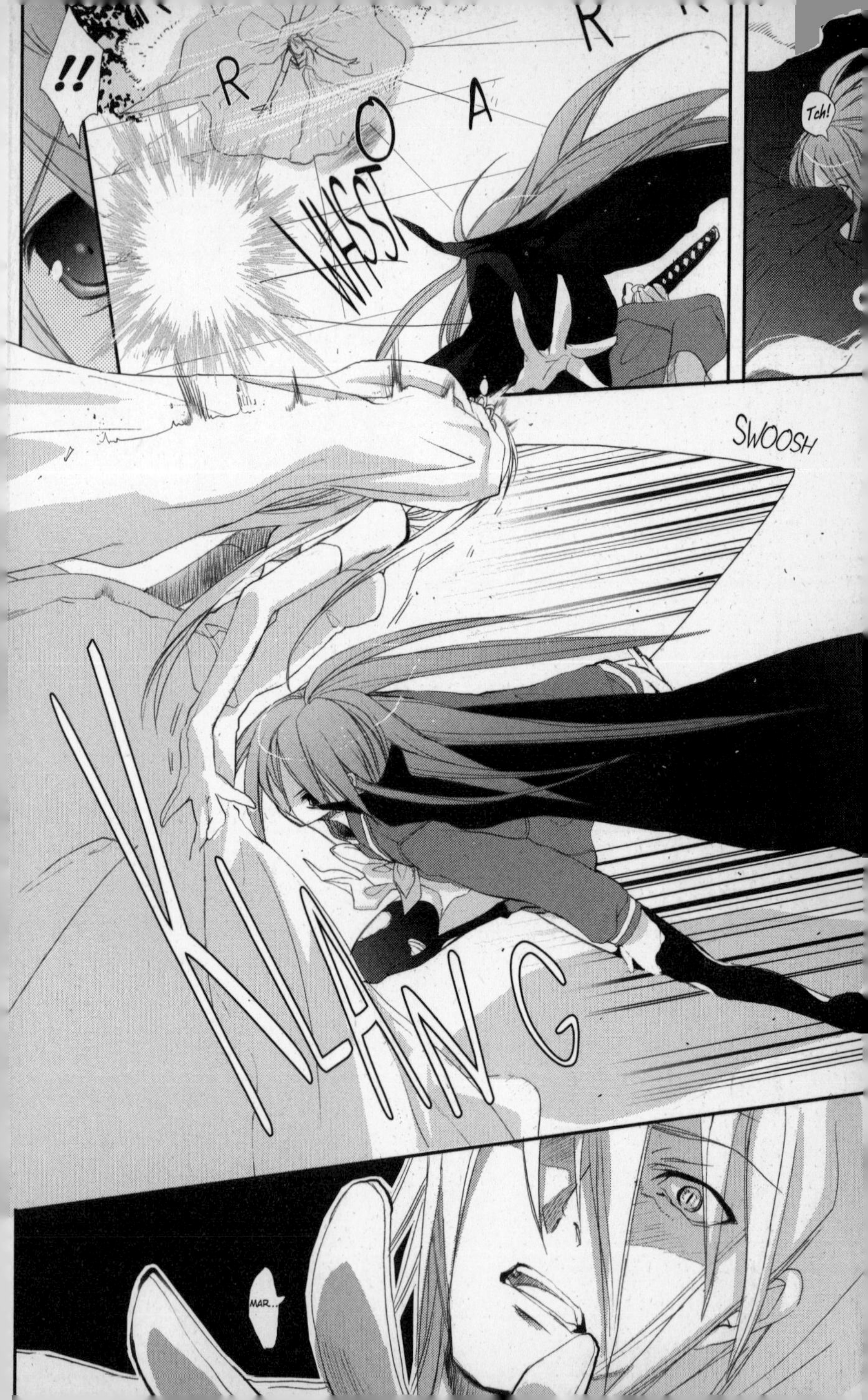
Tch!
!!
R O A R
WHSST
SWOOSH
KLANG
MAR...

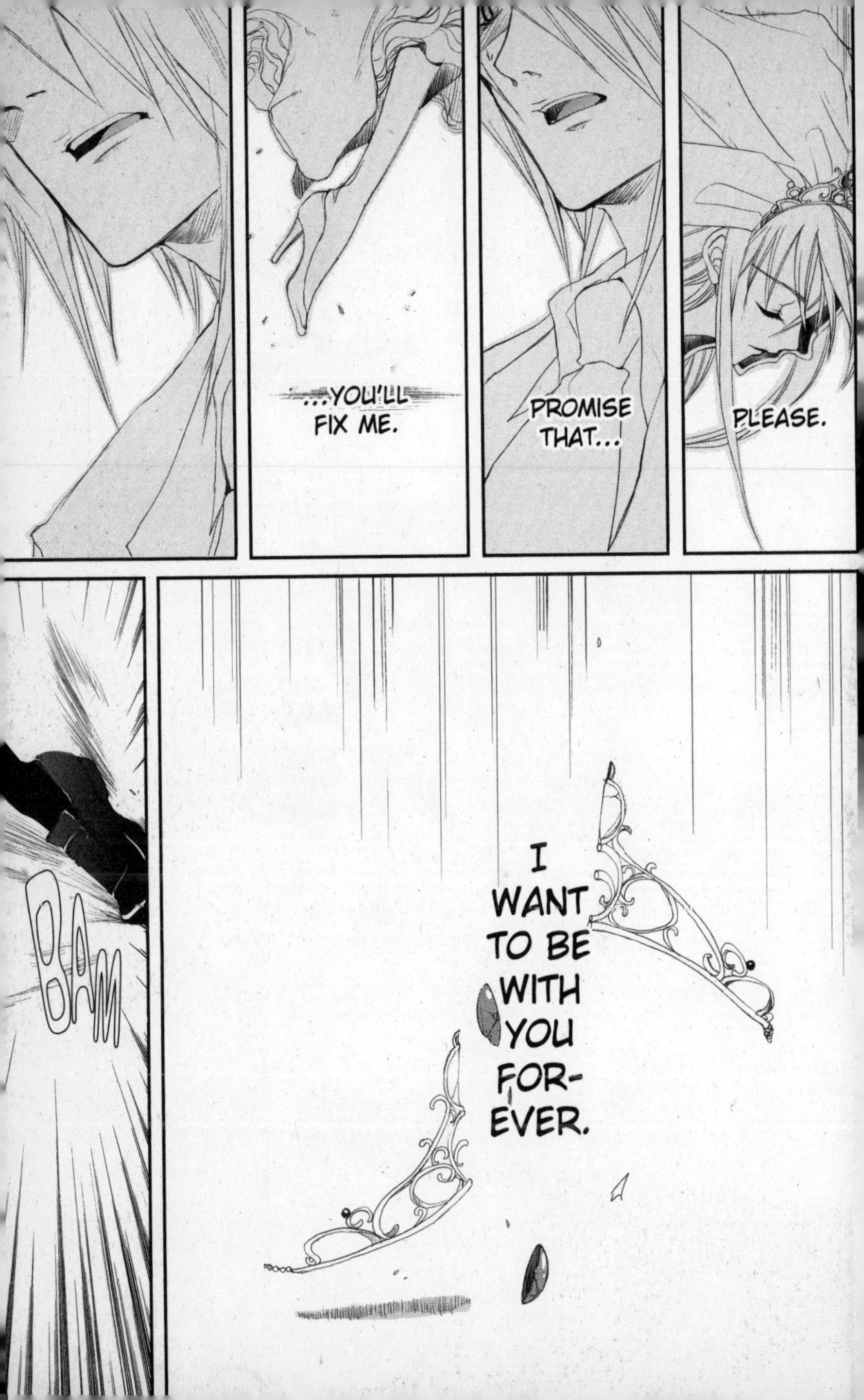
PLEASE.
PROMISE THAT...
...YOU'LL FIX ME.
I WANT TO BE WITH YOU FOR-EVER.
BAM

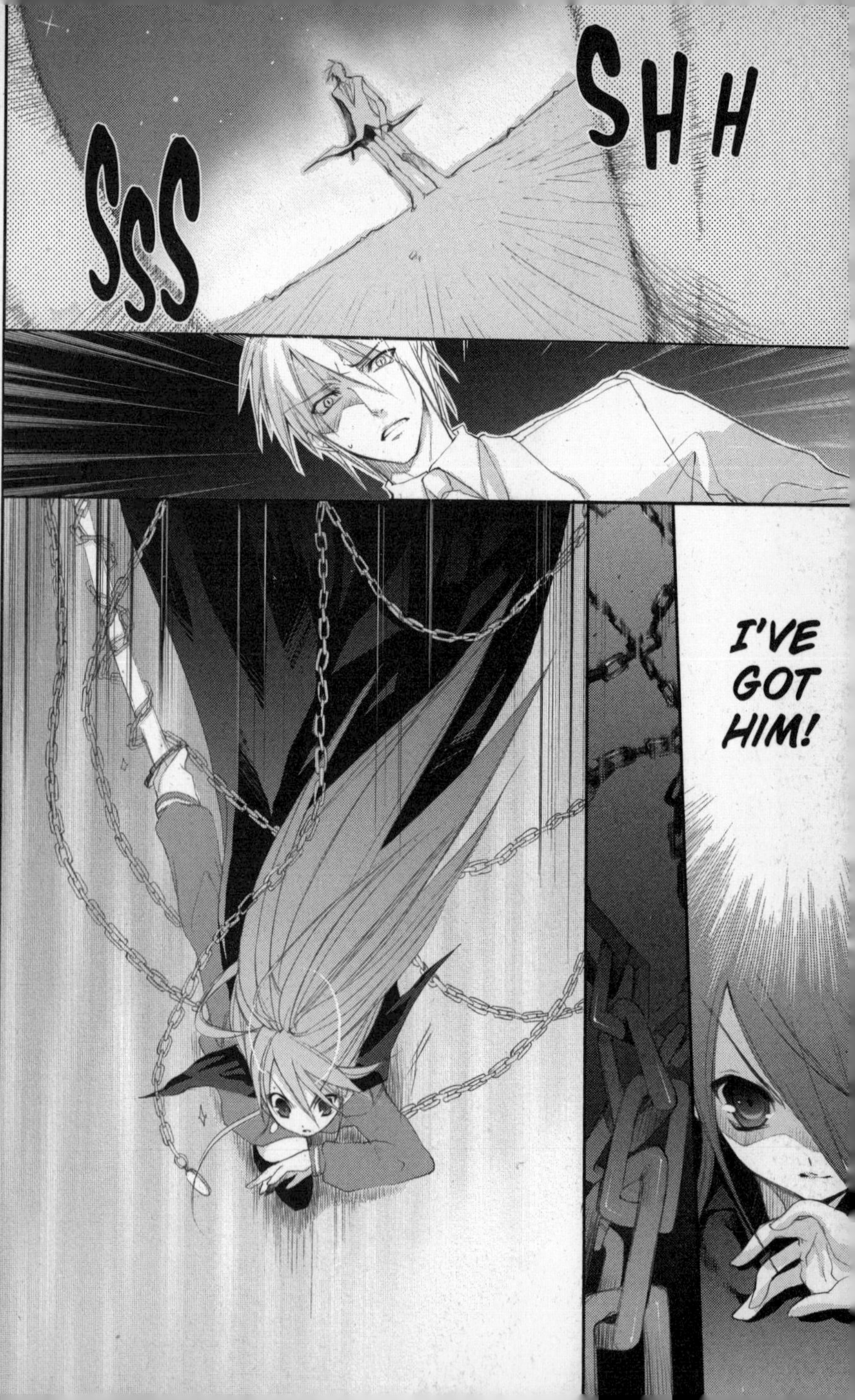
SHH
SSS
I'VE GOT HIM!

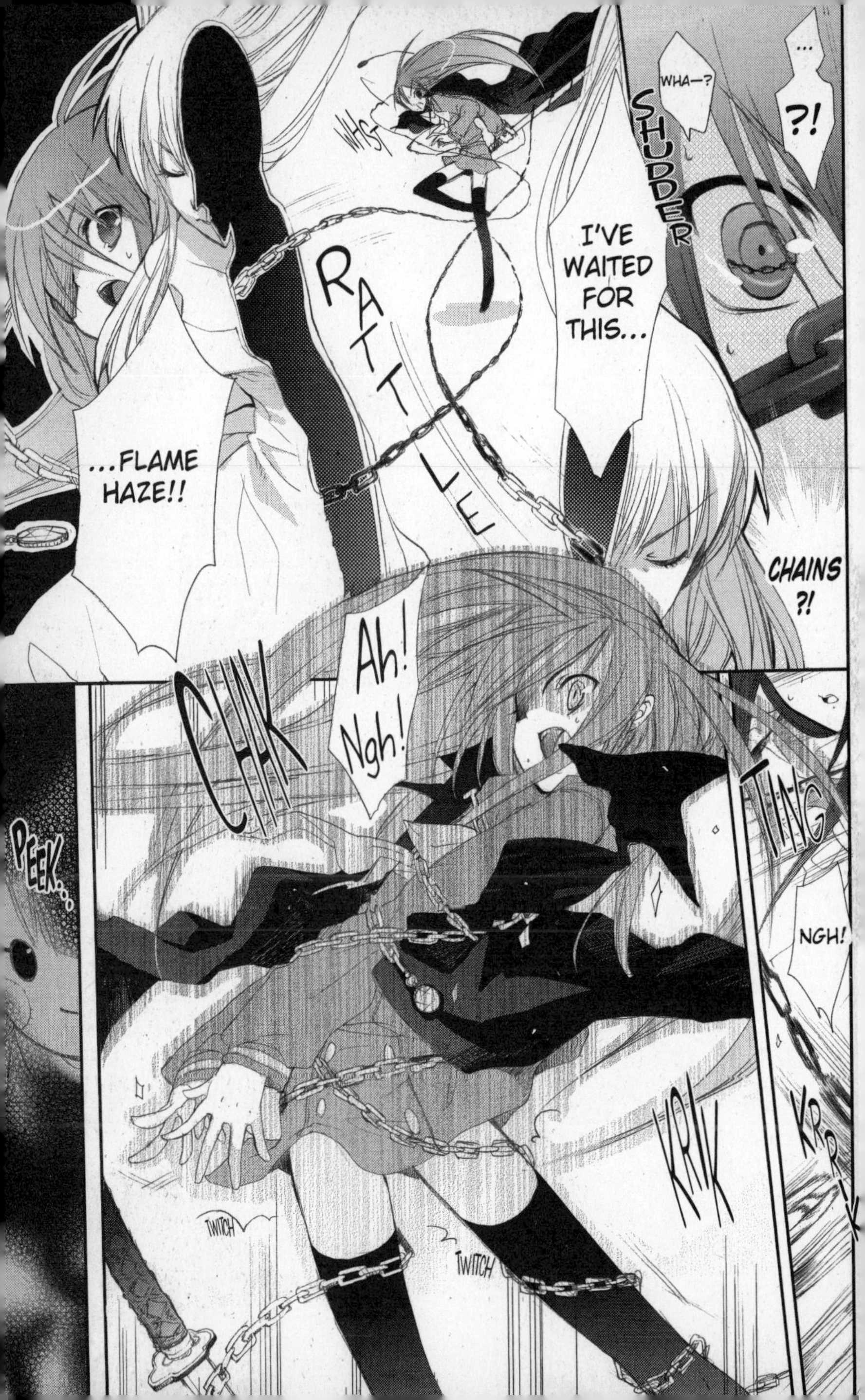
...
?!
WHA—?
SHUDDER
CHAINS ?!
I'VE WAITED FOR THIS...
WHST
RATTLE
...FLAME HAZE!!
TING
NGH!
KRRRIK
Ah! Ngh!
CHK
KRIK
TWITCH
TWITCH
PEEK...

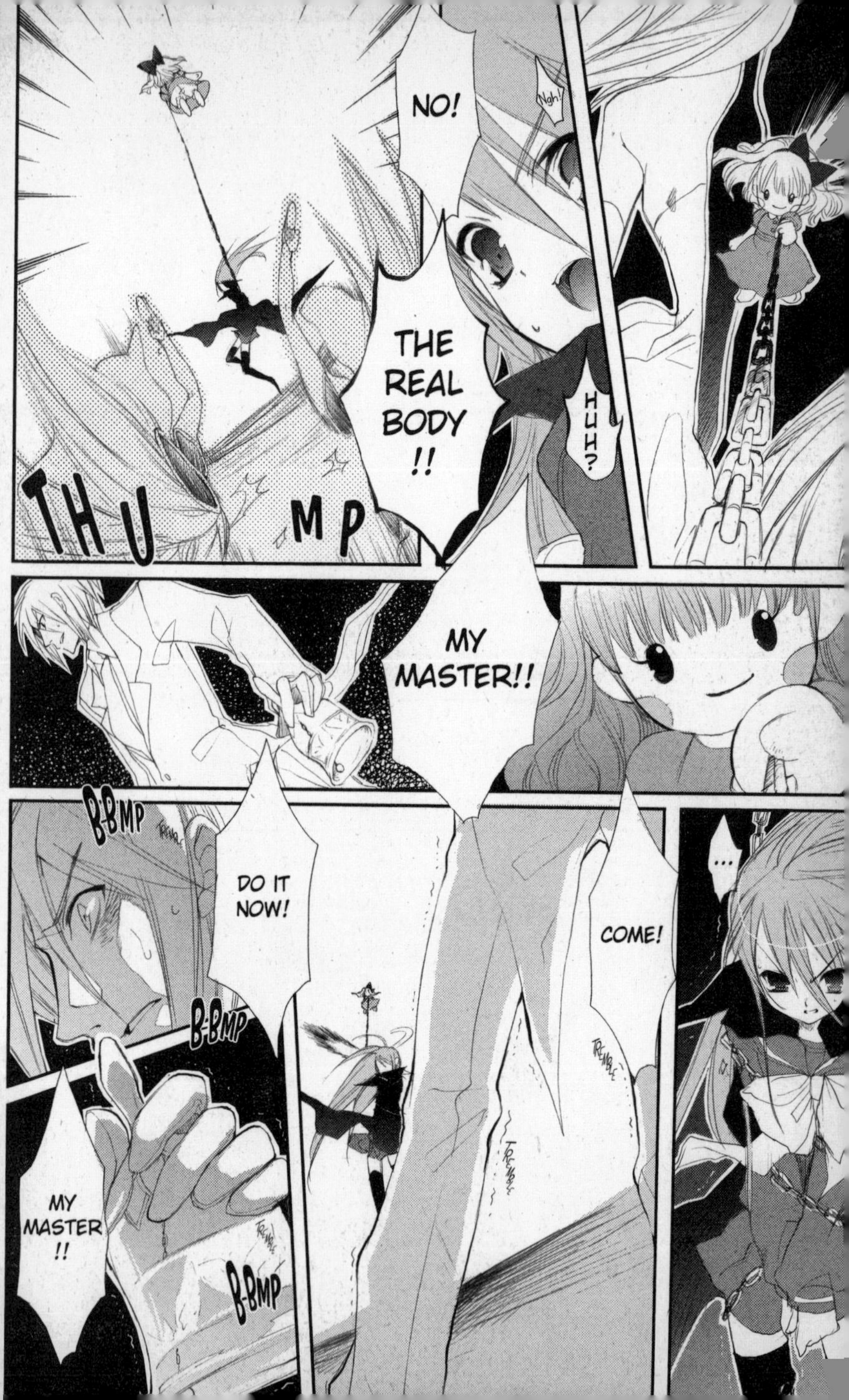

Ngh!
NO!
THE REAL BODY !!
HUH?
THUMP
MY MASTER!!
...
COME!
TREMBLE
DO IT NOW!
TREMBLE
B-BMP
TREMBLE
B-BMP
MY MASTER !!
TREMBLE
B-BMP

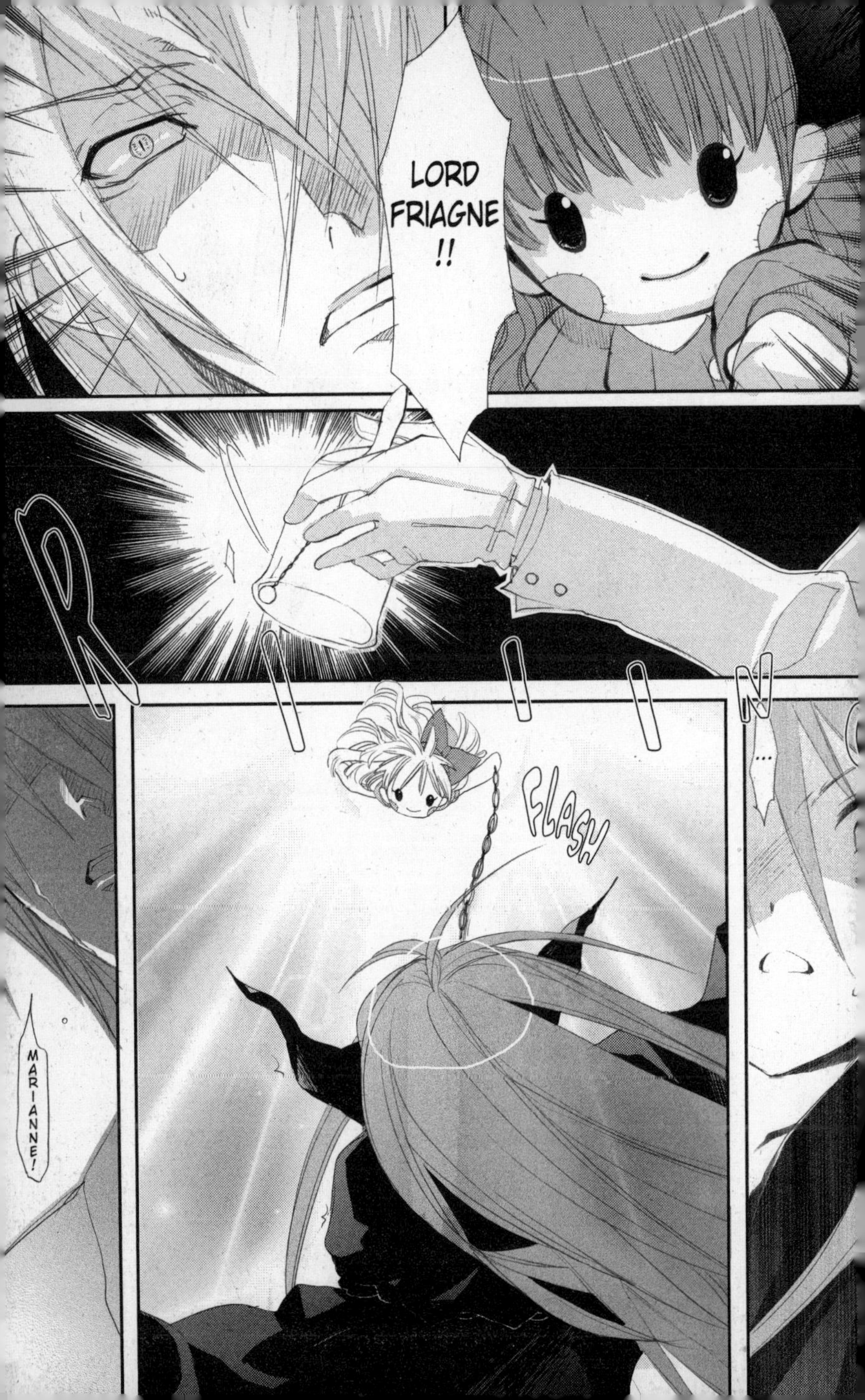
LORD FRIAGNE !!
RIIIIN
FLASH
...
MARIANNE!

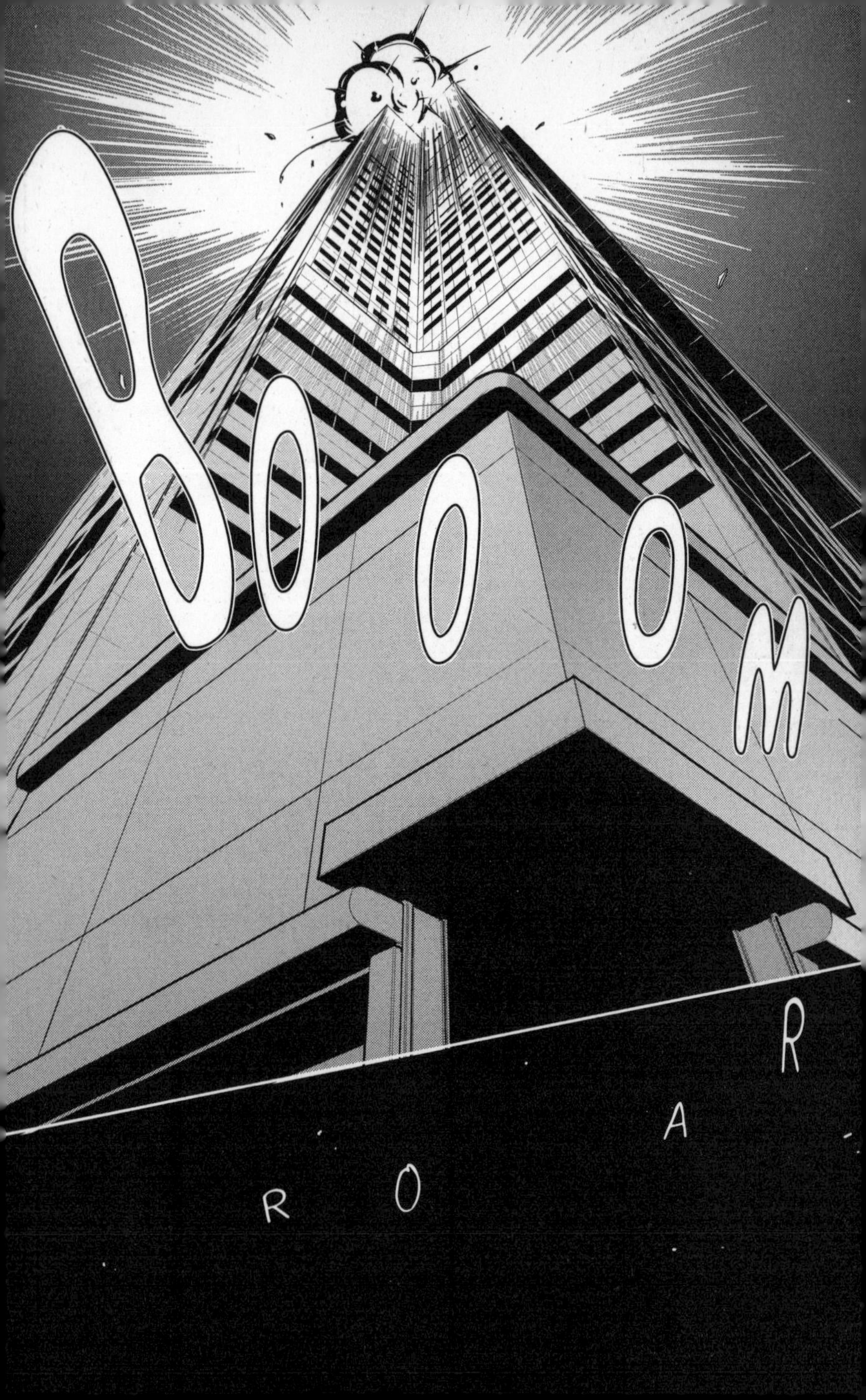
BOOOM
ROAR

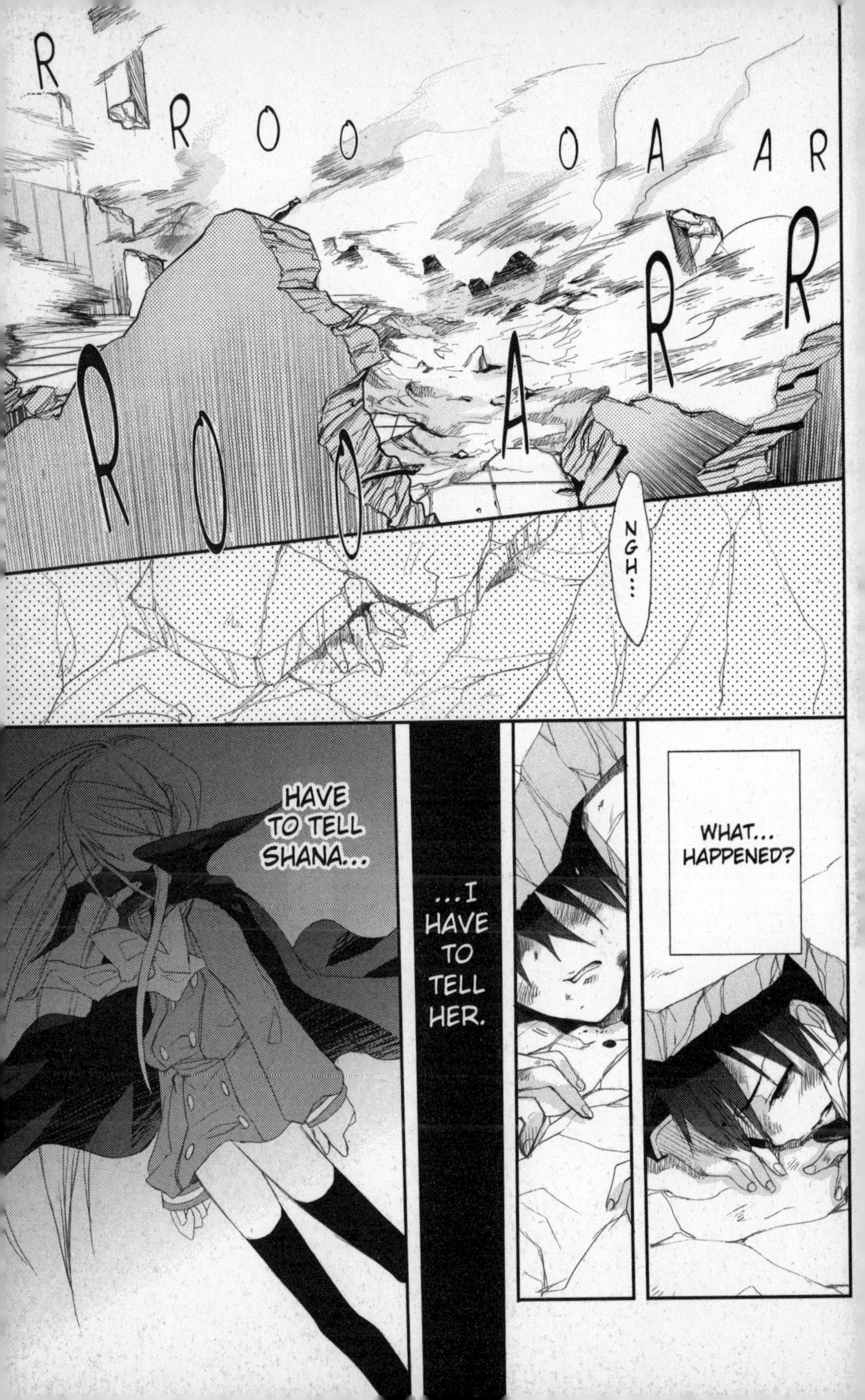
RROOOOAAR
ROOAARR
NGH...
WHAT... HAPPENED?
...I HAVE TO TELL HER.
HAVE TO TELL SHANA...

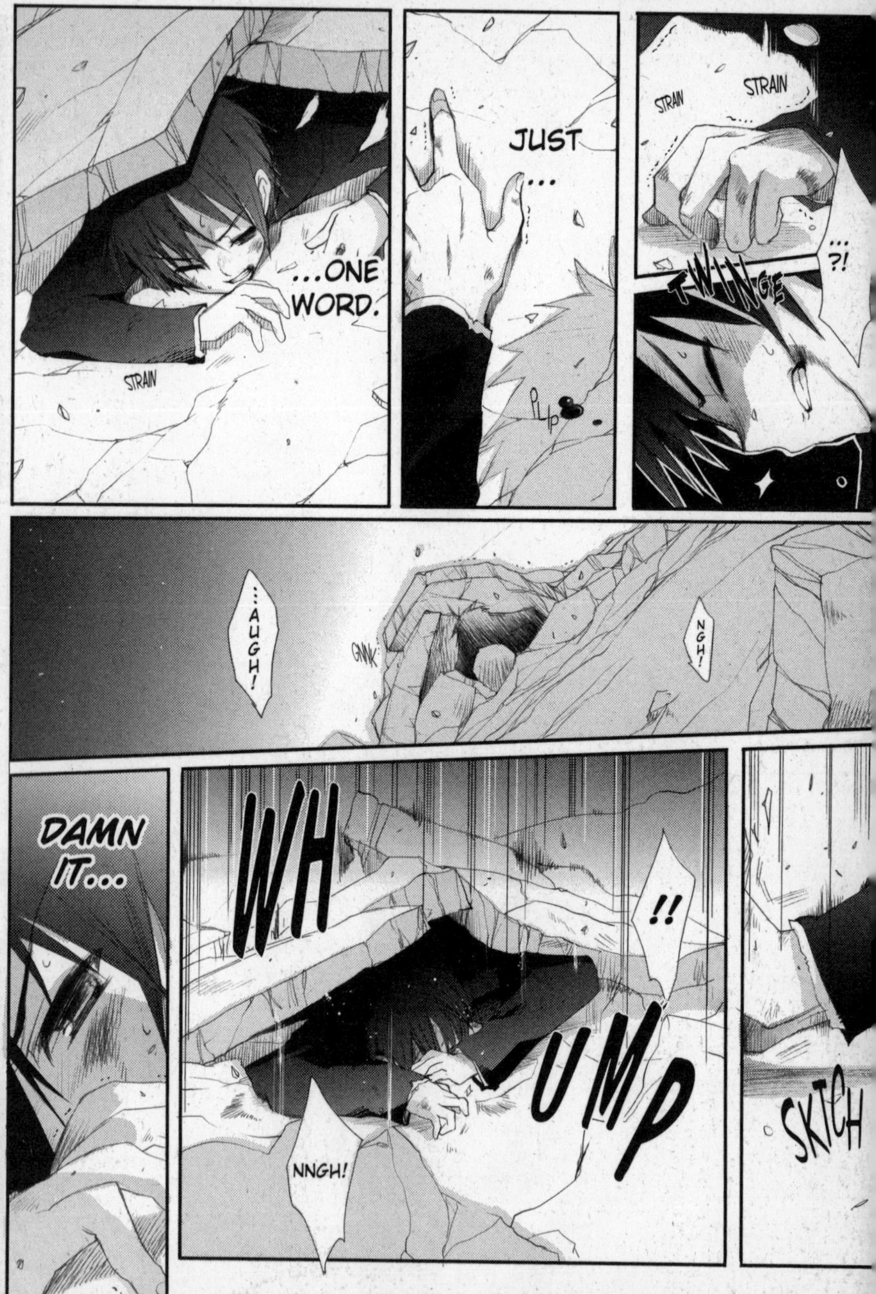
STRAIN
STRAIN
...?!
TWINGE
JUST...
PLIP
...ONE WORD.
STRAIN
NGH!
GNNK
...AUGH!
SKTCH
!!
WHUMP
NNGH!
DAMN IT...

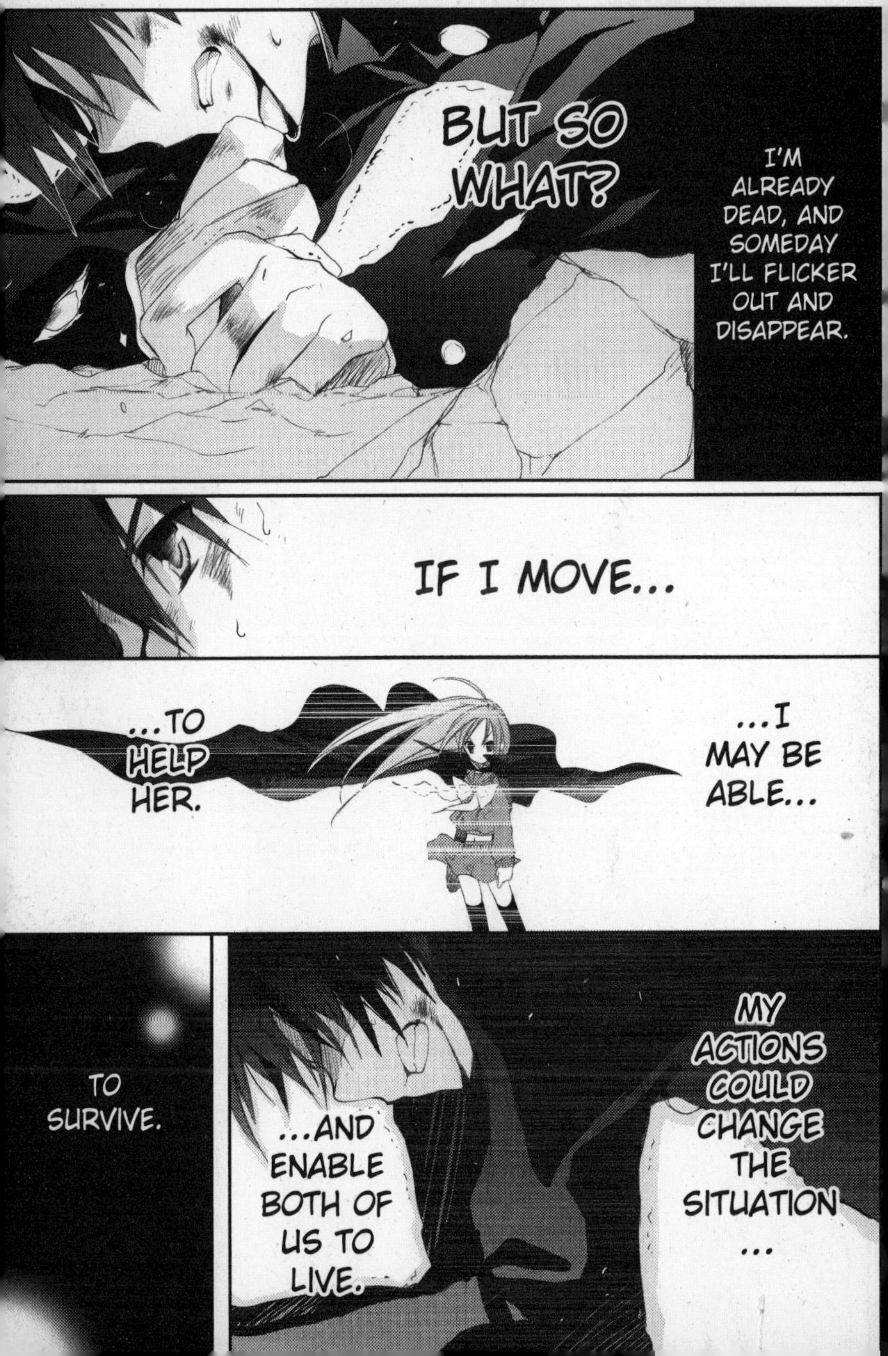
I'M ALREADY DEAD, AND SOMEDAY I'LL FLICKER OUT AND DISAPPEAR.
BUT SO WHAT?
IF I MOVE...
...I MAY BE ABLE...
...TO HELP HER.
MY ACTIONS COULD CHANGE THE SITUATION ...
...AND ENABLE BOTH OF US TO LIVE.
TO SURVIVE.

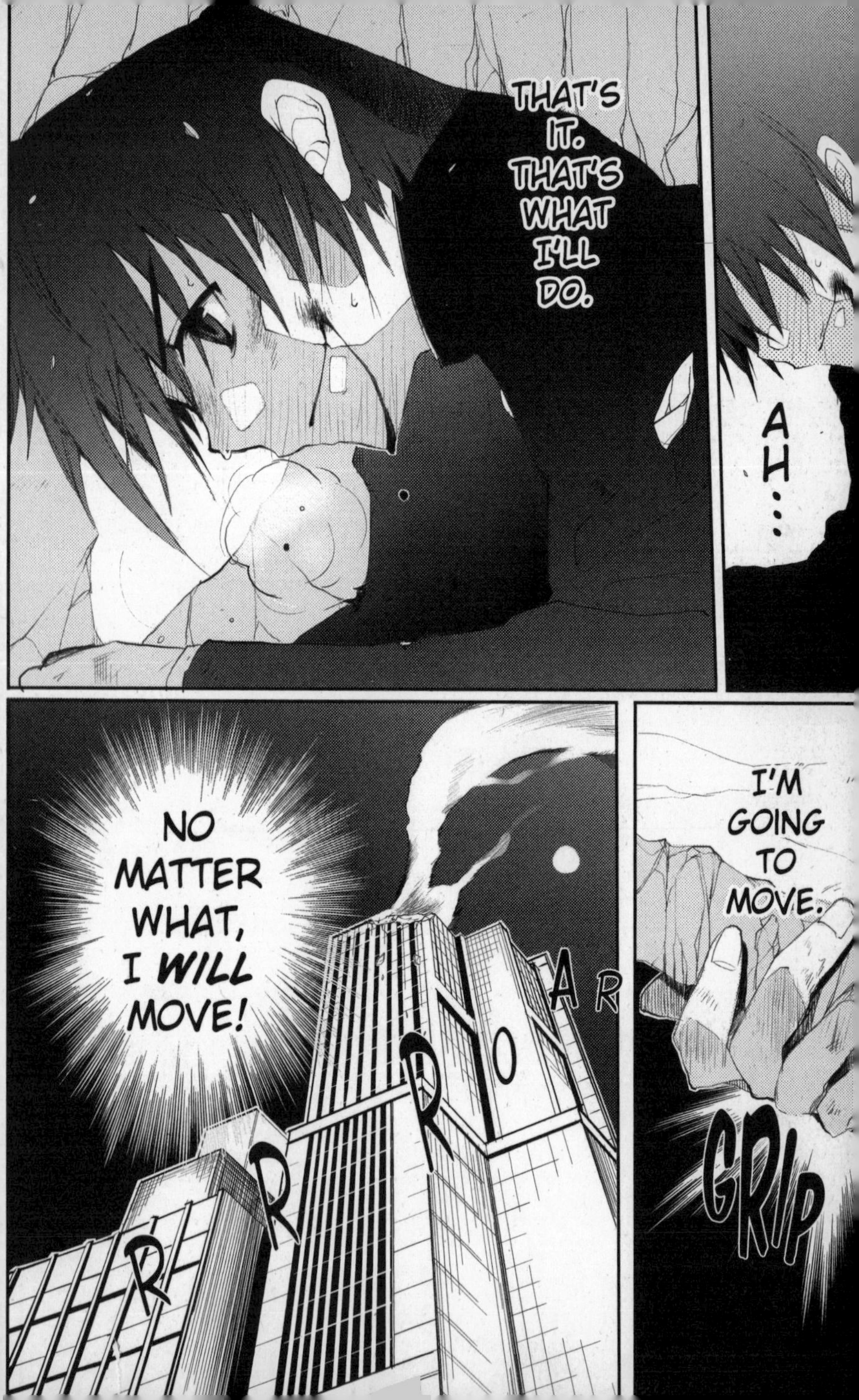
AH...
THAT'S IT. THAT'S WHAT I'LL DO.
I'M GOING TO MOVE.
GRIP
NO MATTER WHAT, I *WILL* MOVE!
RRRROAR

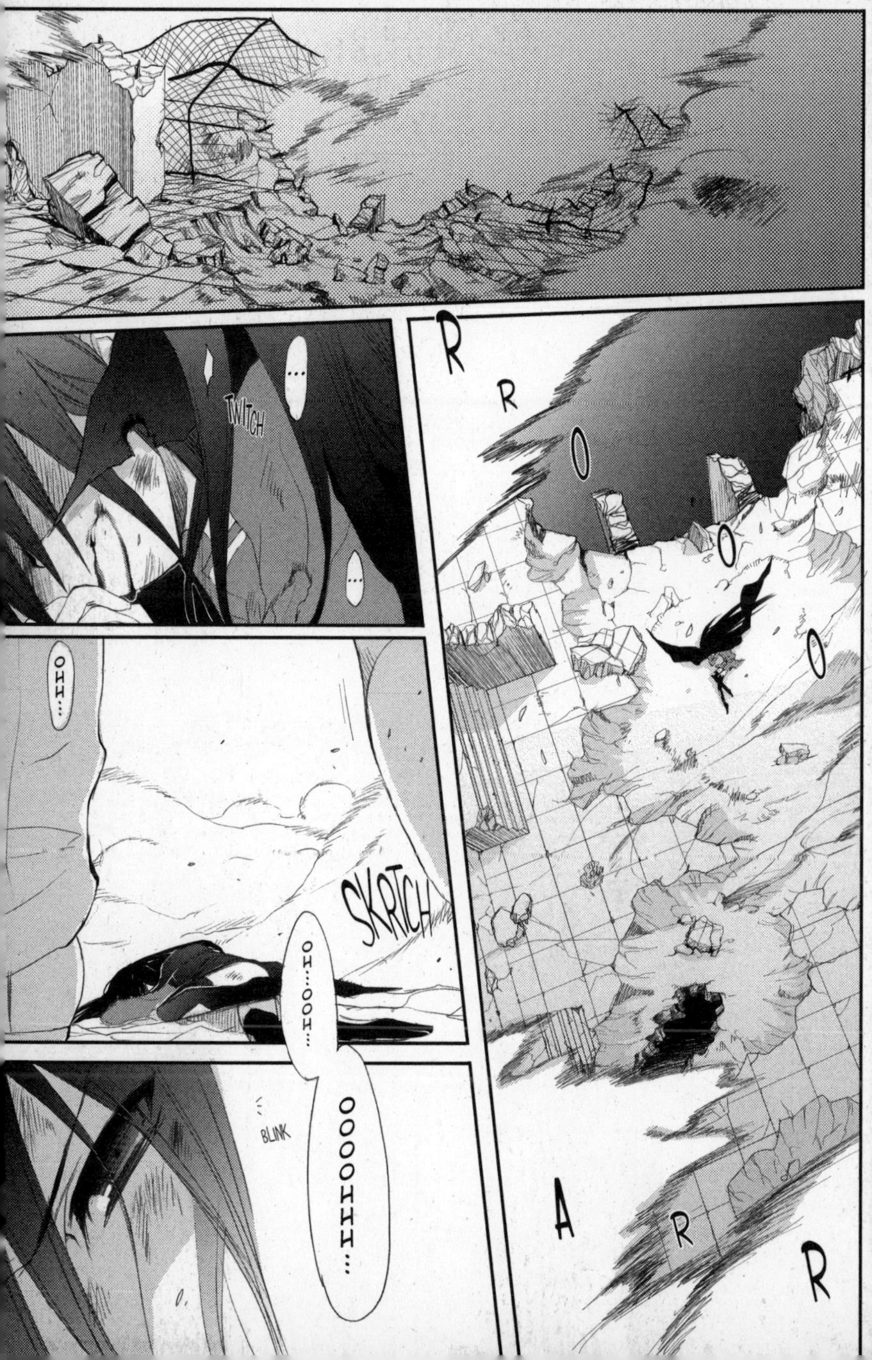

...
TWITCH
...
RROOOO
ARRR
OHH...
SKRTCH
OH...OOH...
OOOOHHH...
BLINK

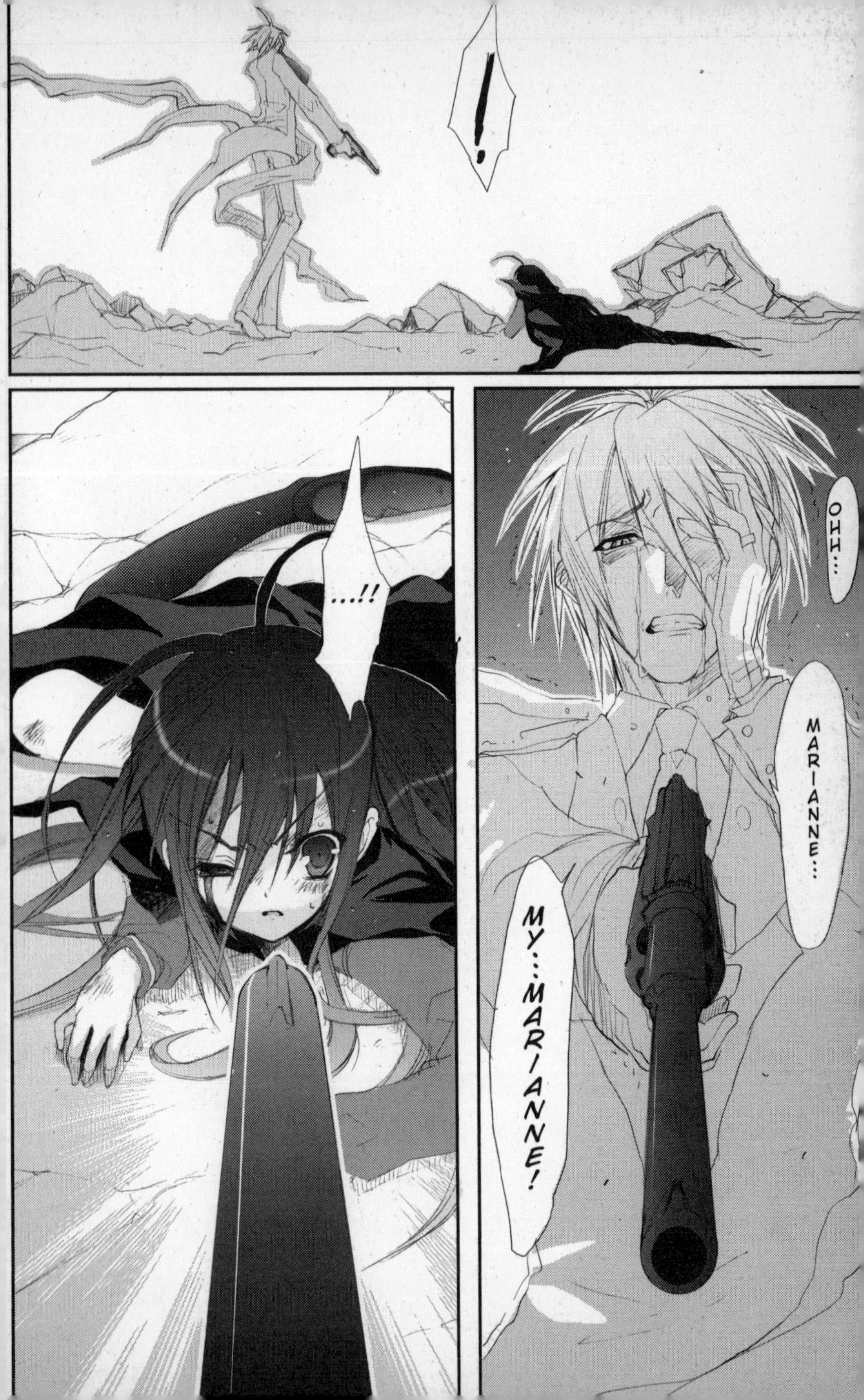
!
OHH...
MARIANNE...
MY...MARIANNE!
...!!

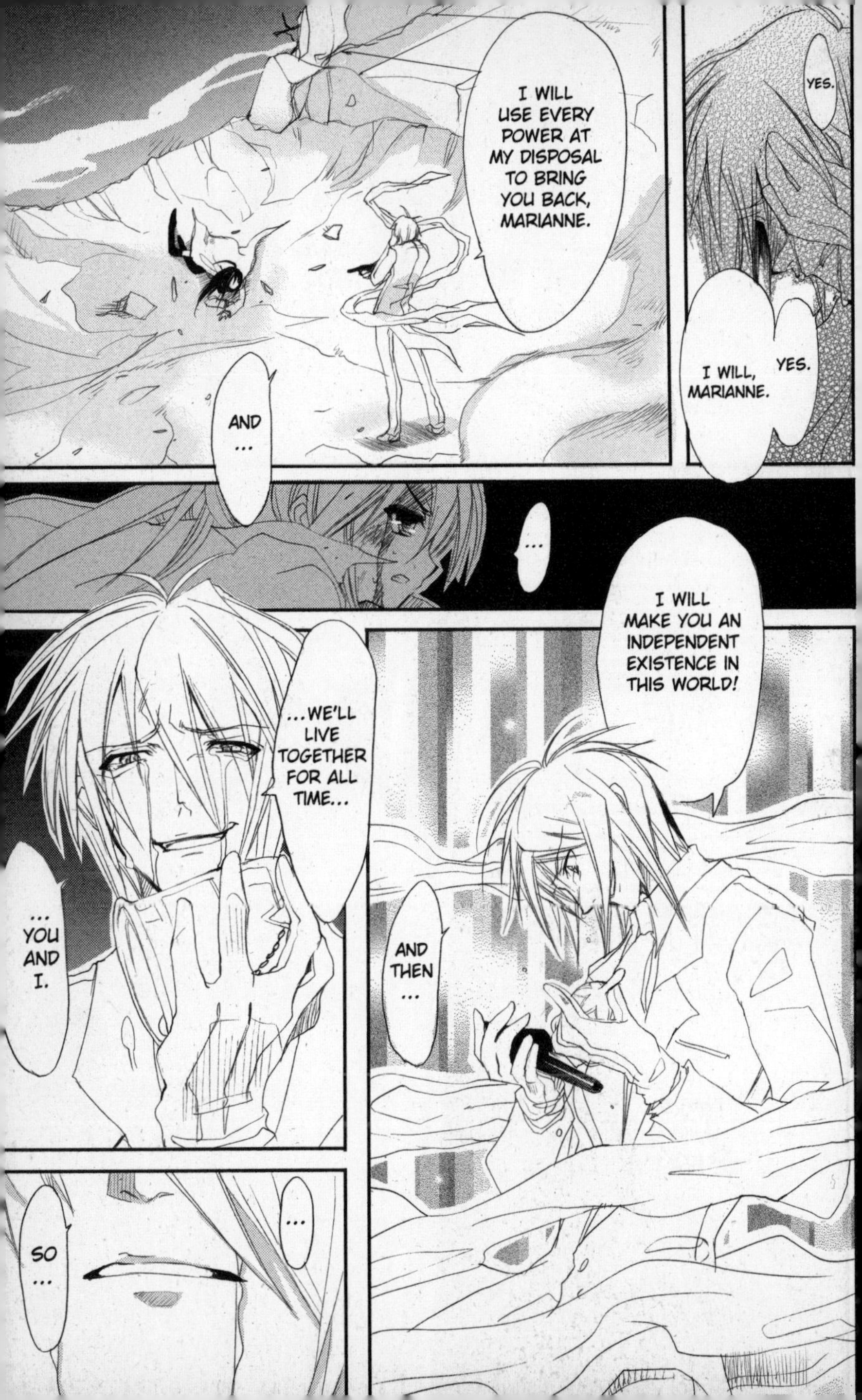
YES.
YES.
I WILL, MARIANNE.
I WILL USE EVERY POWER AT MY DISPOSAL TO BRING YOU BACK, MARIANNE.
AND ...
...
I WILL MAKE YOU AN INDEPENDENT EXISTENCE IN THIS WORLD!
AND THEN ...
...WE'LL LIVE TOGETHER FOR ALL TIME...
... YOU AND I.
...
SO ...

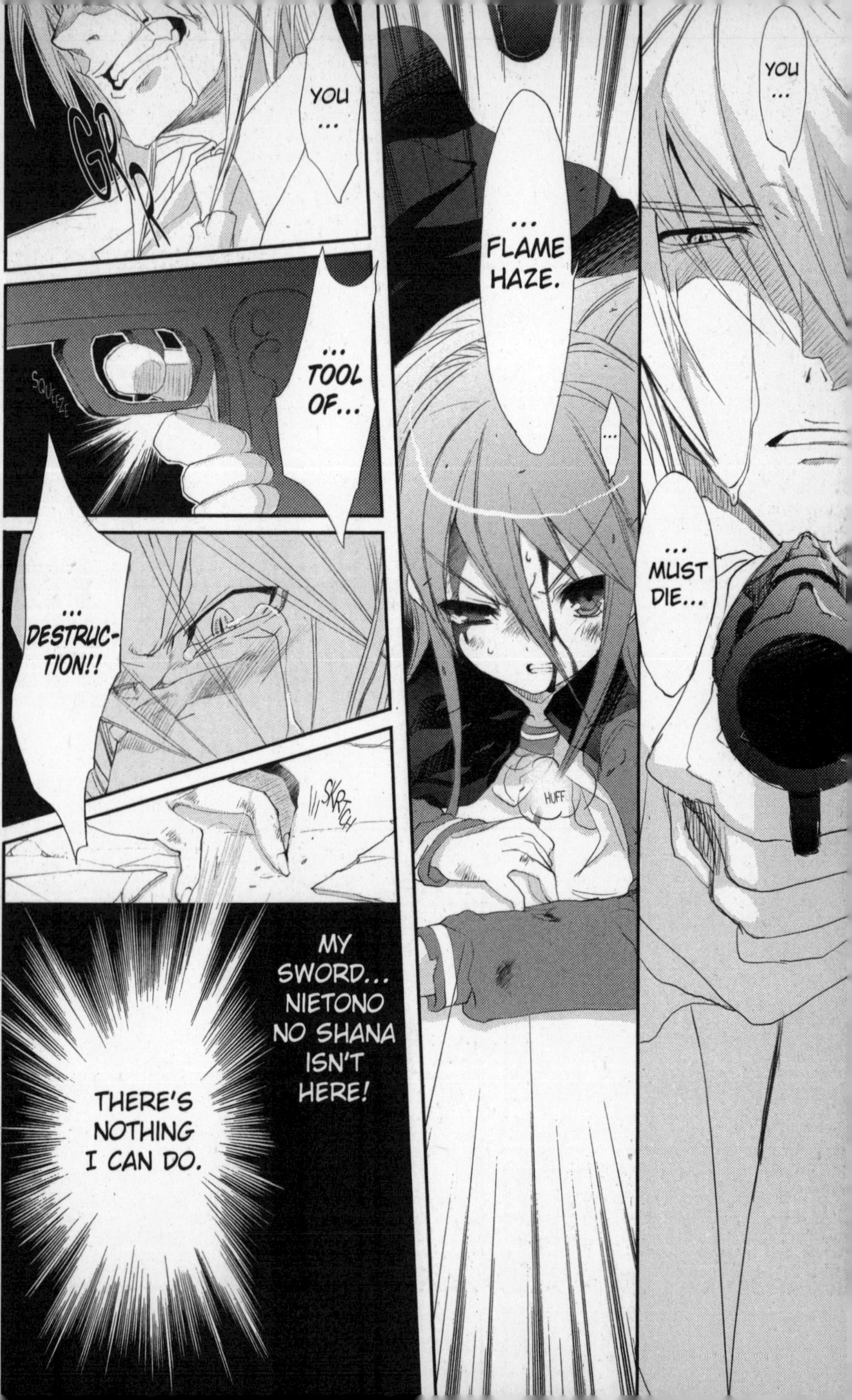
YOU ...
... MUST DIE...
... FLAME HAZE.
...
HUFF
YOU ...
... TOOL OF...
SQUEEZE
... DESTRUCTION!!
SKRTCH
MY SWORD... NIETONO NO SHANA ISN'T HERE!
THERE'S NOTHING I CAN DO.

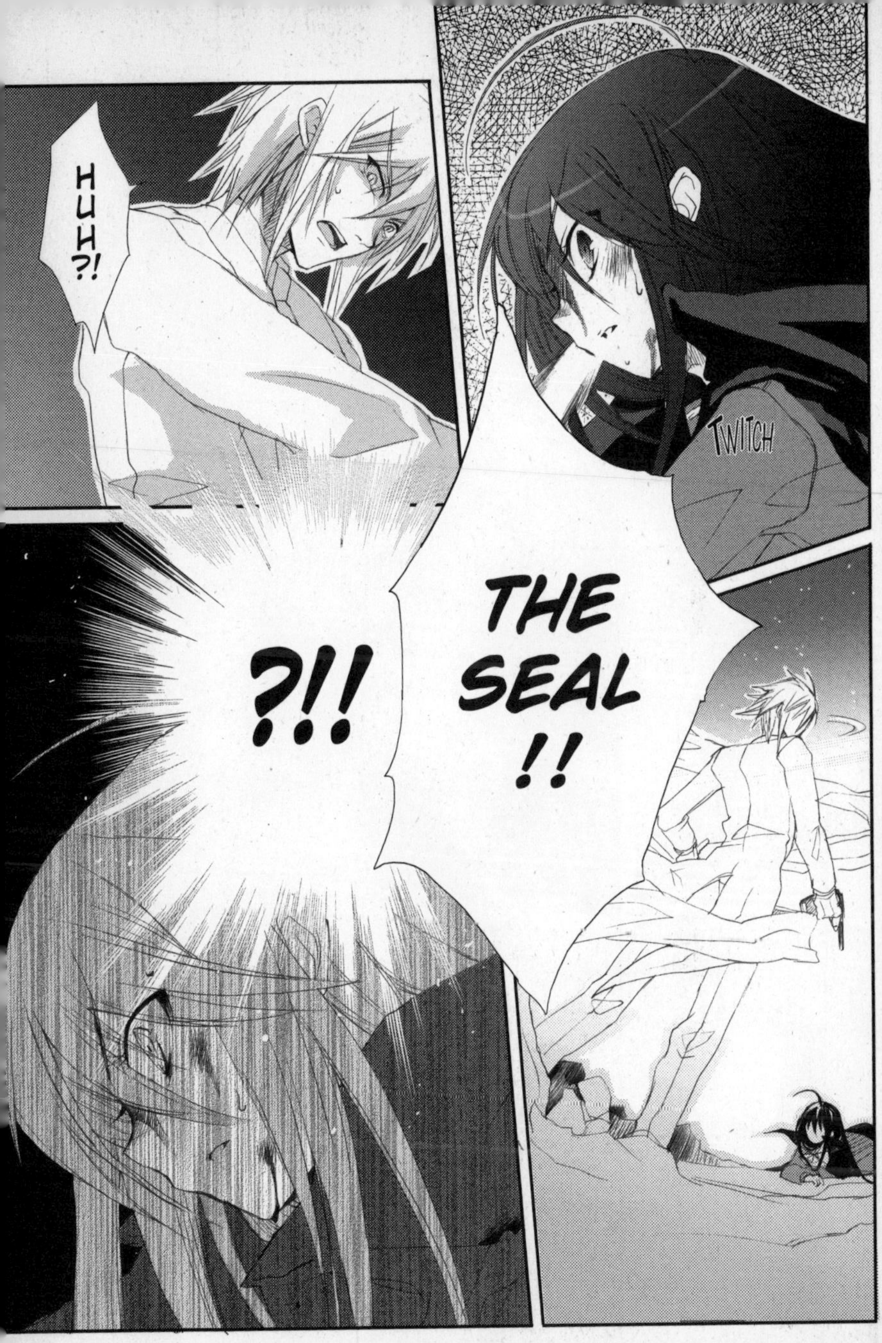
TWITCH
HUH?!
THE SEAL !!
?!!

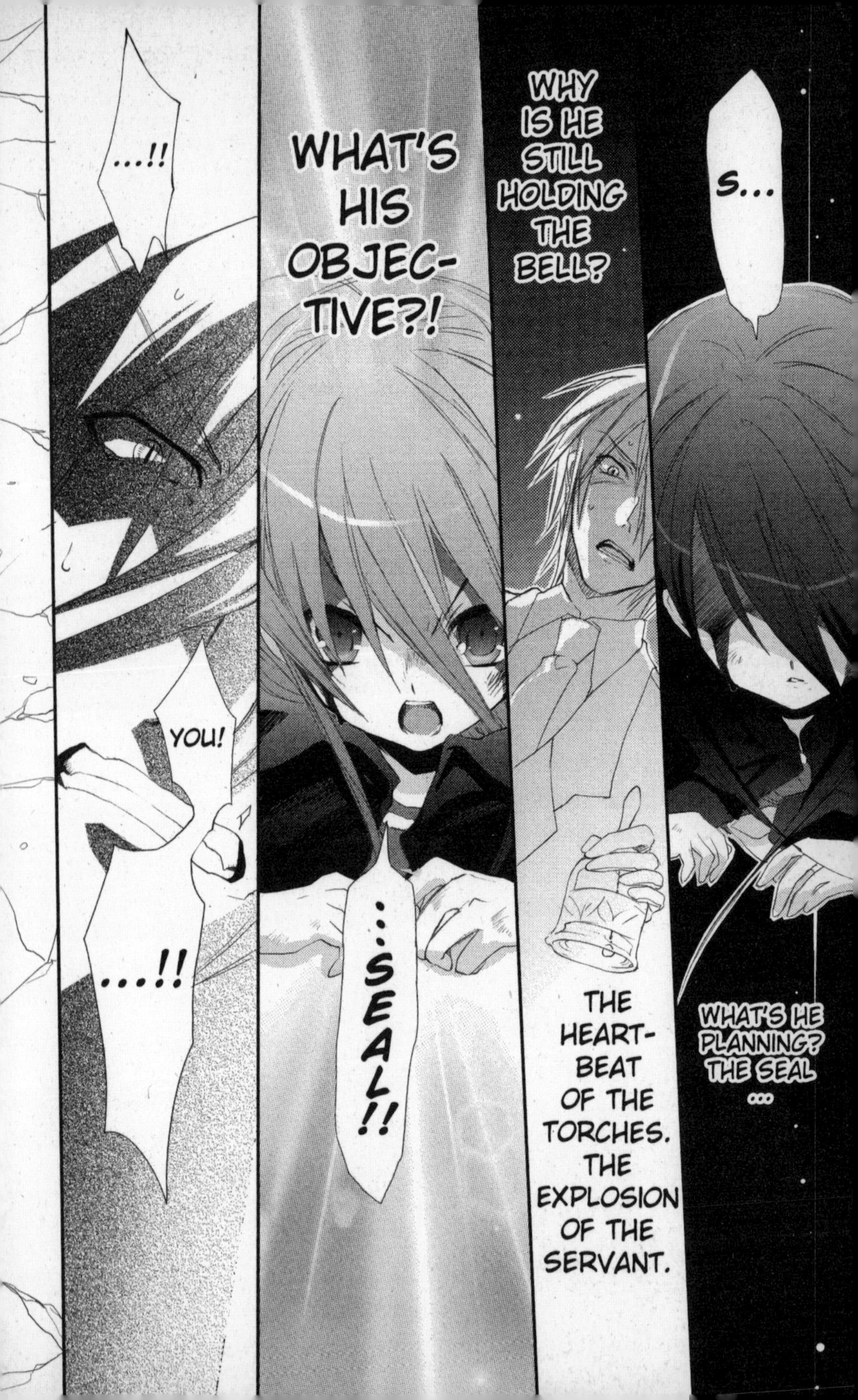
S...
WHAT'S HE PLANNING? THE SEAL ...
WHY IS HE STILL HOLDING THE BELL?
THE HEART-BEAT OF THE TORCHES. THE EXPLOSION OF THE SERVANT.
WHAT'S HIS OBJEC-TIVE?!
...SEAL!!
...!!
YOU!
...!!

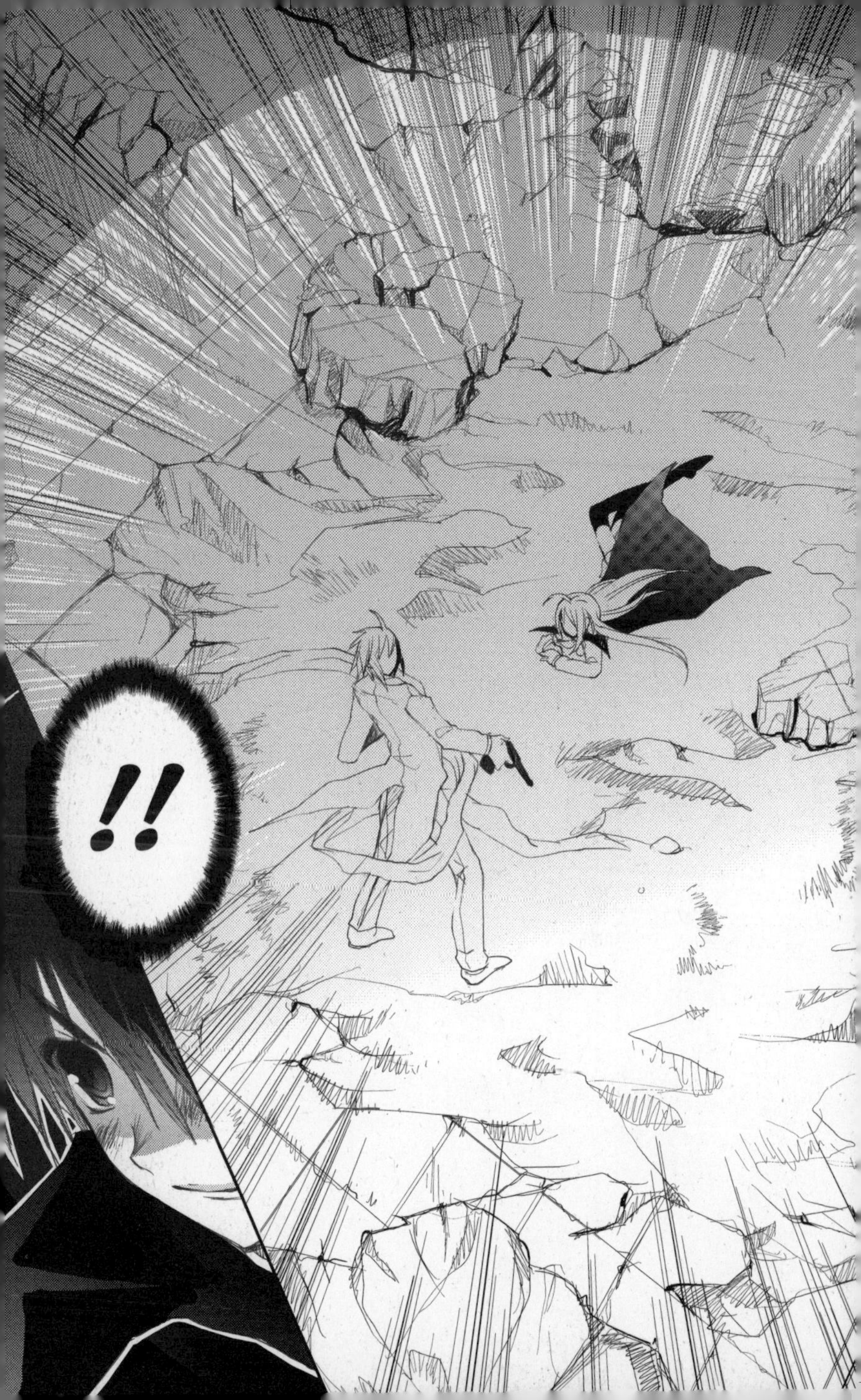
!!

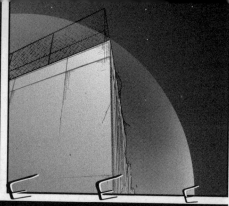

SKREEEE

SKR EEE

NOW THE SOUND OF HIS BELL

IT CAN'T BE!

A

R

A

R

74

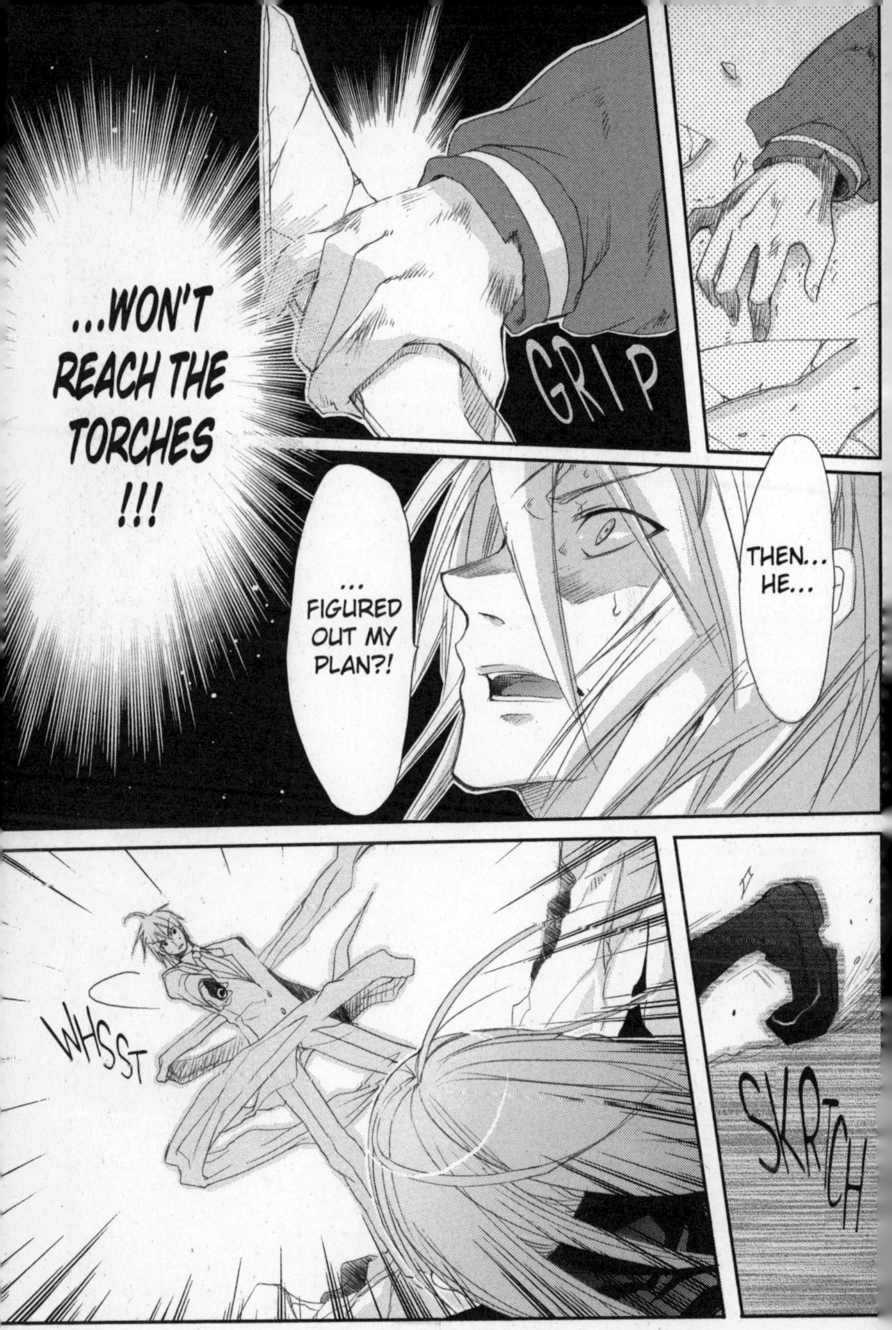
GRIP
...WON'T REACH THE TORCHES!!!
THEN... HE...
...FIGURED OUT MY PLAN?!
SKRTCH
WHSST

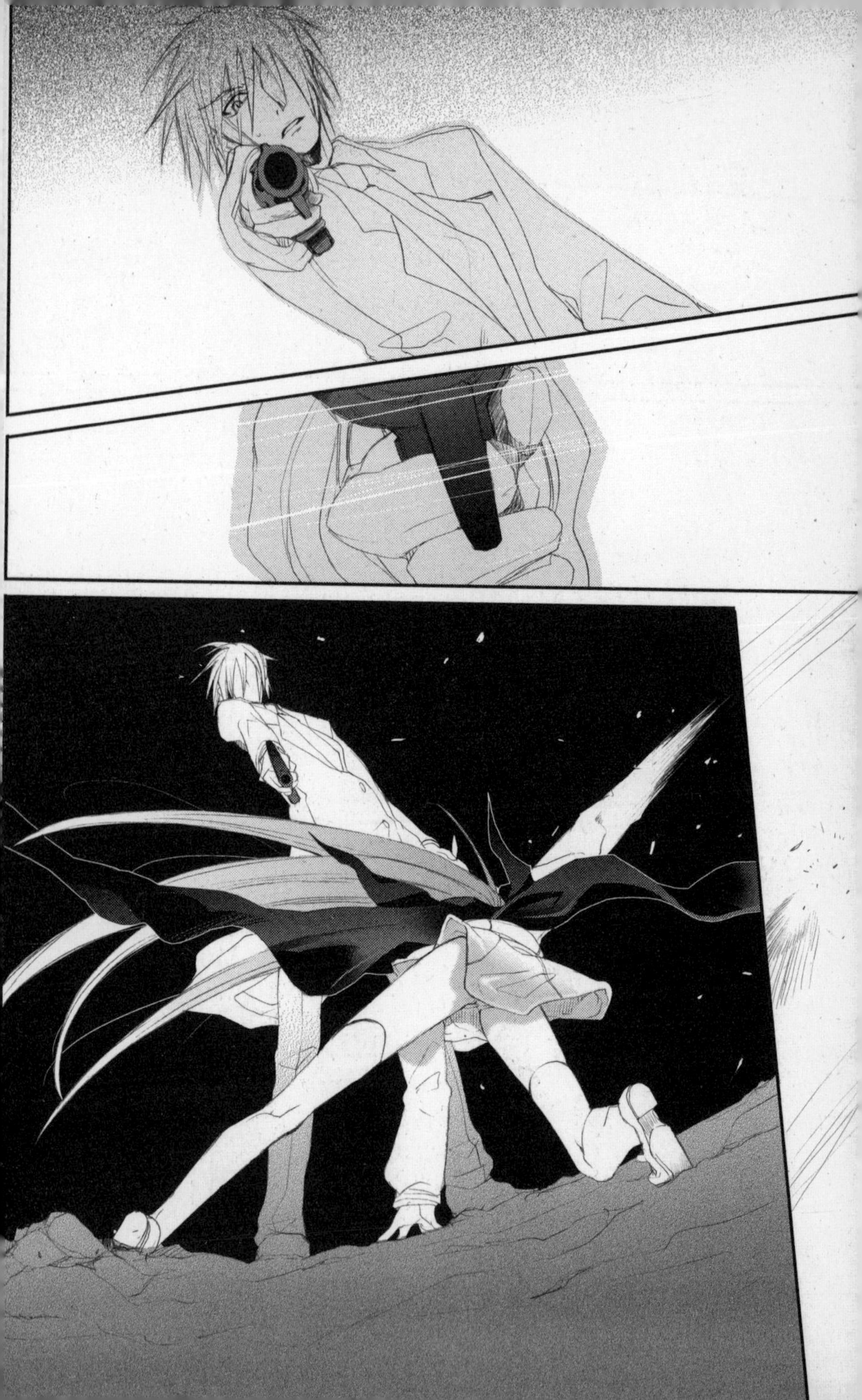

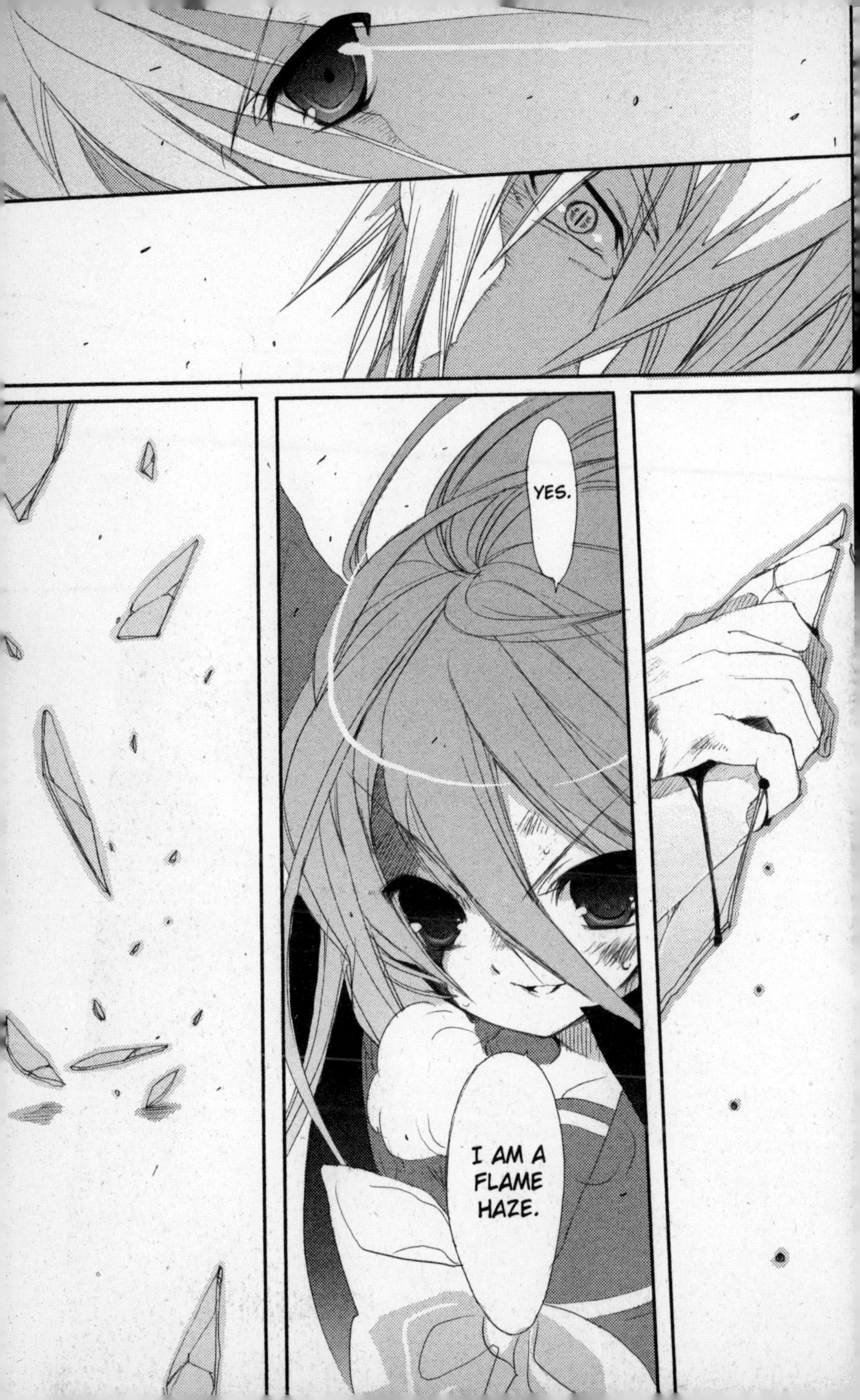
YES.
I AM A FLAME HAZE.

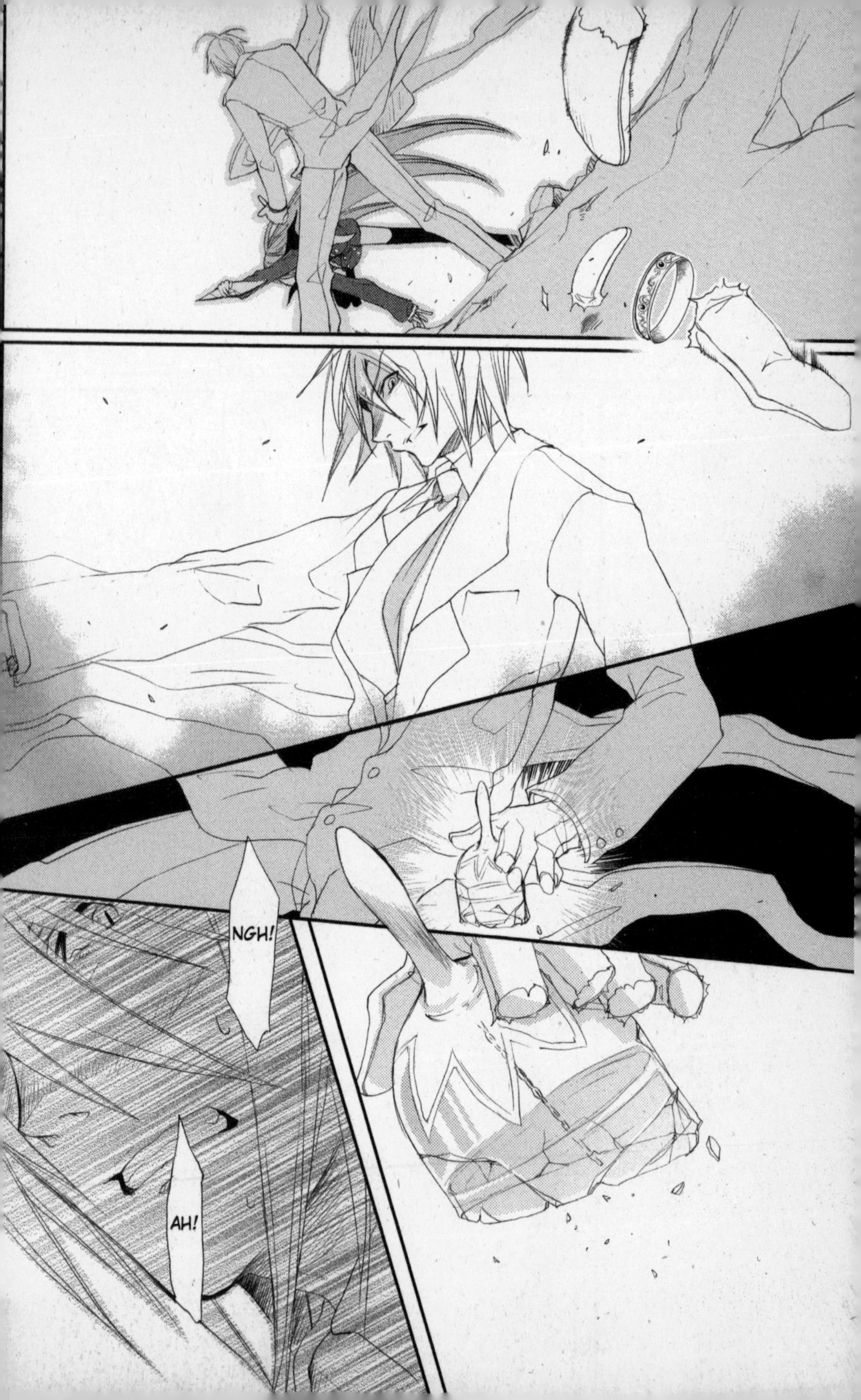
NGH!
AH!

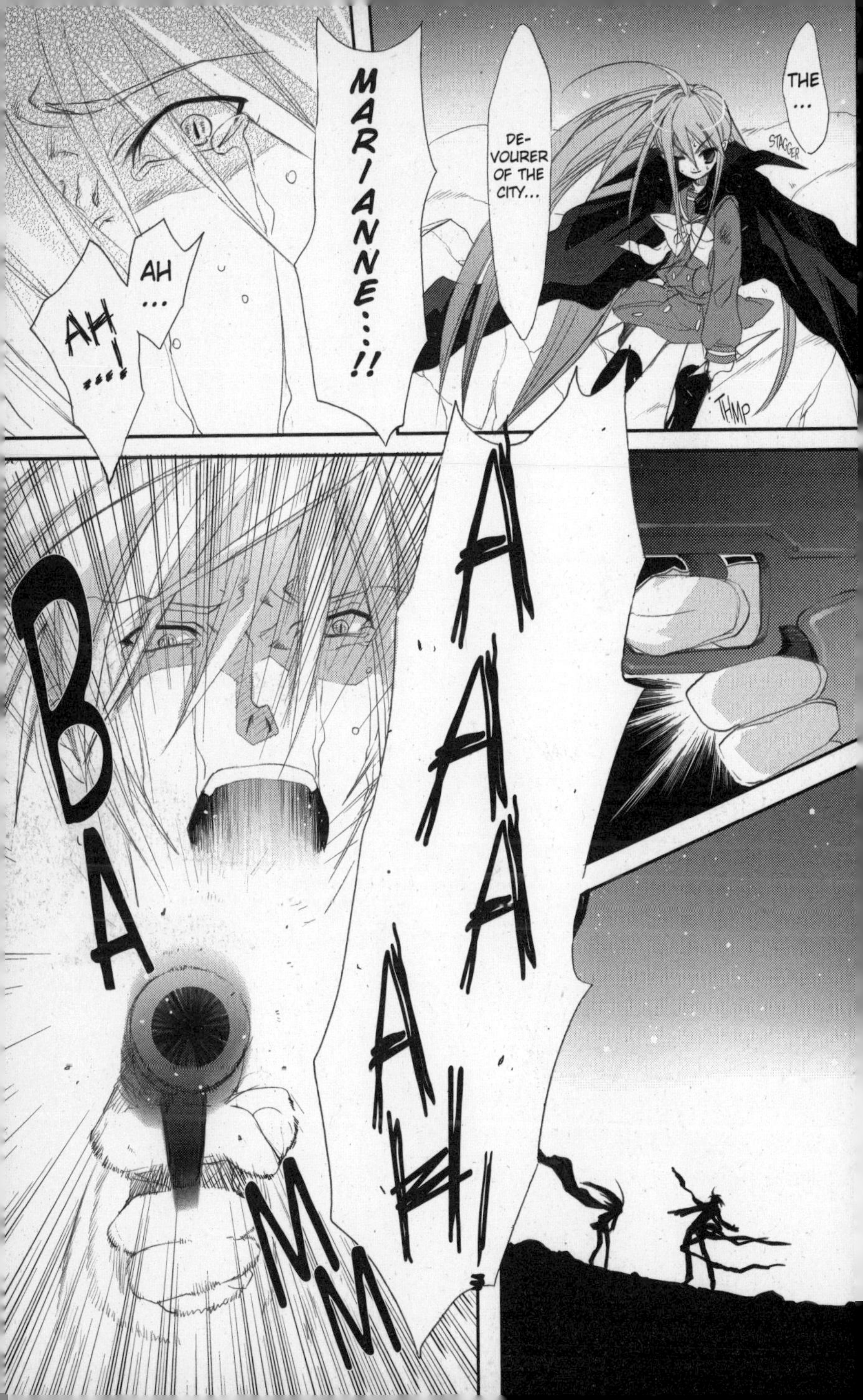
THE ...
STAGGER
DE-VOURER OF THE CITY...
THMP
MARIANNE...!!
AH ...
AH ...!
AAAAH!
BAMM

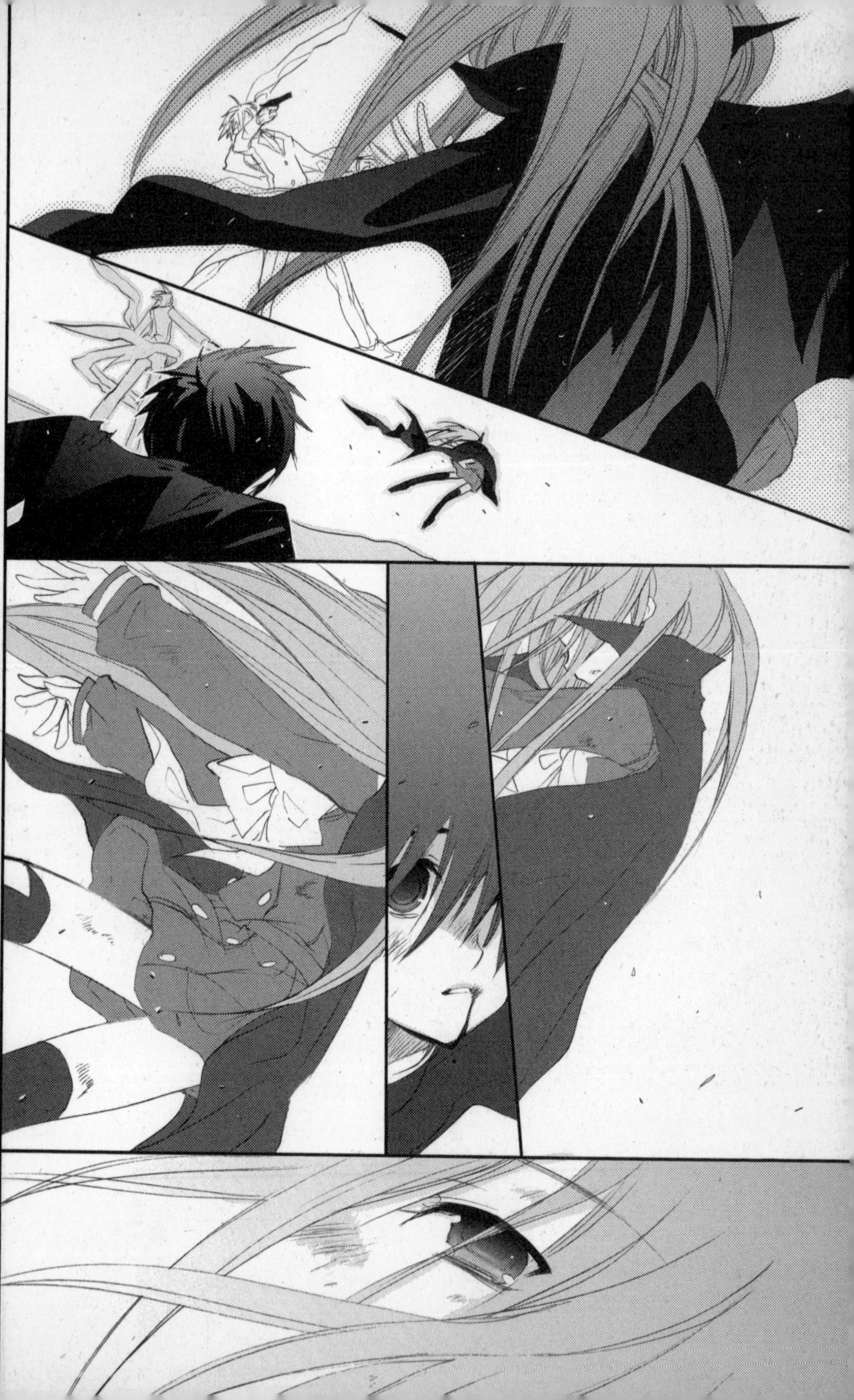

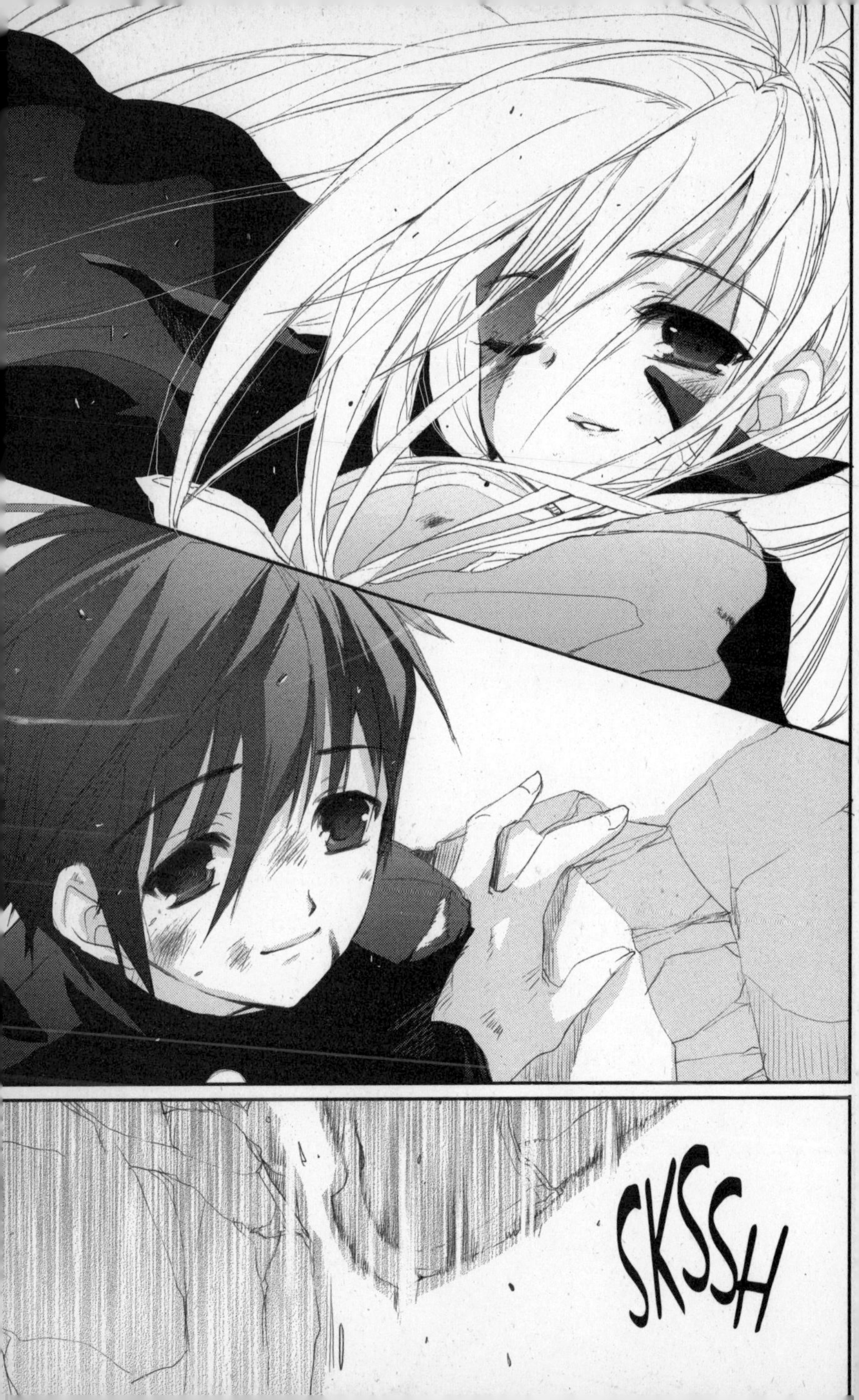
SKSSH

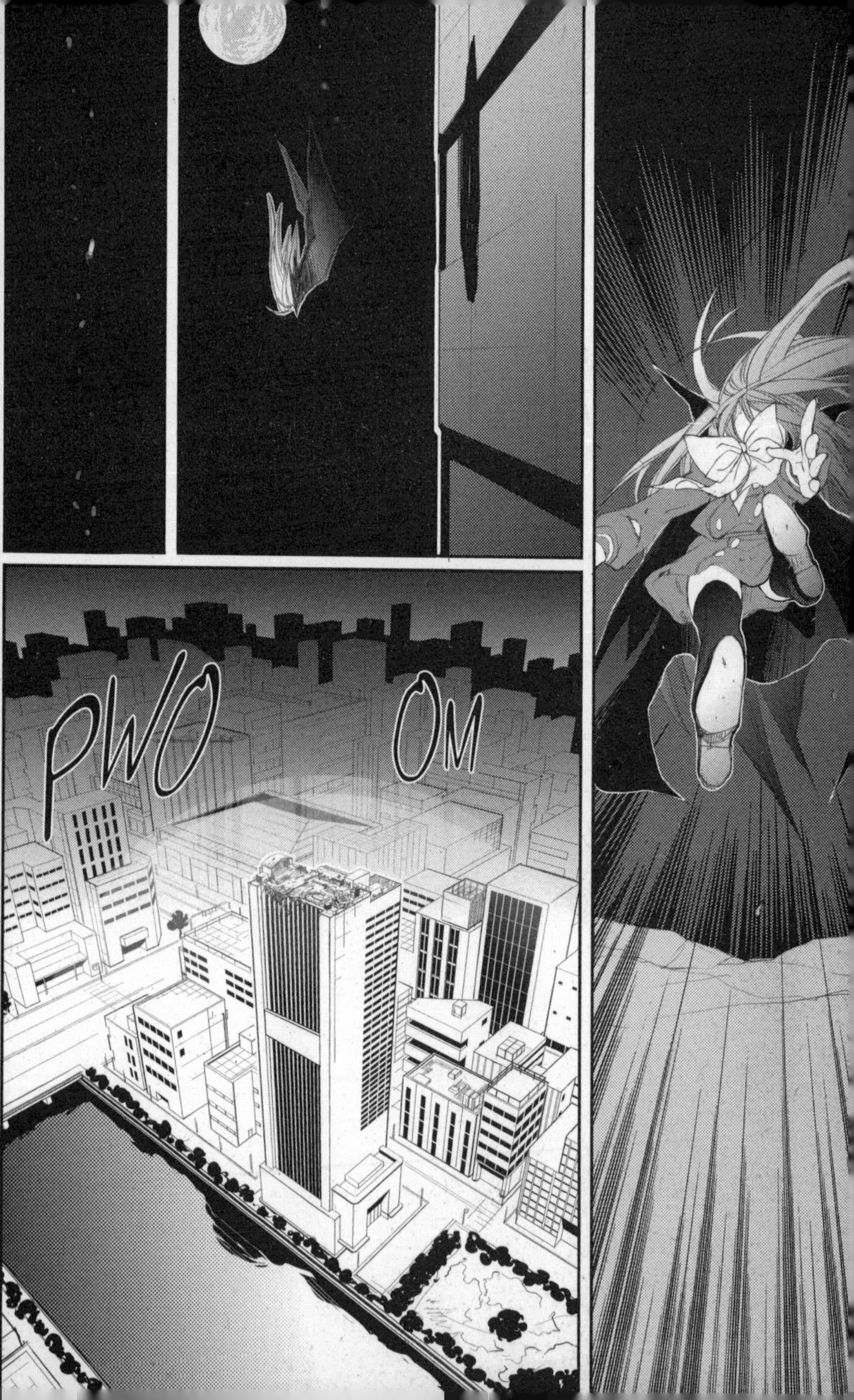
PWO OM

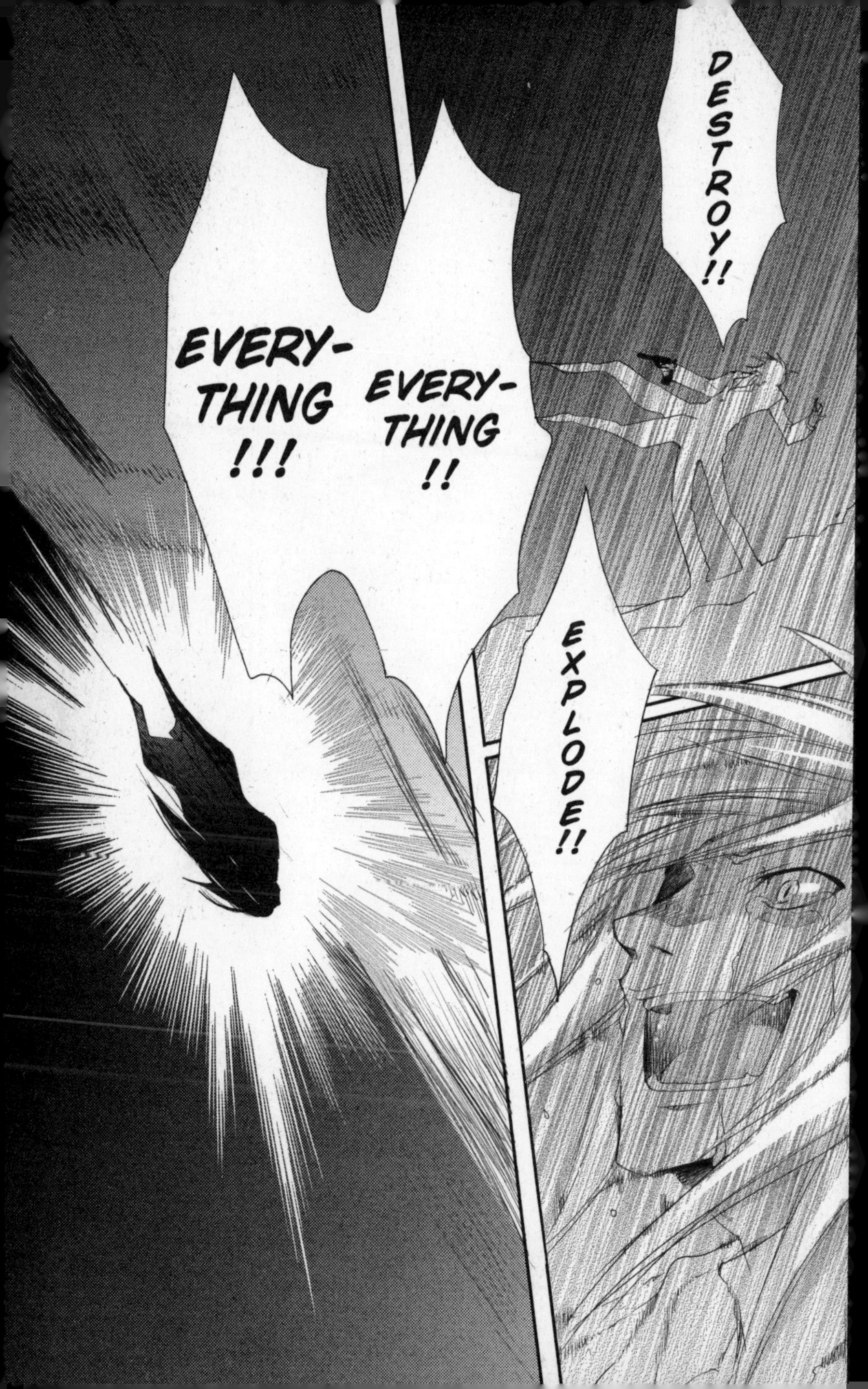
DESTROY!!
EVERYTHING!!
EVERYTHING!!!
EXPLODE!!

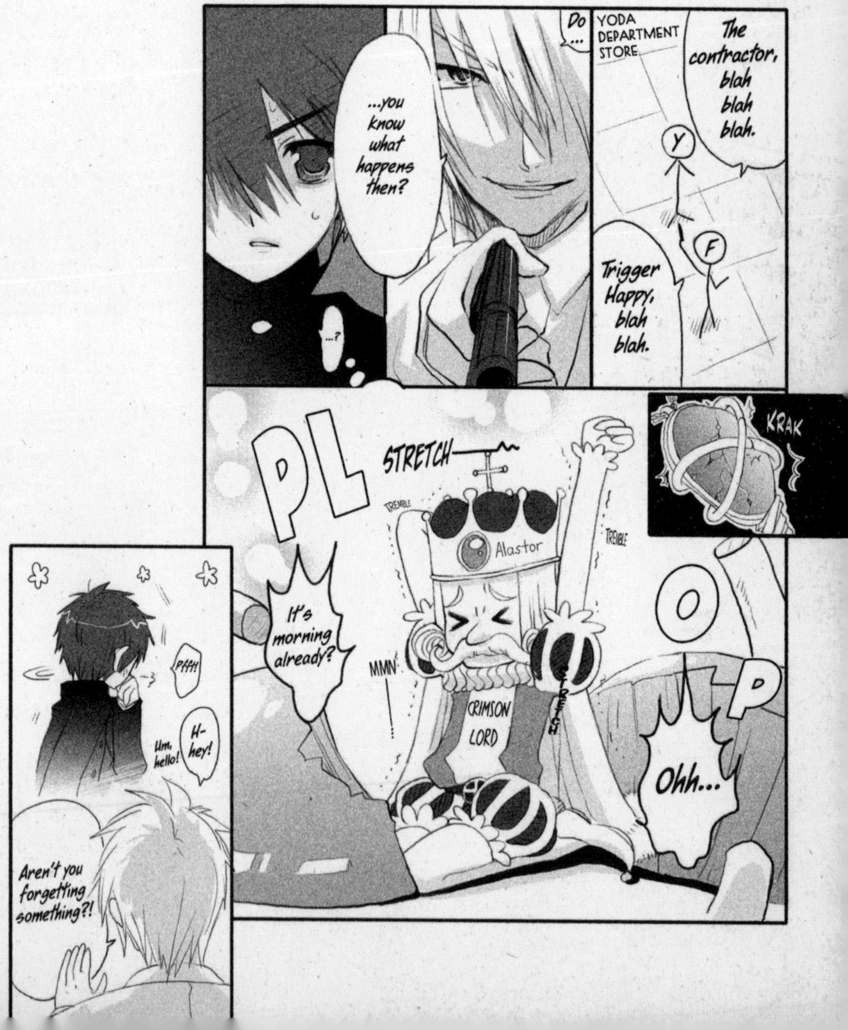
YODA DEPARTMENT STORE
The contractor, blah blah blah.
Y
F
Trigger Happy, blah blah.
Do...
...you know what happens then?
...?
KRAK
PL
O
O
P
Ohh...
STRETCH
TREMBLE
TREMBLE
Alastor
CRIMSON LORD
STRETCH
It's morning already?
MMN
Pfft!
H-hey!
Um, hello!
Aren't you forgetting something?!

Episode 19
Flame Haze IV

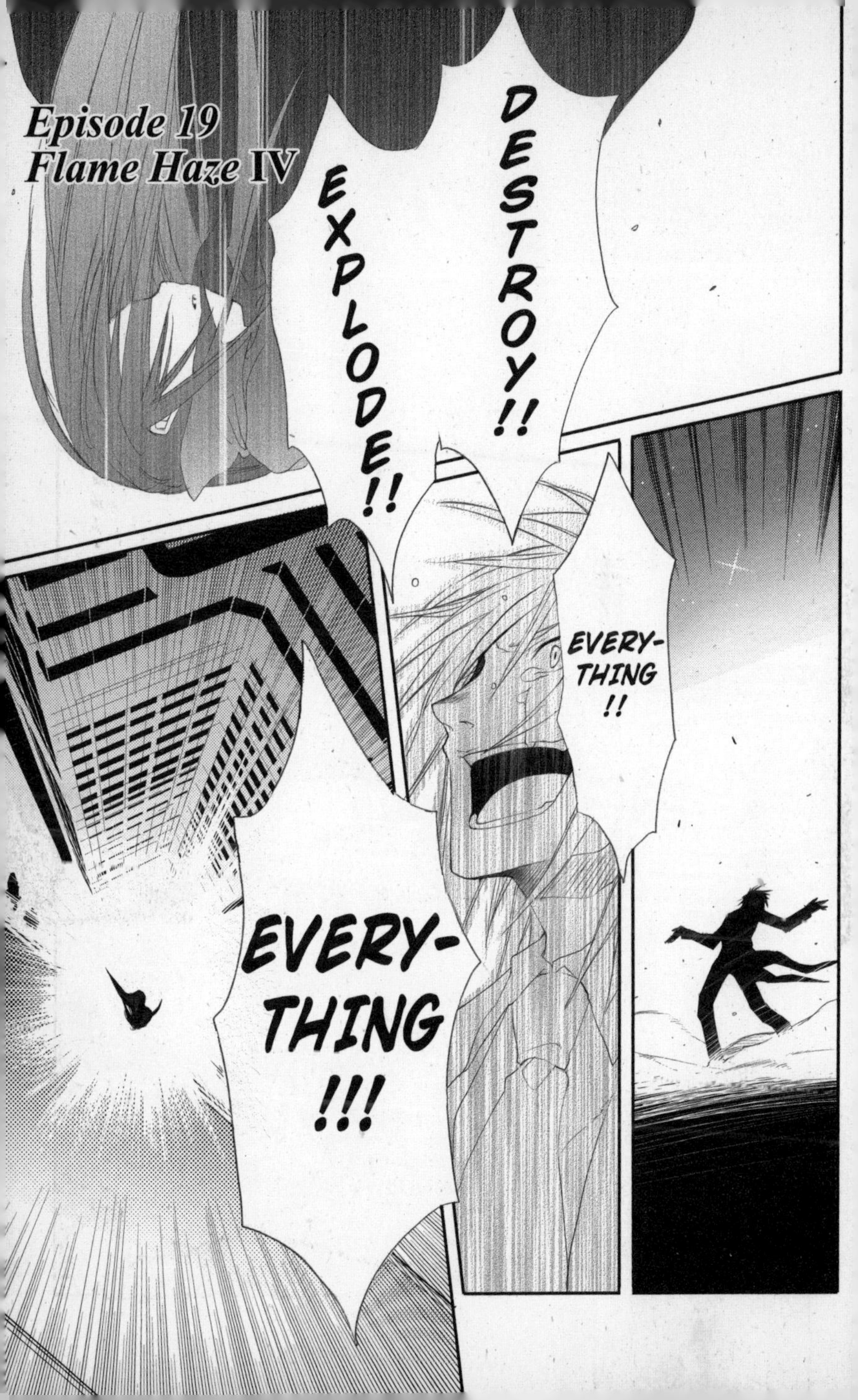
DESTROY!!
EXPLODE!!
EVERY-THING!!
EVERY-THING!!!

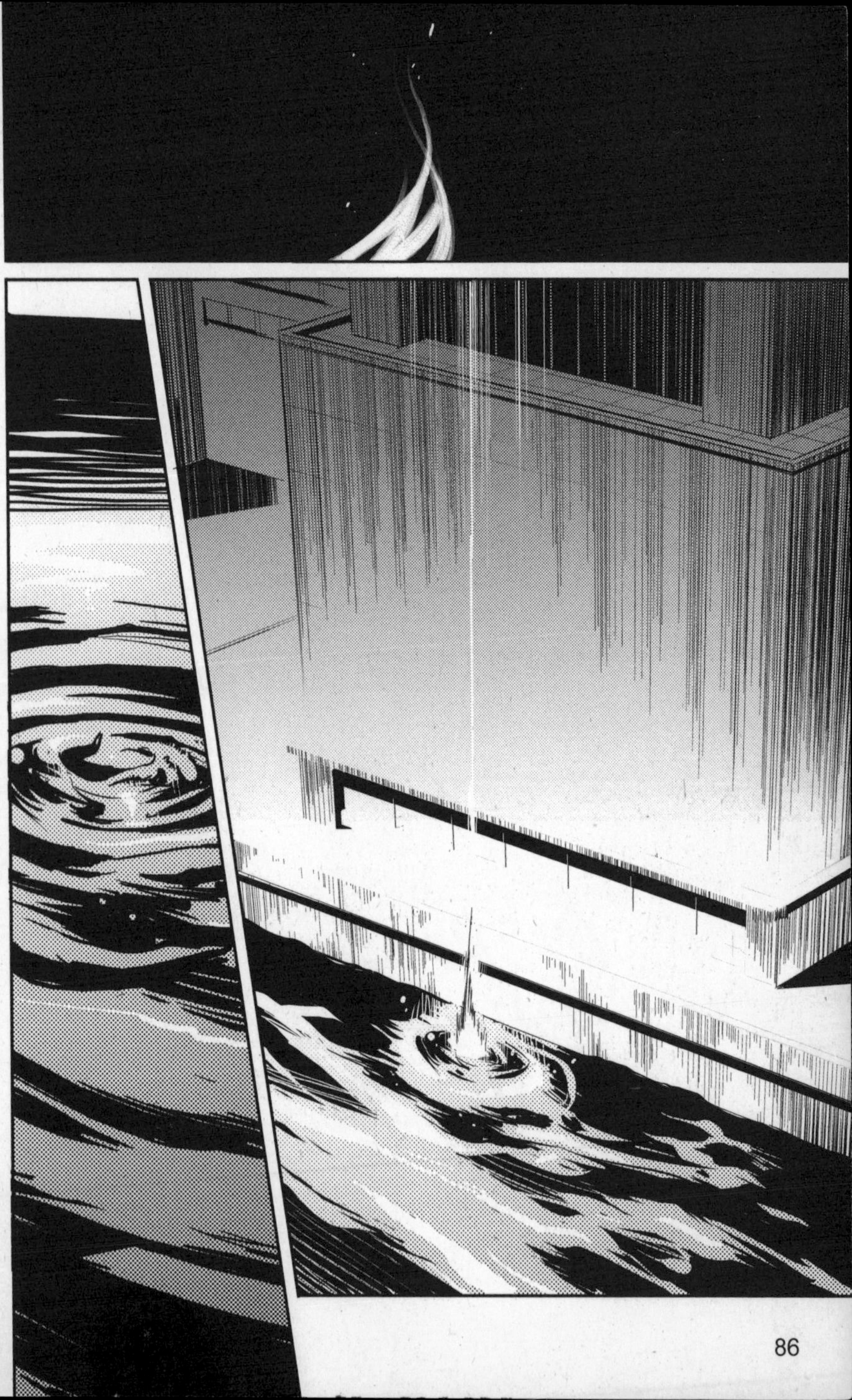

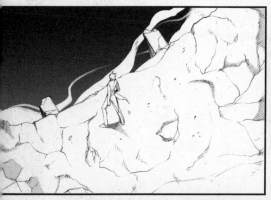

····

SHE... DIDN'T EXPLODE?

?!

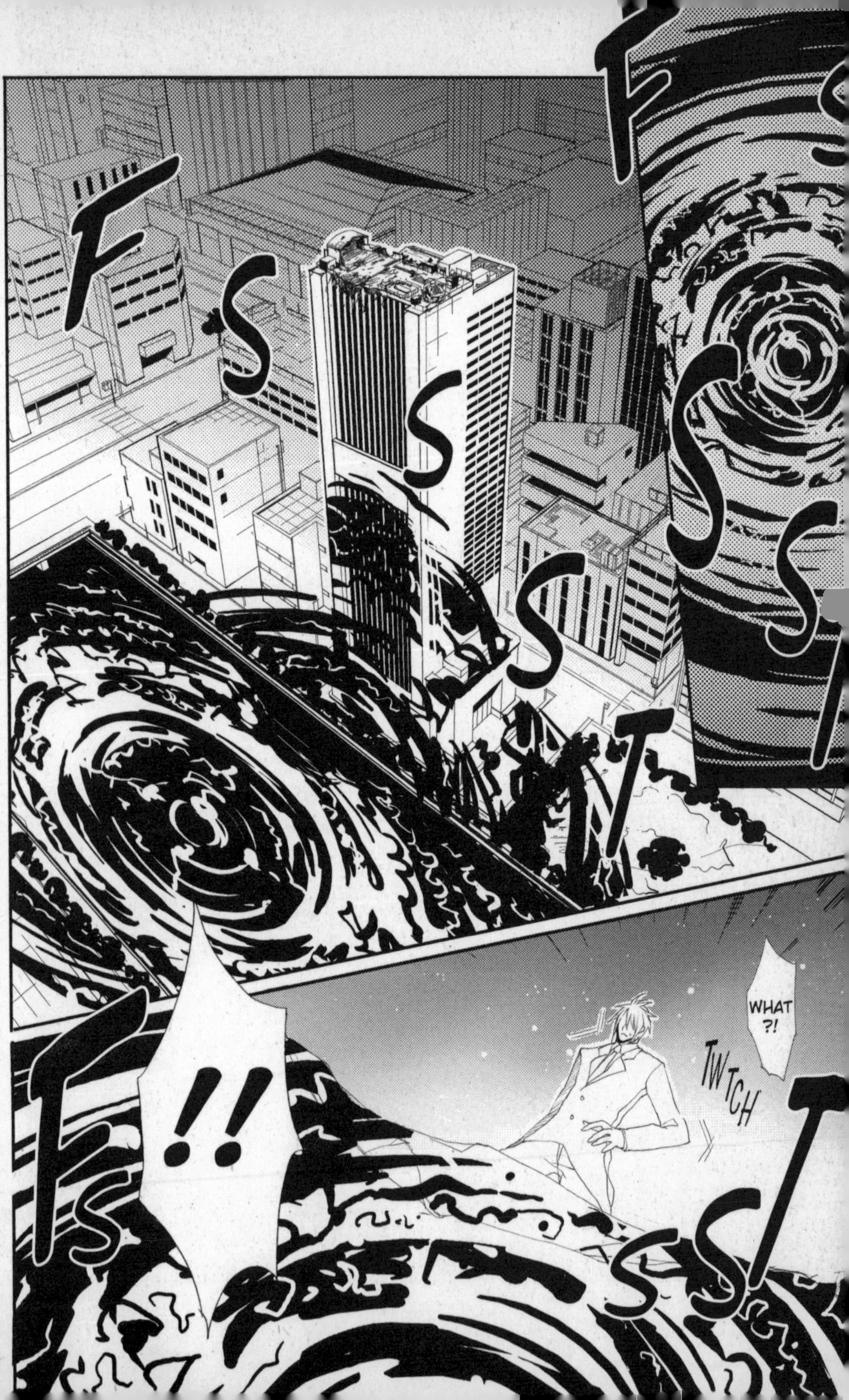

FSSSST
FSSST
WHAT ?!
TWITCH
!!
FSSSST

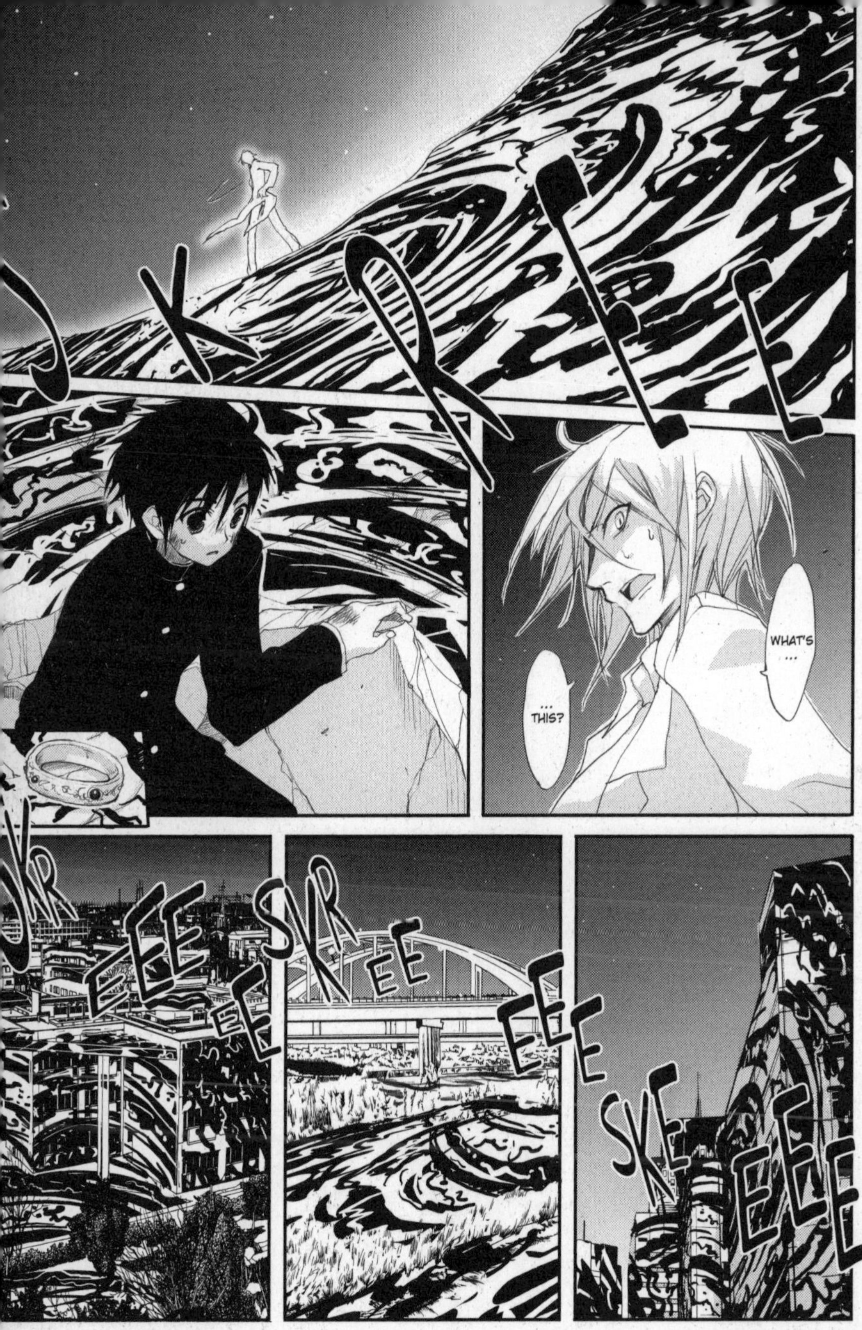
WHAT'S...
...THIS?

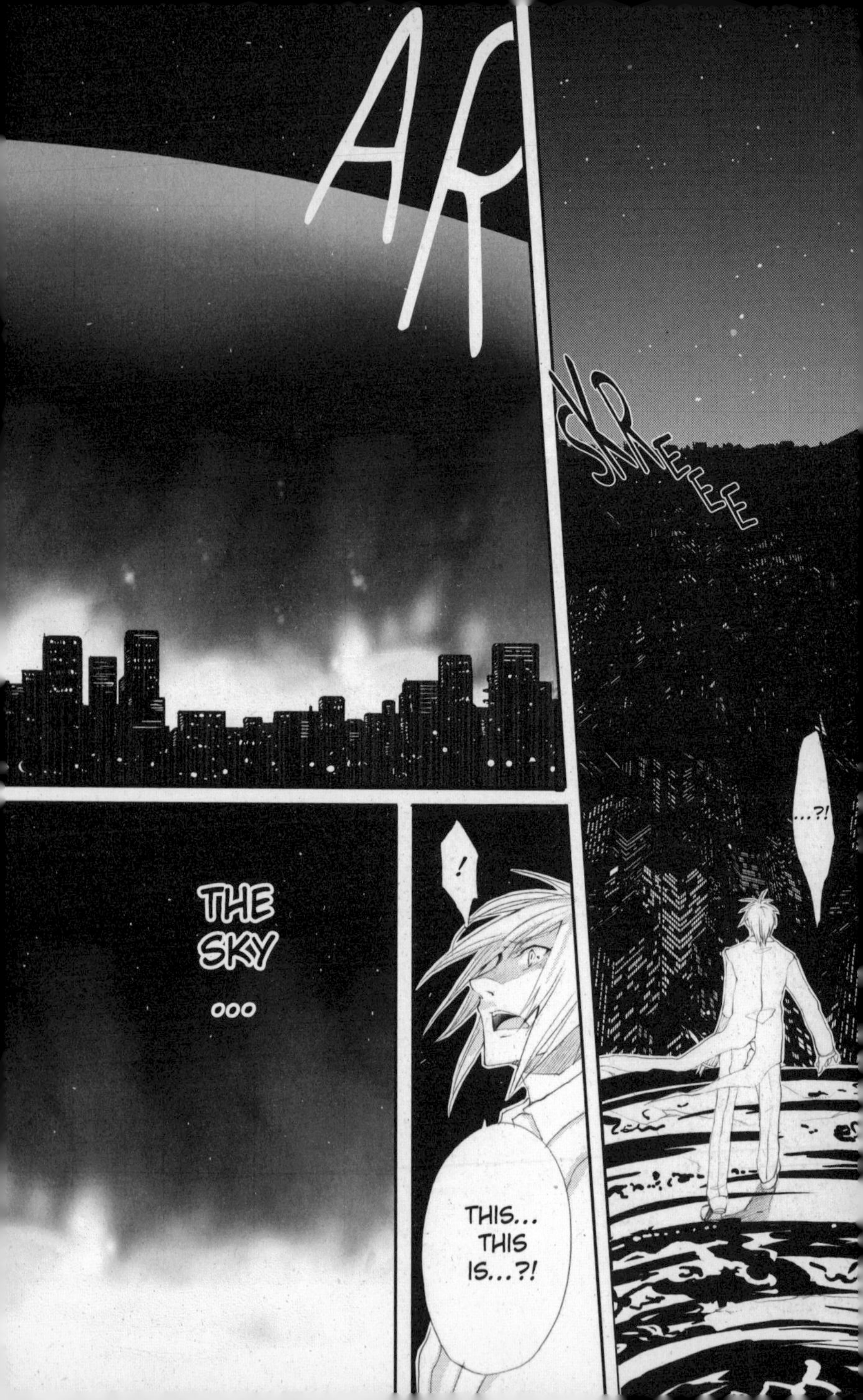

SKREEEE
...?!
AR
!
THIS... THIS IS...?!
THE SKY ...

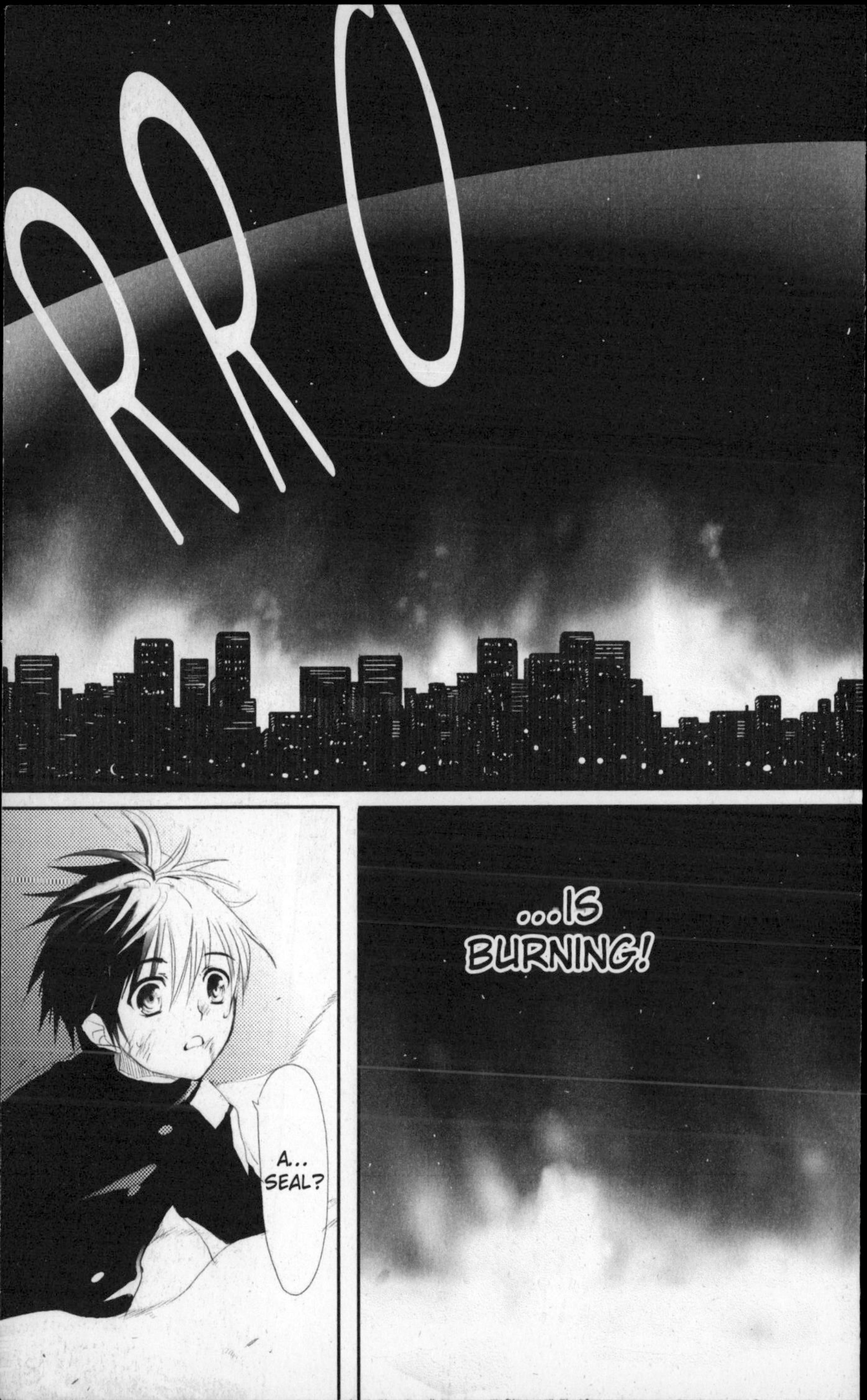
RRO
...IS BURNING!
A... SEAL?

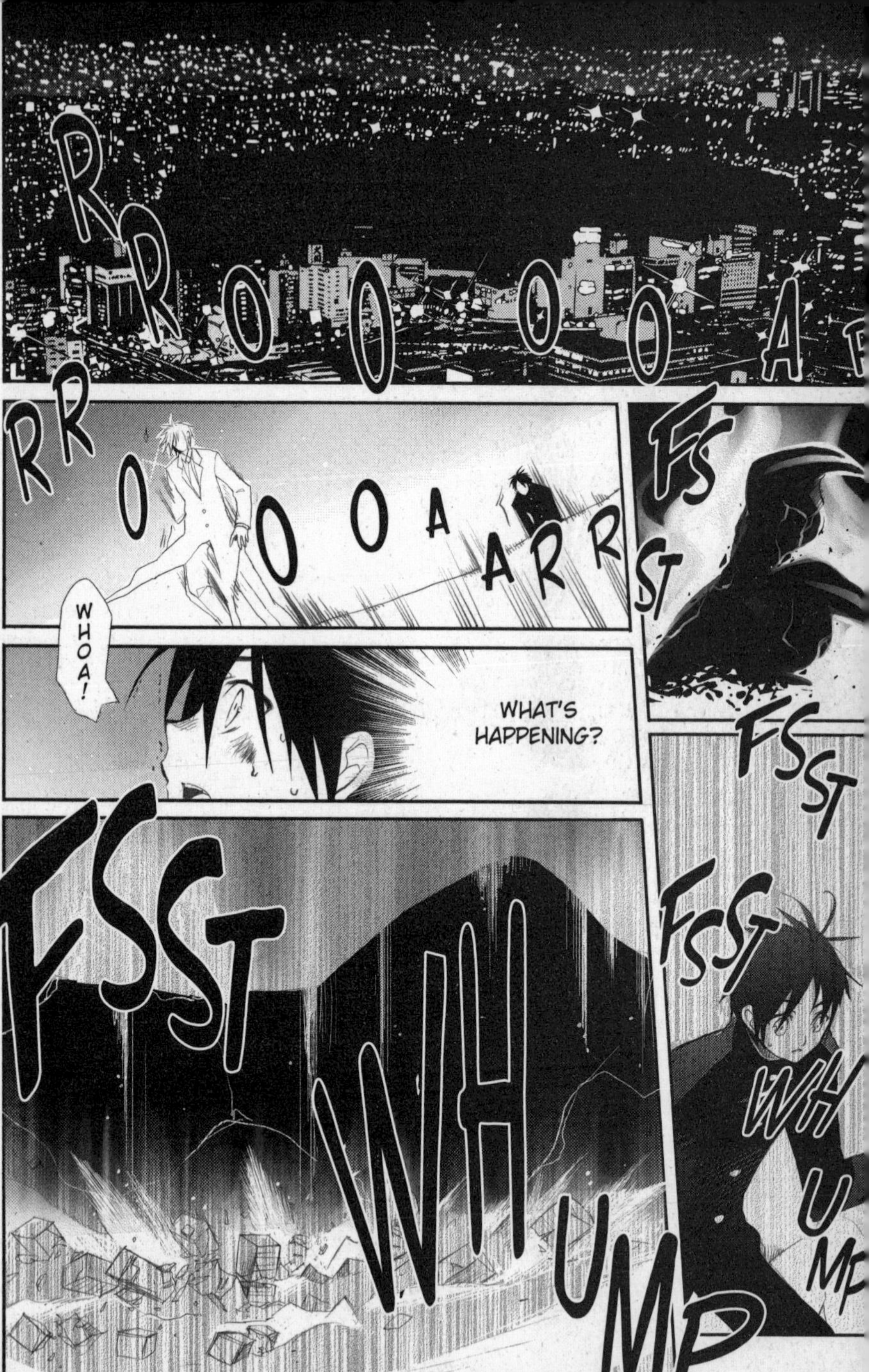
RROOOOAR
FSST
RROOOAARR
WHOA!
WHAT'S HAPPENING?
FSST
FSST WHUMP
FSST WHUMP

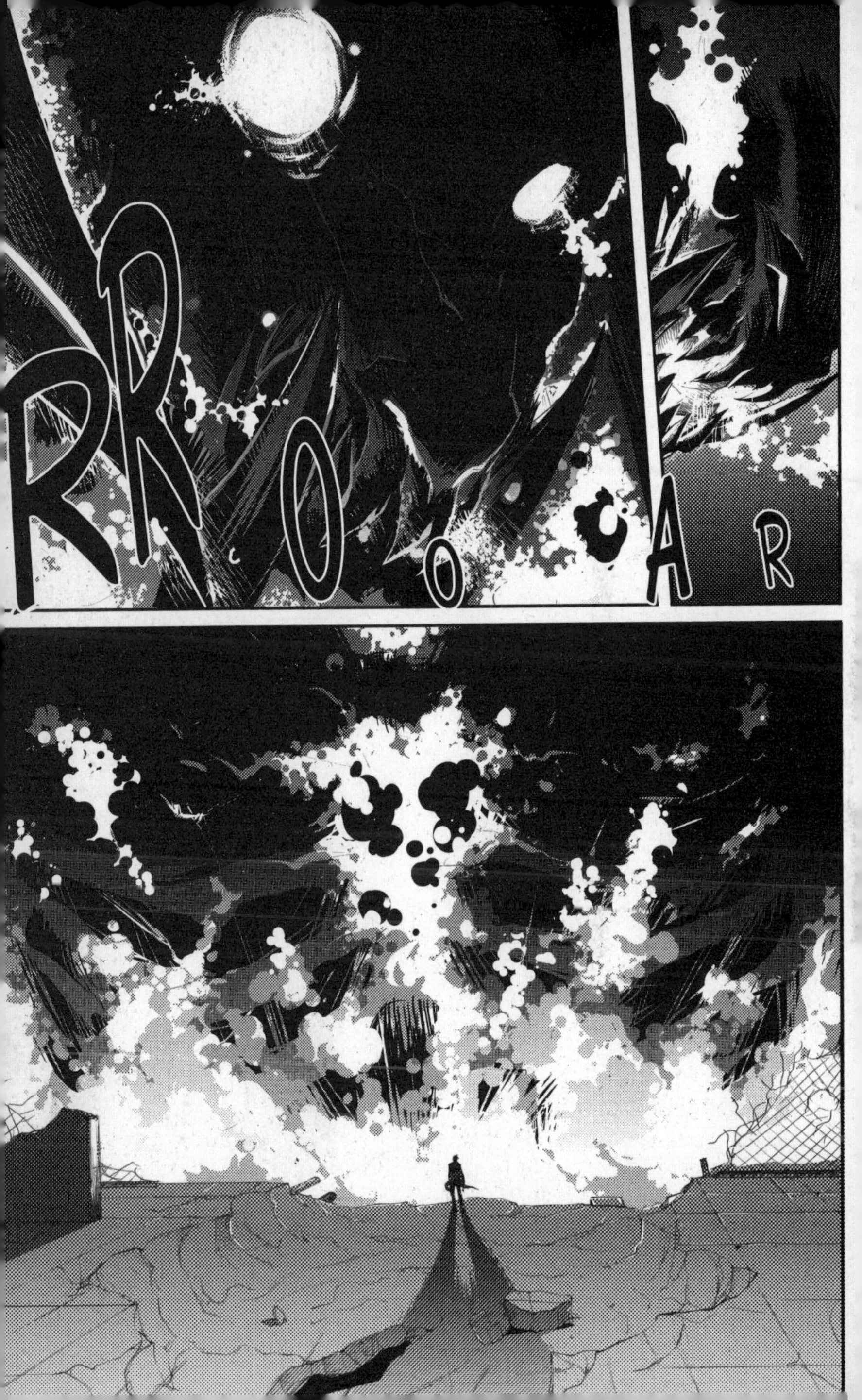
RROOOAR

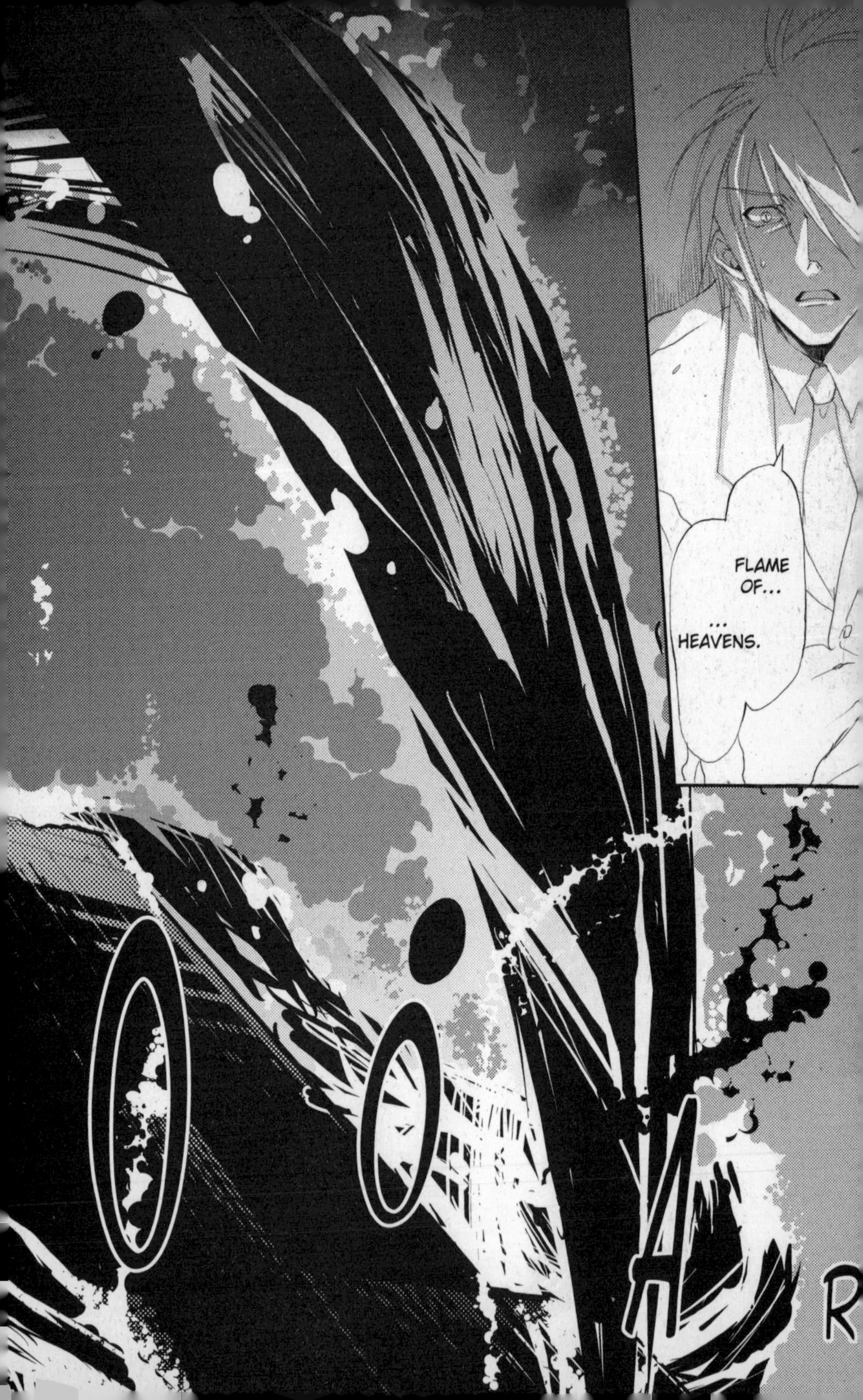
FLAME OF...
...HEAVENS.
R

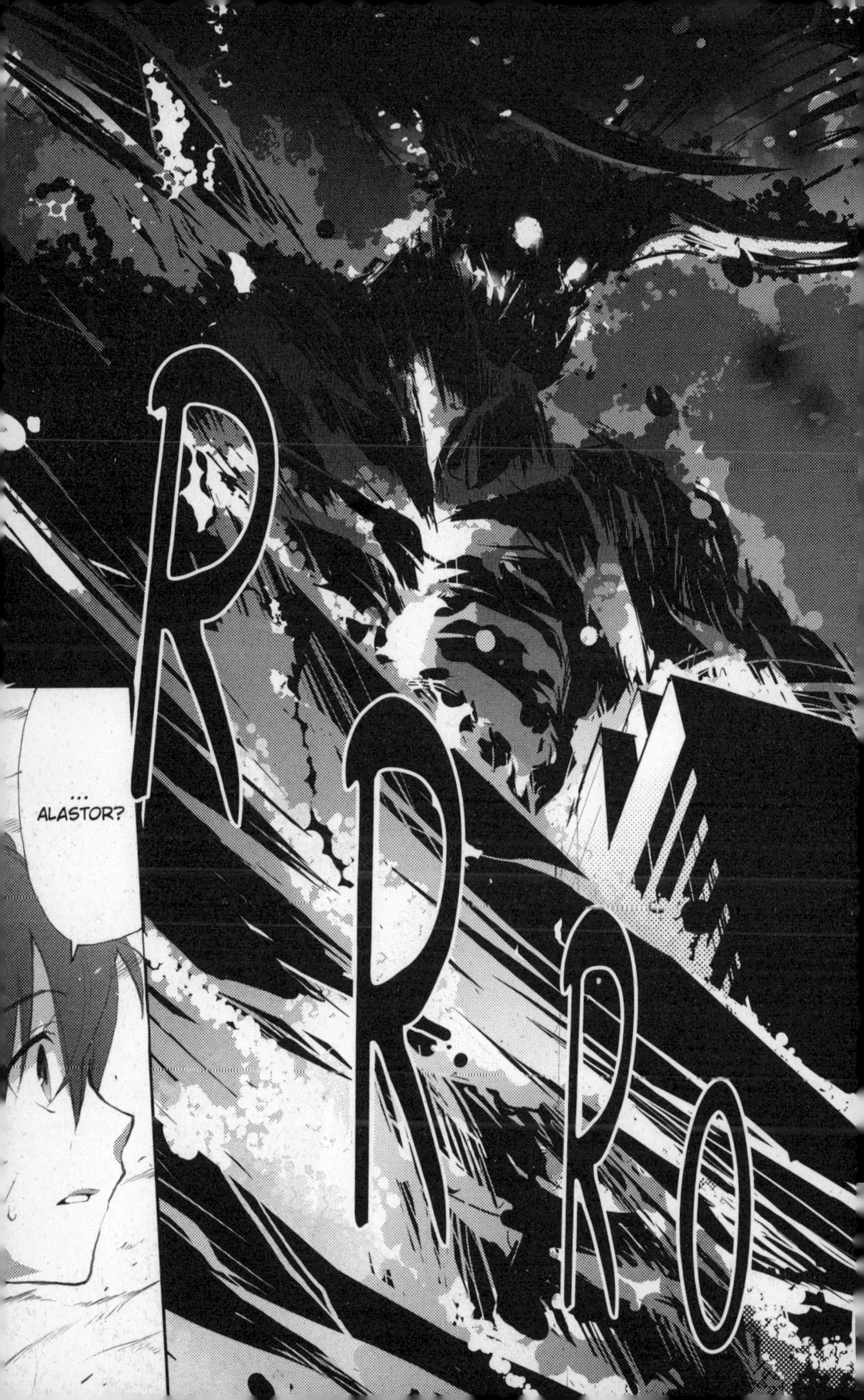

RRRO
... ALASTOR?

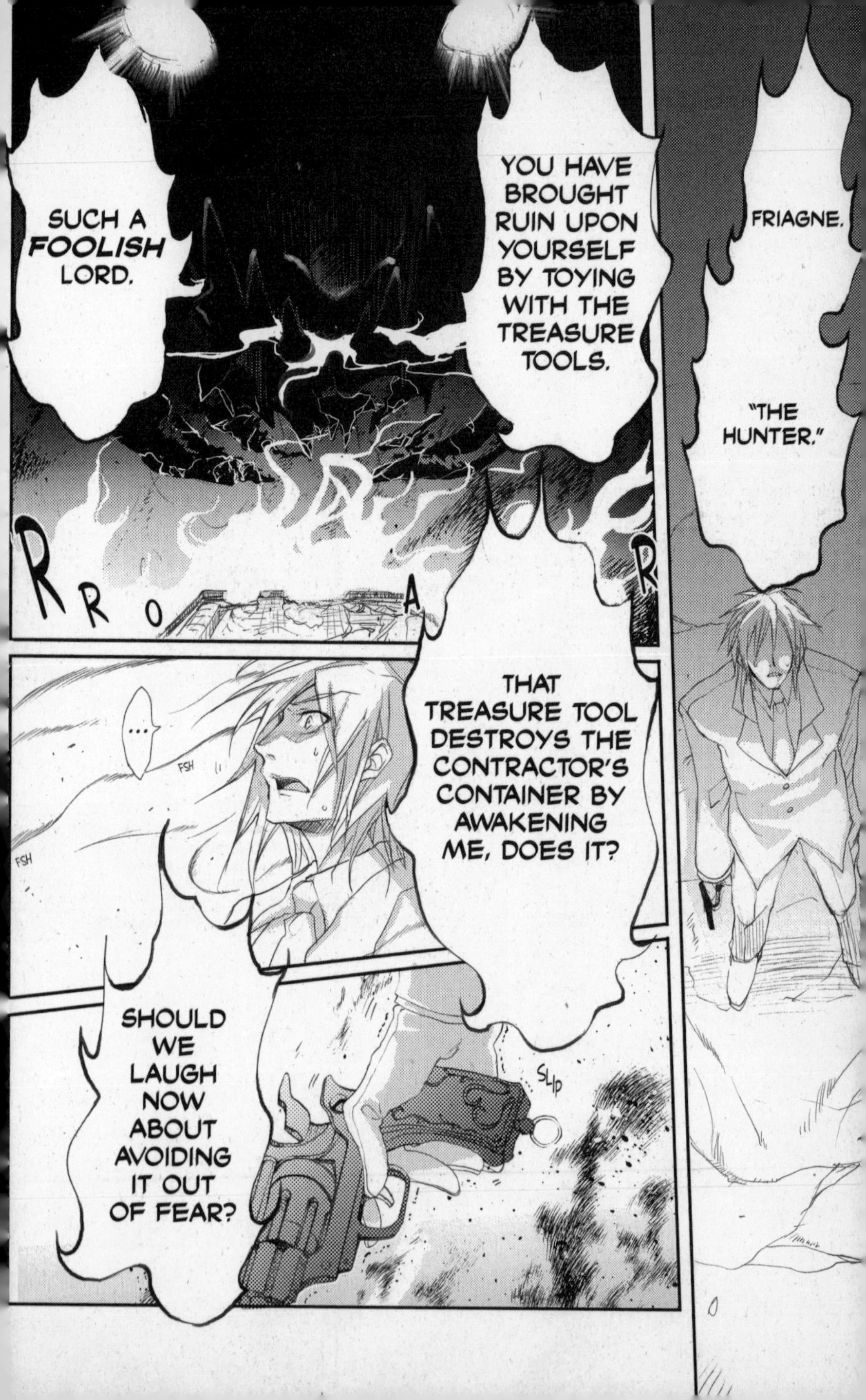
FRIAGNE.
"THE HUNTER."
YOU HAVE BROUGHT RUIN UPON YOURSELF BY TOYING WITH THE TREASURE TOOLS.
SUCH A FOOLISH LORD.
RROAR
THAT TREASURE TOOL DESTROYS THE CONTRACTOR'S CONTAINER BY AWAKENING ME, DOES IT?
...
FSH
FSH
SHOULD WE LAUGH NOW ABOUT AVOIDING IT OUT OF FEAR?
SLIP

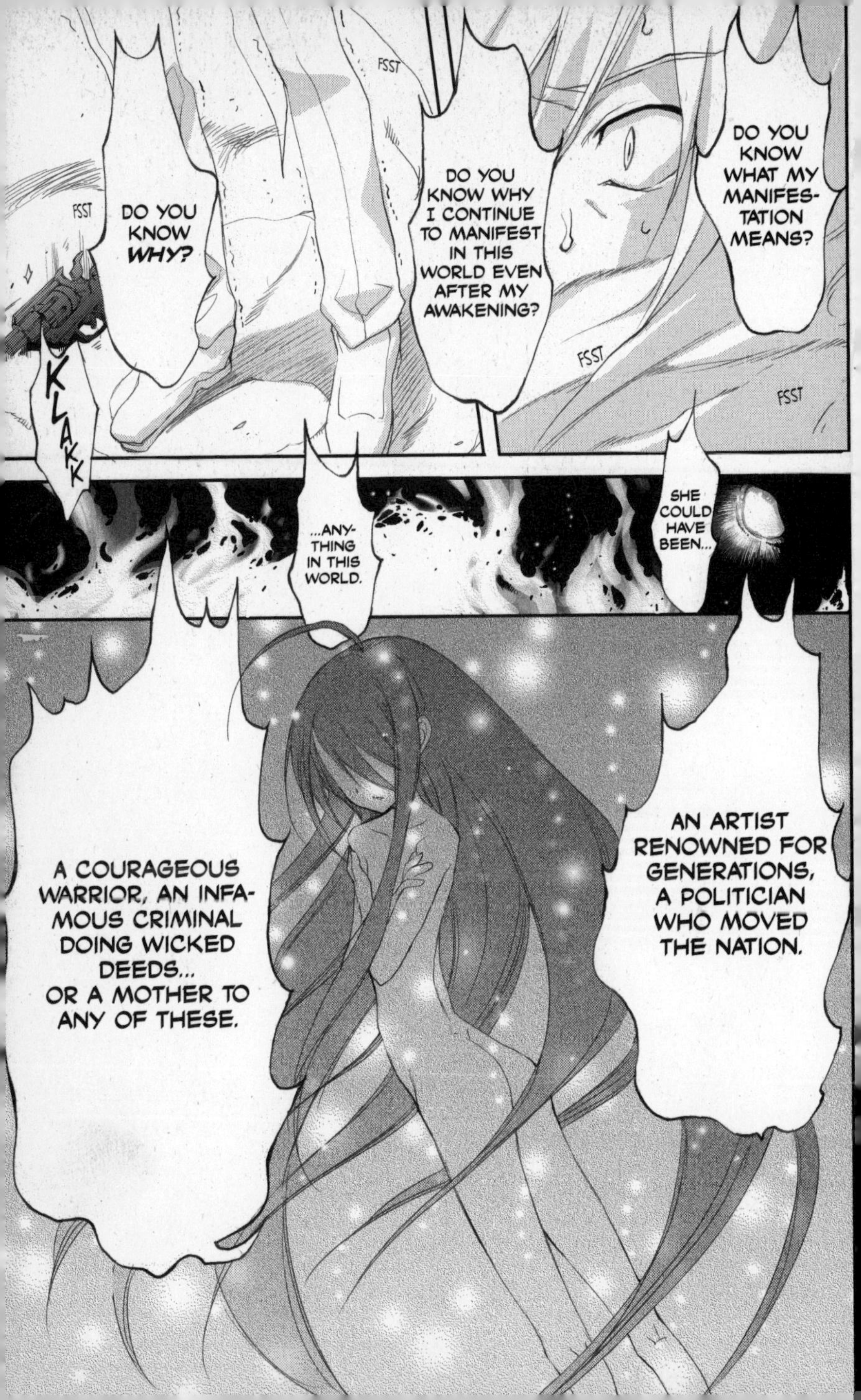
DO YOU KNOW WHAT MY MANIFESTATION MEANS?
FSST
FSST
DO YOU KNOW WHY I CONTINUE TO MANIFEST IN THIS WORLD EVEN AFTER MY AWAKENING?
FSST
DO YOU KNOW *WHY?*
FSST
FSST
KLAKK
SHE COULD HAVE BEEN...
...ANYTHING IN THIS WORLD.
AN ARTIST RENOWNED FOR GENERATIONS, A POLITICIAN WHO MOVED THE NATION.
A COURAGEOUS WARRIOR, AN INFAMOUS CRIMINAL DOING WICKED DEEDS... OR A MOTHER TO ANY OF THESE.

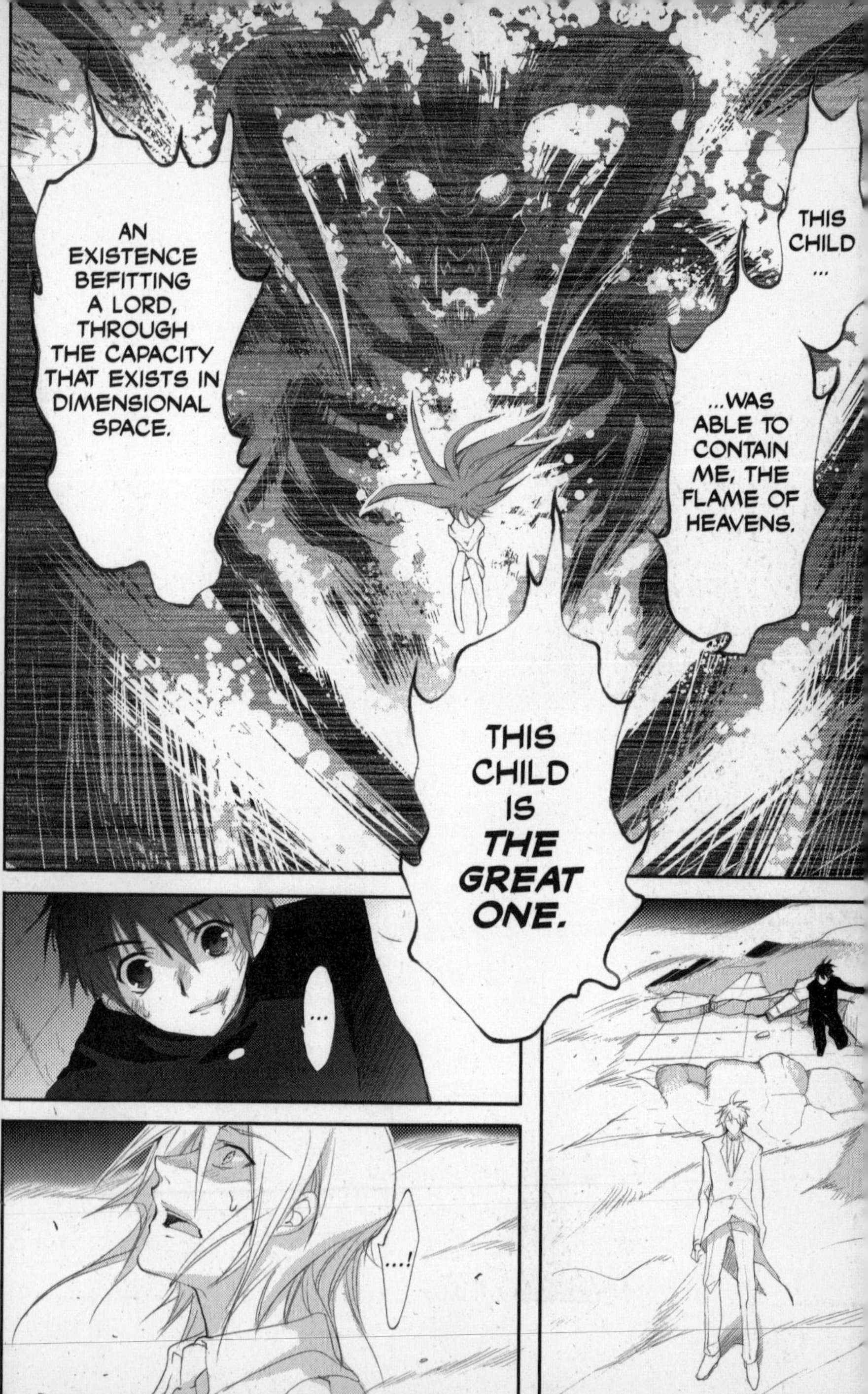

THIS CHILD ...
...WAS ABLE TO CONTAIN ME, THE FLAME OF HEAVENS.
AN EXISTENCE BEFITTING A LORD, THROUGH THE CAPACITY THAT EXISTS IN DIMENSIONAL SPACE.
THIS CHILD IS ***THE GREAT ONE.***
...
...!

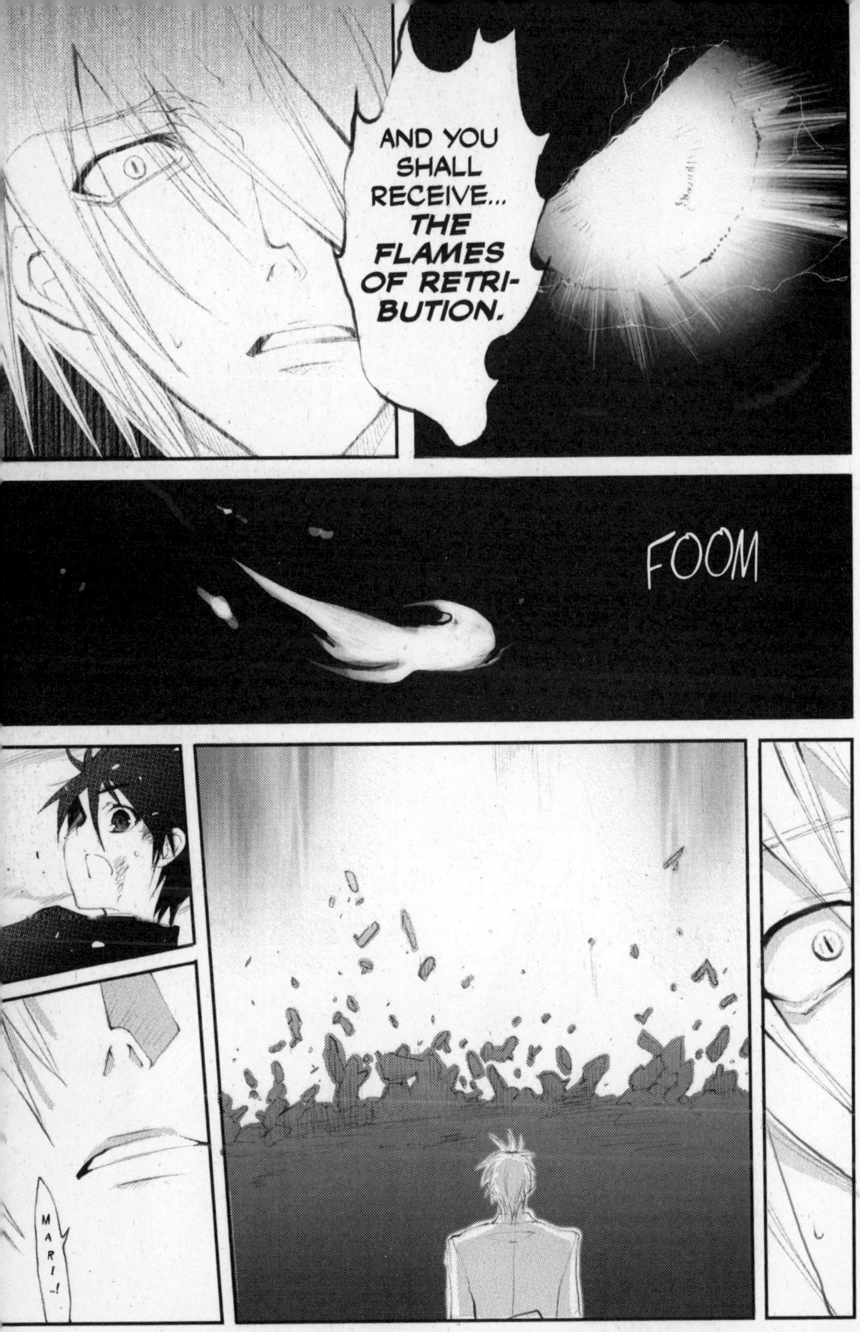
AND YOU SHALL RECEIVE... THE FLAMES OF RETRI- BUTION.
FOOM
MARI...!

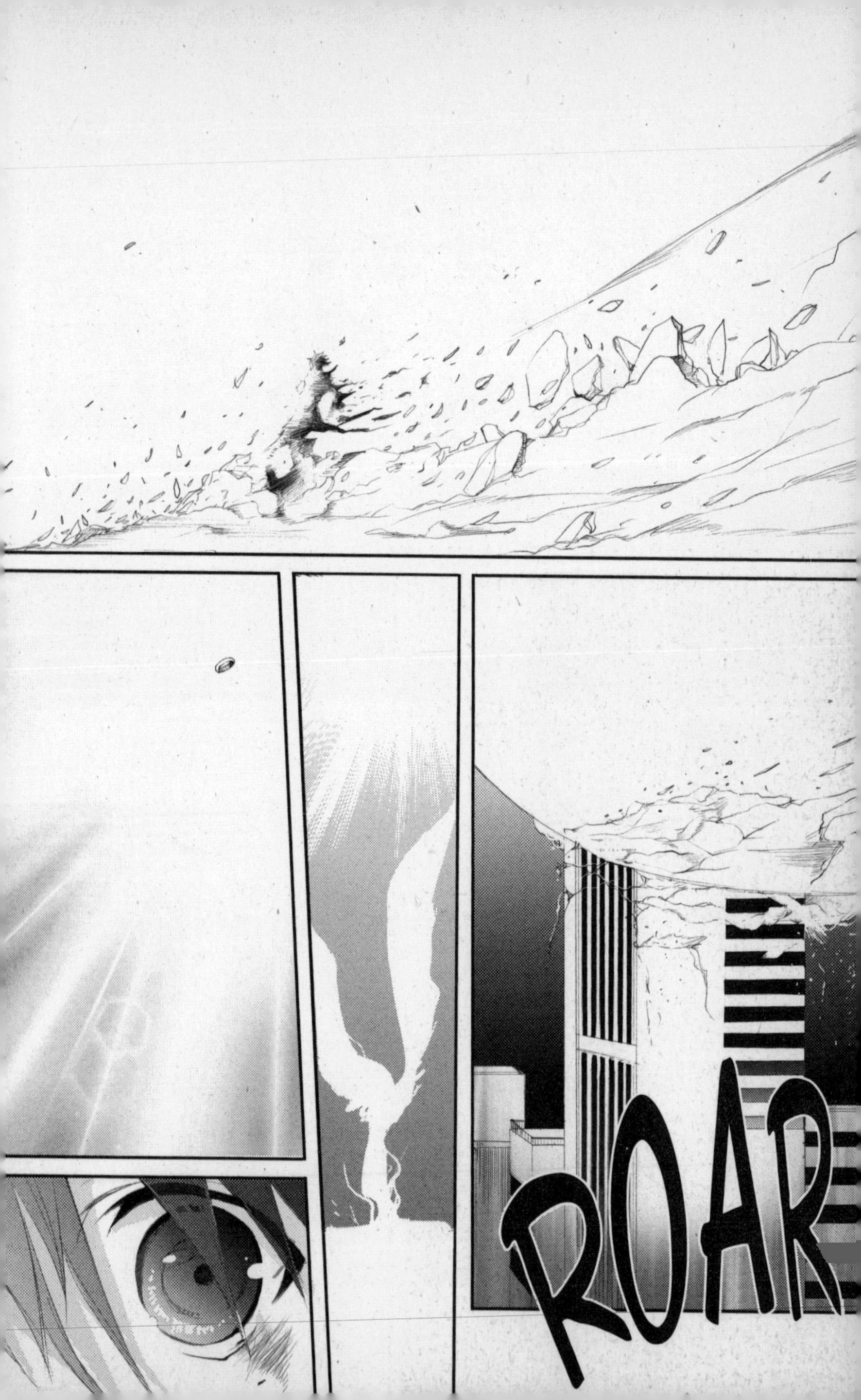
ROAR

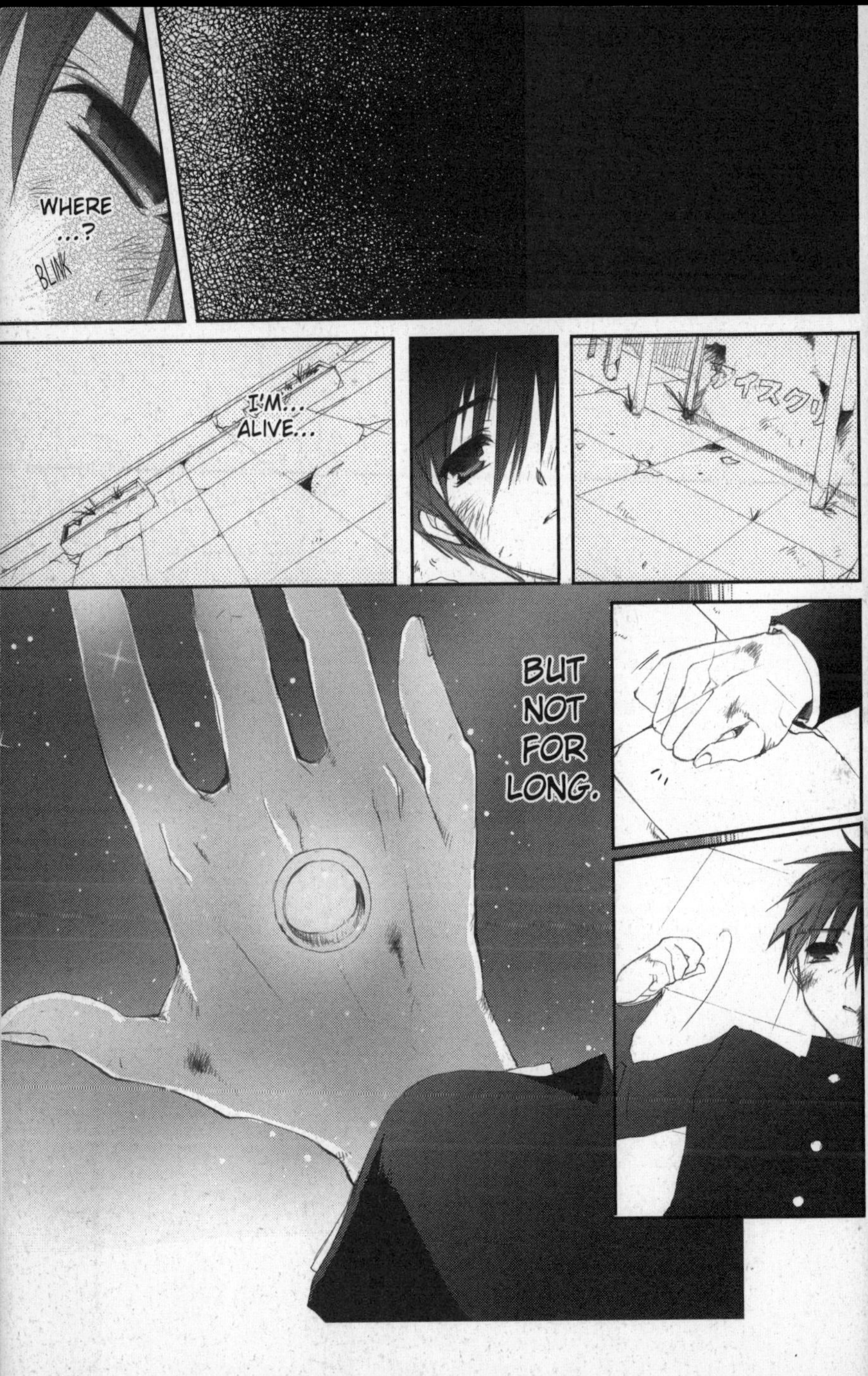
WHERE ...?
BLINK
アイスクリ
I'M... ALIVE...
BUT NOT FOR LONG.

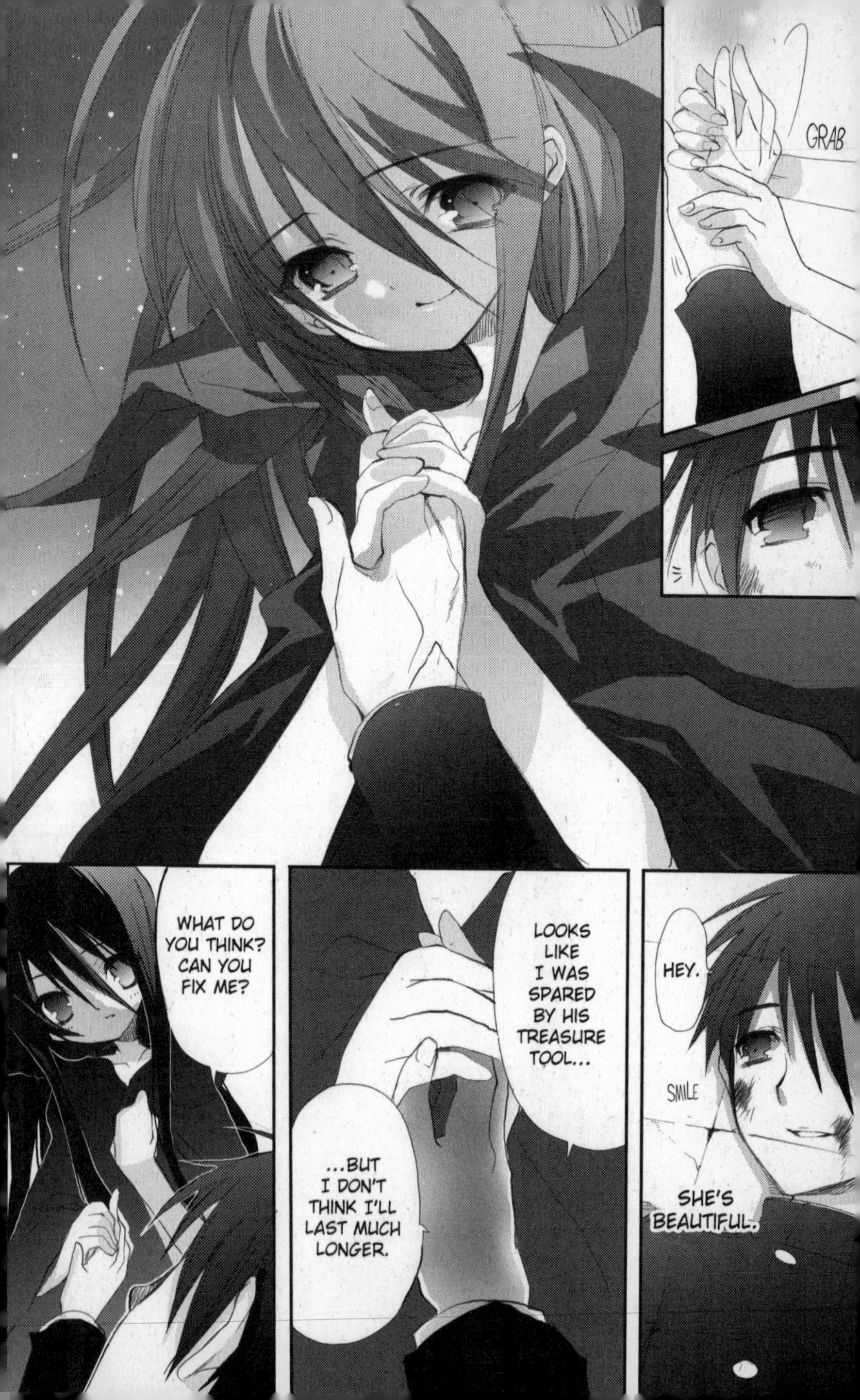
GRAB
HEY.
SMILE
SHE'S BEAUTIFUL.
LOOKS LIKE I WAS SPARED BY HIS TREASURE TOOL...
...BUT I DON'T THINK I'LL LAST MUCH LONGER.
WHAT DO YOU THINK? CAN YOU FIX ME?

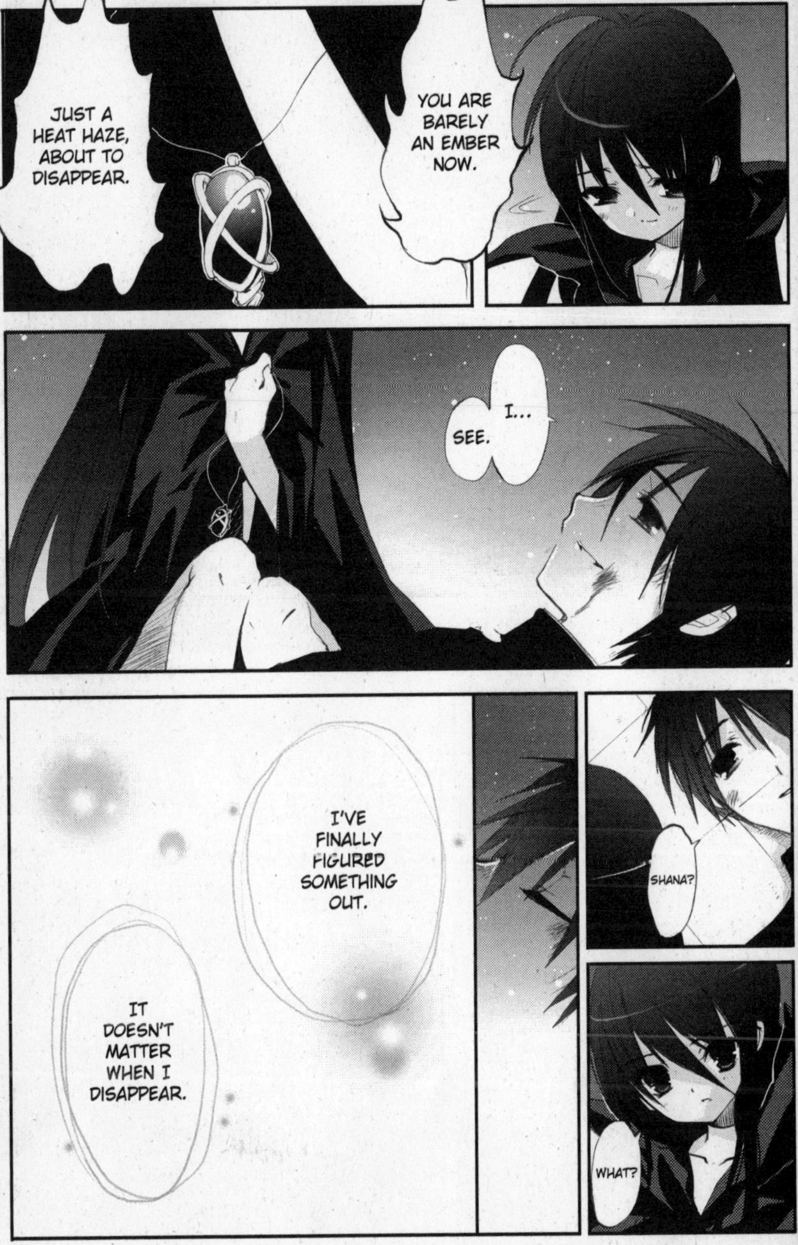
YOU ARE BARELY AN EMBER NOW.
JUST A HEAT HAZE, ABOUT TO DISAPPEAR.
I... SEE.
SHANA?
WHAT?
I'VE FINALLY FIGURED SOMETHING OUT.
IT DOESN'T MATTER WHEN I DISAPPEAR.

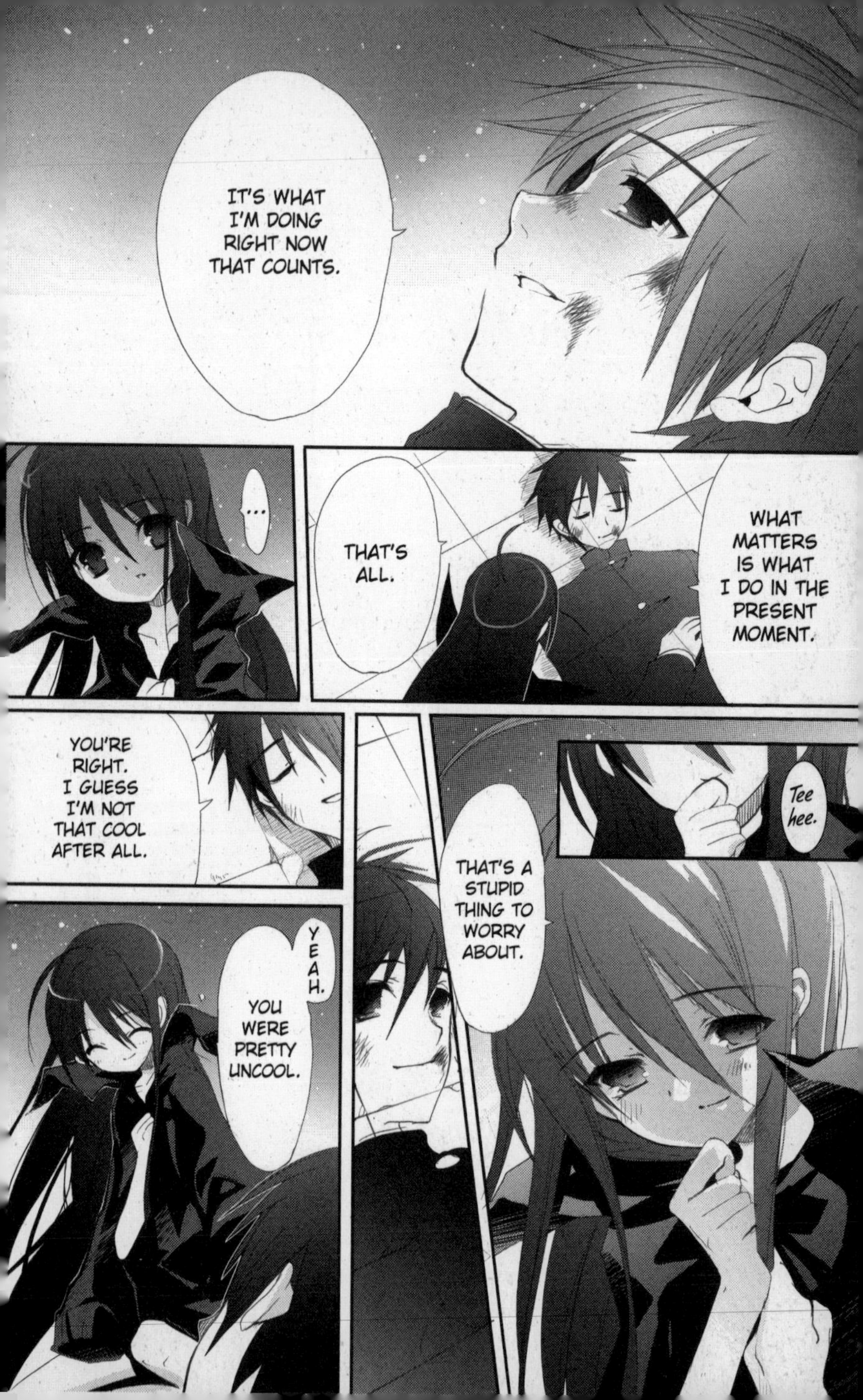
IT'S WHAT I'M DOING RIGHT NOW THAT COUNTS.
WHAT MATTERS IS WHAT I DO IN THE PRESENT MOMENT.
THAT'S ALL.
...
Tee hee.
YOU'RE RIGHT. I GUESS I'M NOT THAT COOL AFTER ALL.
THAT'S A STUPID THING TO WORRY ABOUT.
YEAH.
YOU WERE PRETTY UNCOOL.

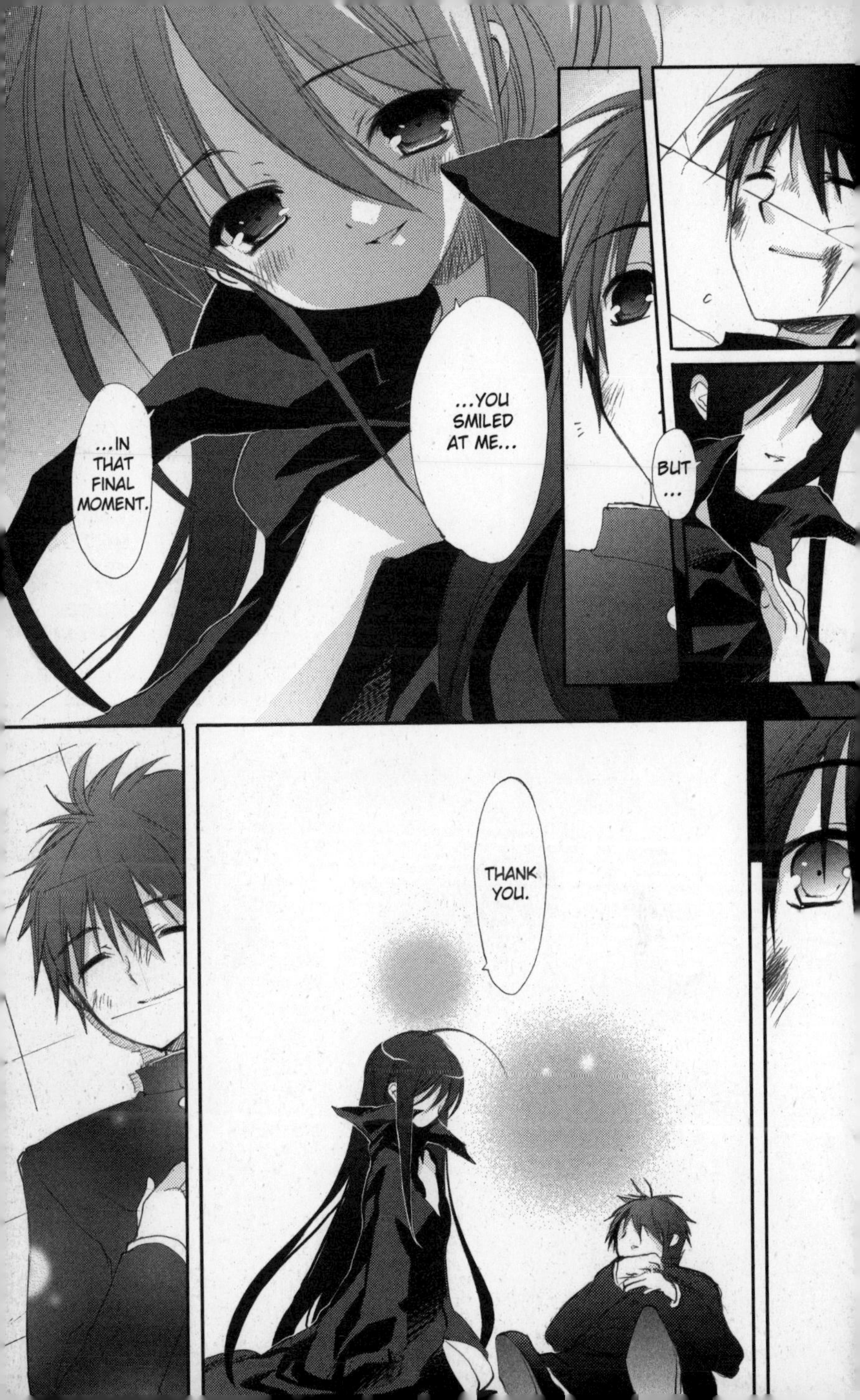

BUT...
...YOU SMILED AT ME...
...IN THAT FINAL MOMENT.
THANK YOU.

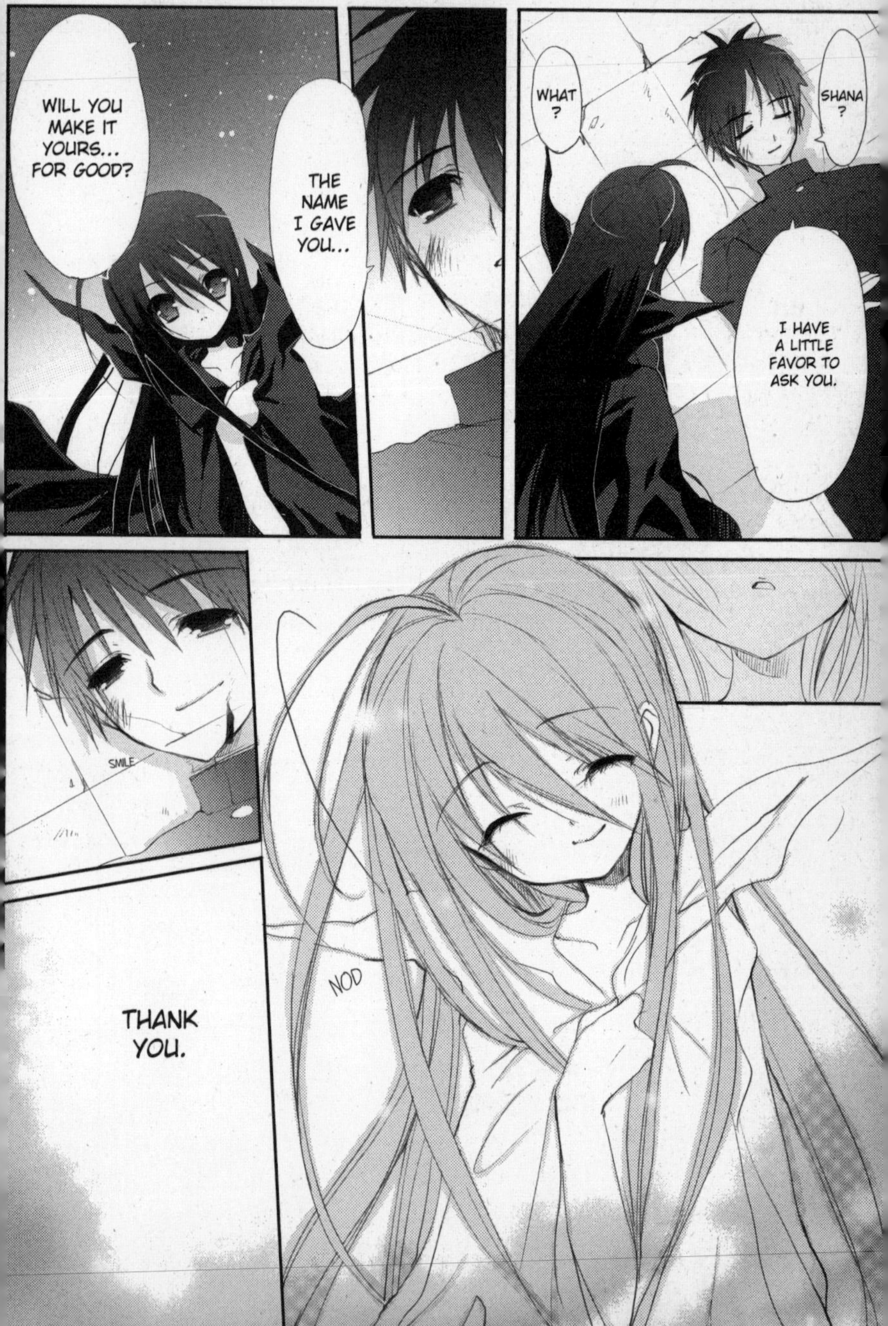
SHANA?
WHAT?
I HAVE A LITTLE FAVOR TO ASK YOU.
THE NAME I GAVE YOU...
WILL YOU MAKE IT YOURS... FOR GOOD?
NOD
SMILE
THANK YOU.

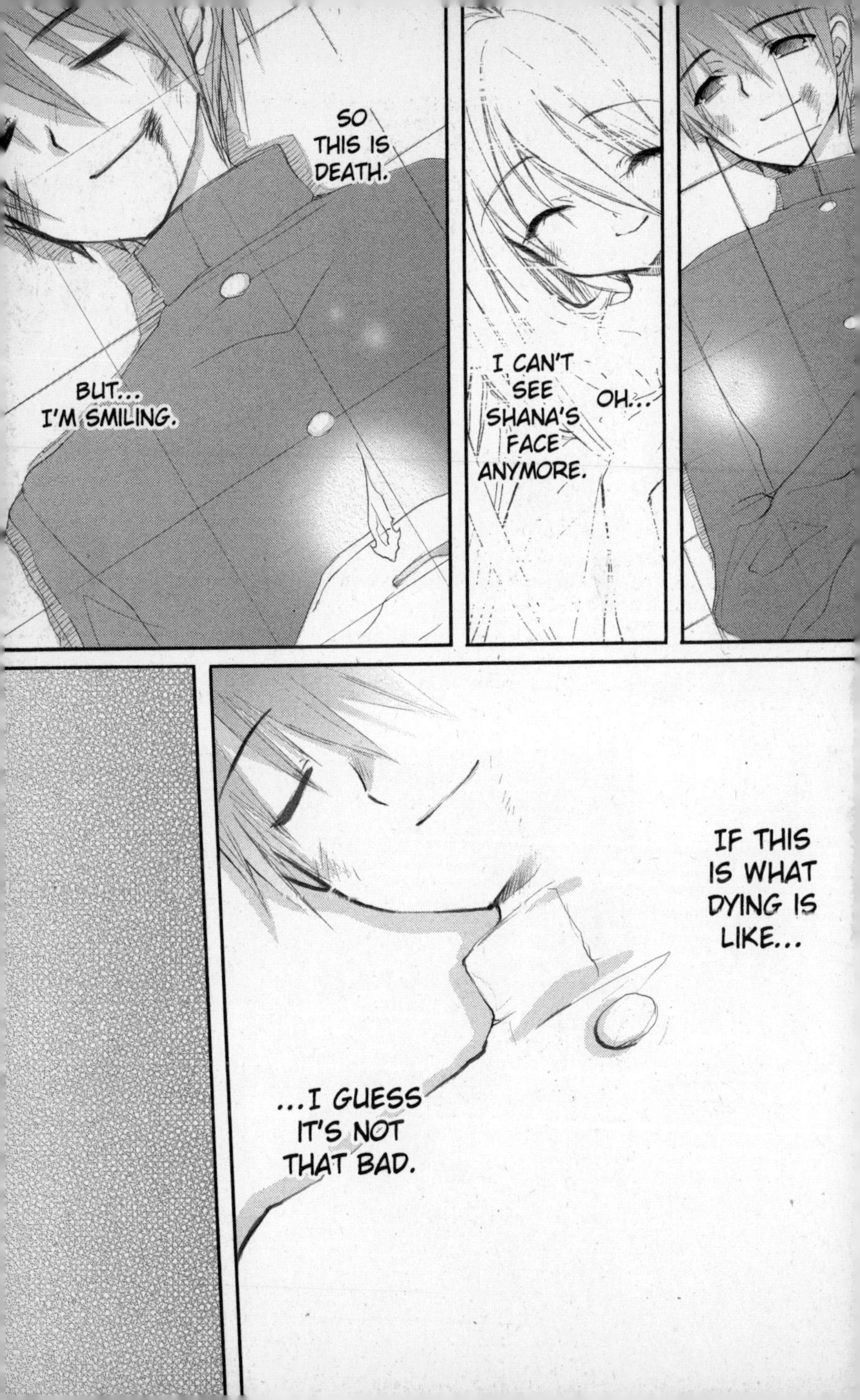
OH...
I CAN'T SEE SHANA'S FACE ANYMORE.
SO THIS IS DEATH.
BUT... I'M SMILING.
IF THIS IS WHAT DYING IS LIKE...
...I GUESS IT'S NOT THAT BAD.

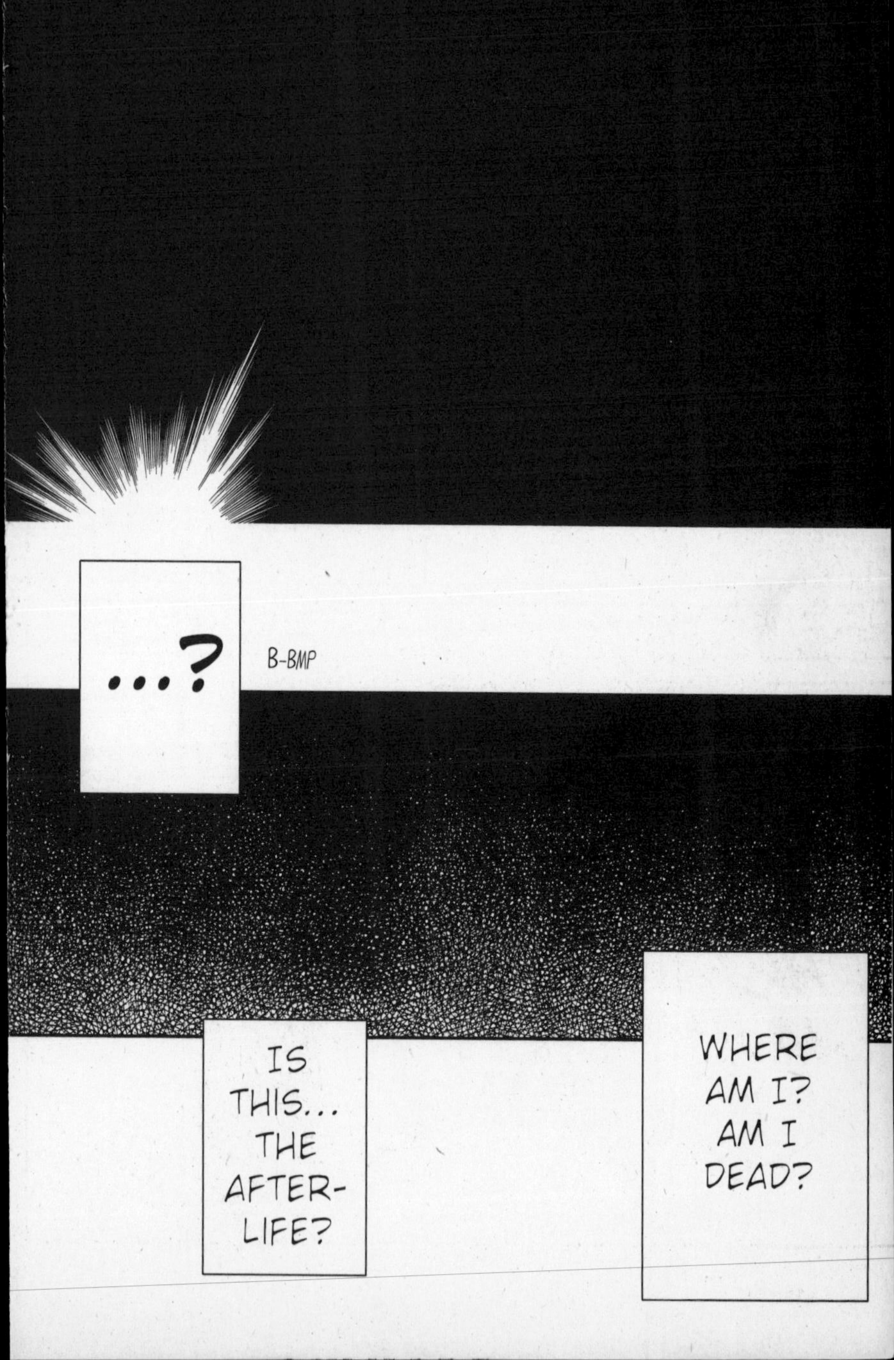
B-BMP
...?
WHERE AM I? AM I DEAD?
IS THIS... THE AFTER-LIFE?

...CAN HEAR...

I...

...THE WIND... THE CITY...

AND...

B-BMP

B-BMP

A HEART-BEAT?

B-BMP

...

AH HA HA HA HA HA HA HA!!

HA HA!

?!

TWTCH

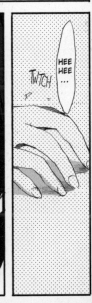

HEE HEE...

TWITCH

111

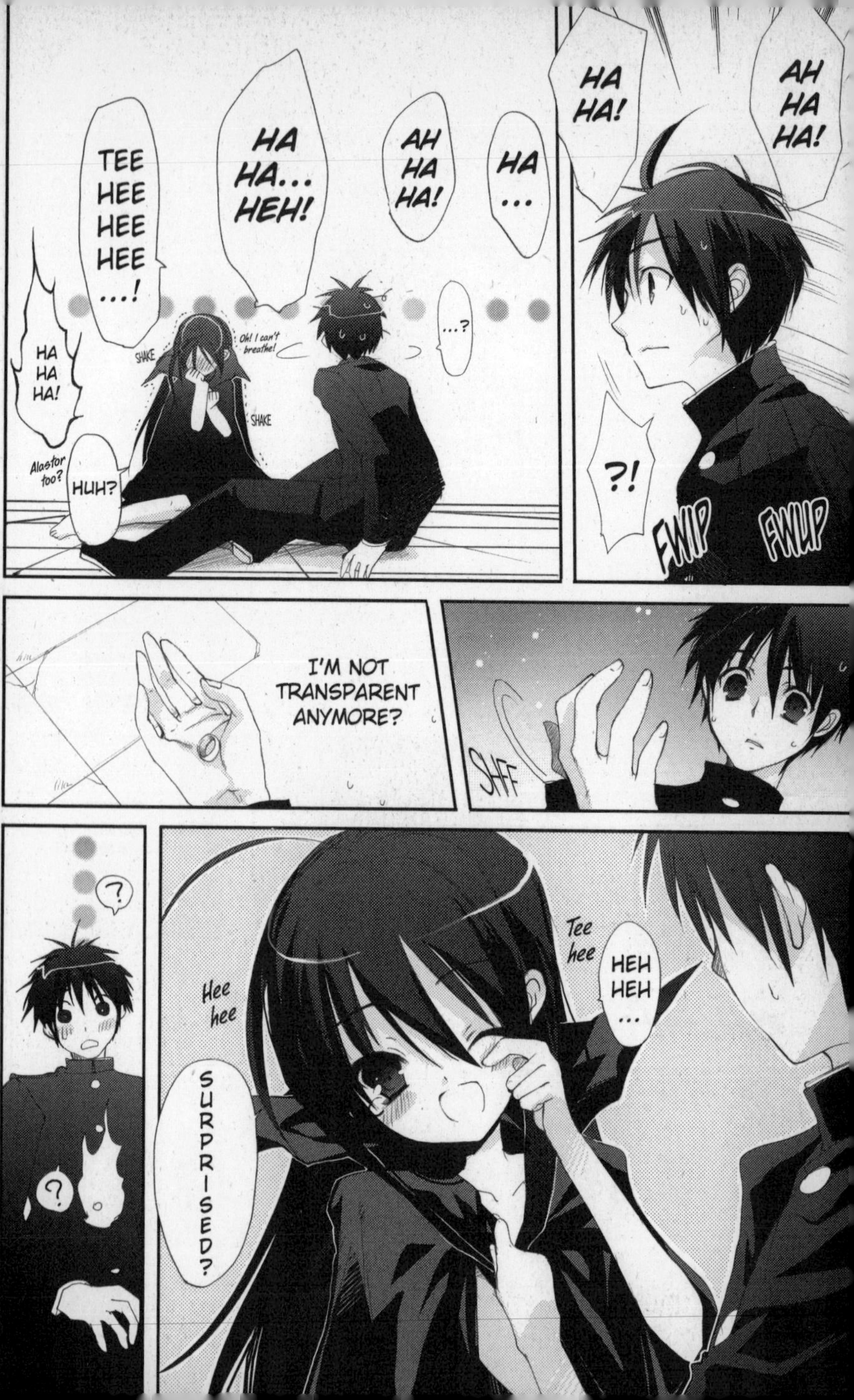
AH HA HA!
HA HA!
?!
FWIP
FWLIP
HA ...
AH HA HA!
HA HA... HEH!
TEE HEE HEE HEE ...!
...?
Oh! I can't breathe!
SHAKE
SHAKE
HA HA HA!
Alastor too?
HUH?
SHFF
I'M NOT TRANSPARENT ANYMORE?
Tee hee
HEH HEH ...
Hee hee
SURPRISED?
?
?

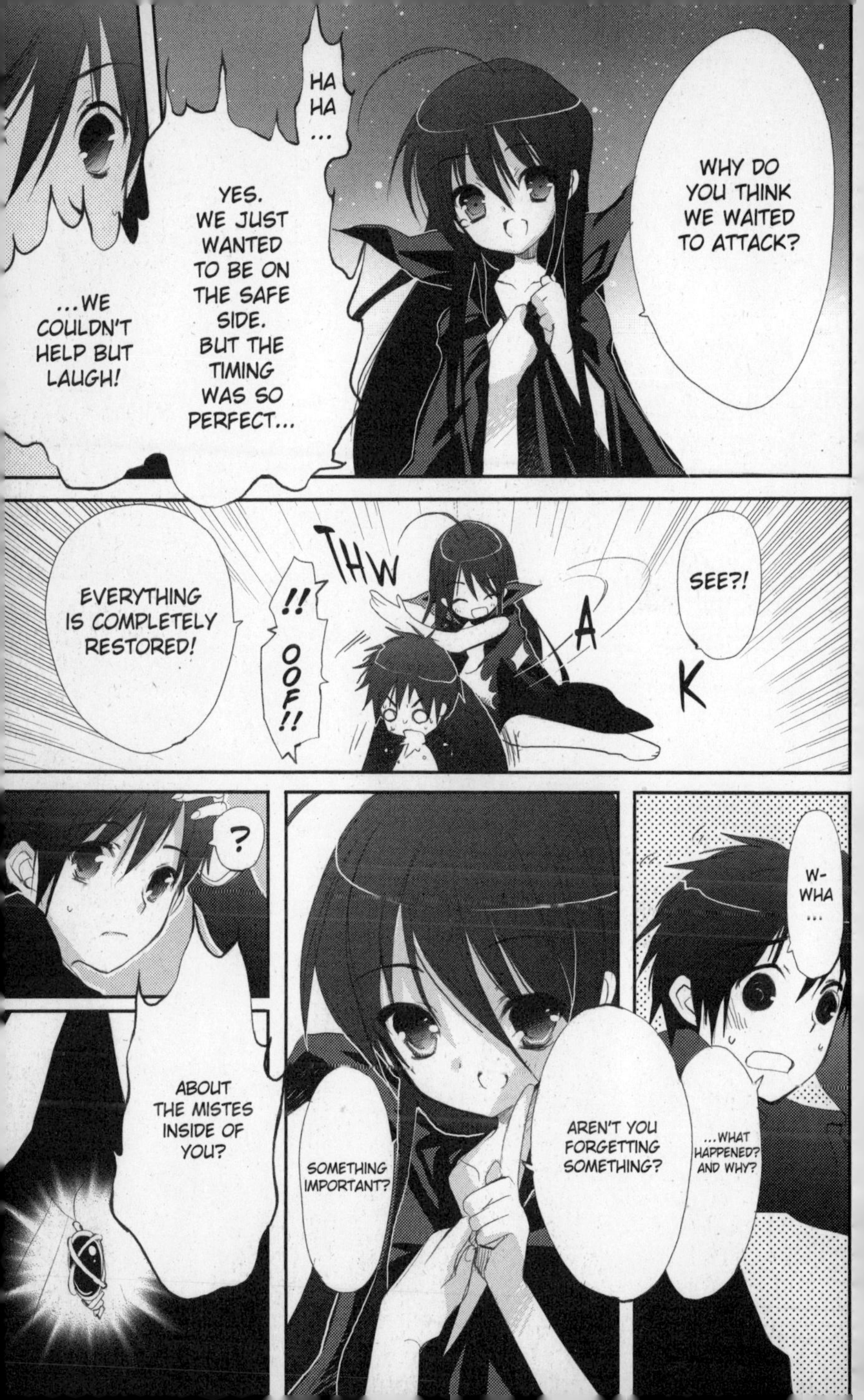
WHY DO YOU THINK WE WAITED TO ATTACK?
HA HA ...
YES. WE JUST WANTED TO BE ON THE SAFE SIDE. BUT THE TIMING WAS SO PERFECT...
...WE COULDN'T HELP BUT LAUGH!
SEE?!
THWACK
!! OOF!!
EVERYTHING IS COMPLETELY RESTORED!
W-WHA ...
...WHAT HAPPENED? AND WHY?
AREN'T YOU FORGETTING SOMETHING?
SOMETHING IMPORTANT?
?
ABOUT THE MISTES INSIDE OF YOU?

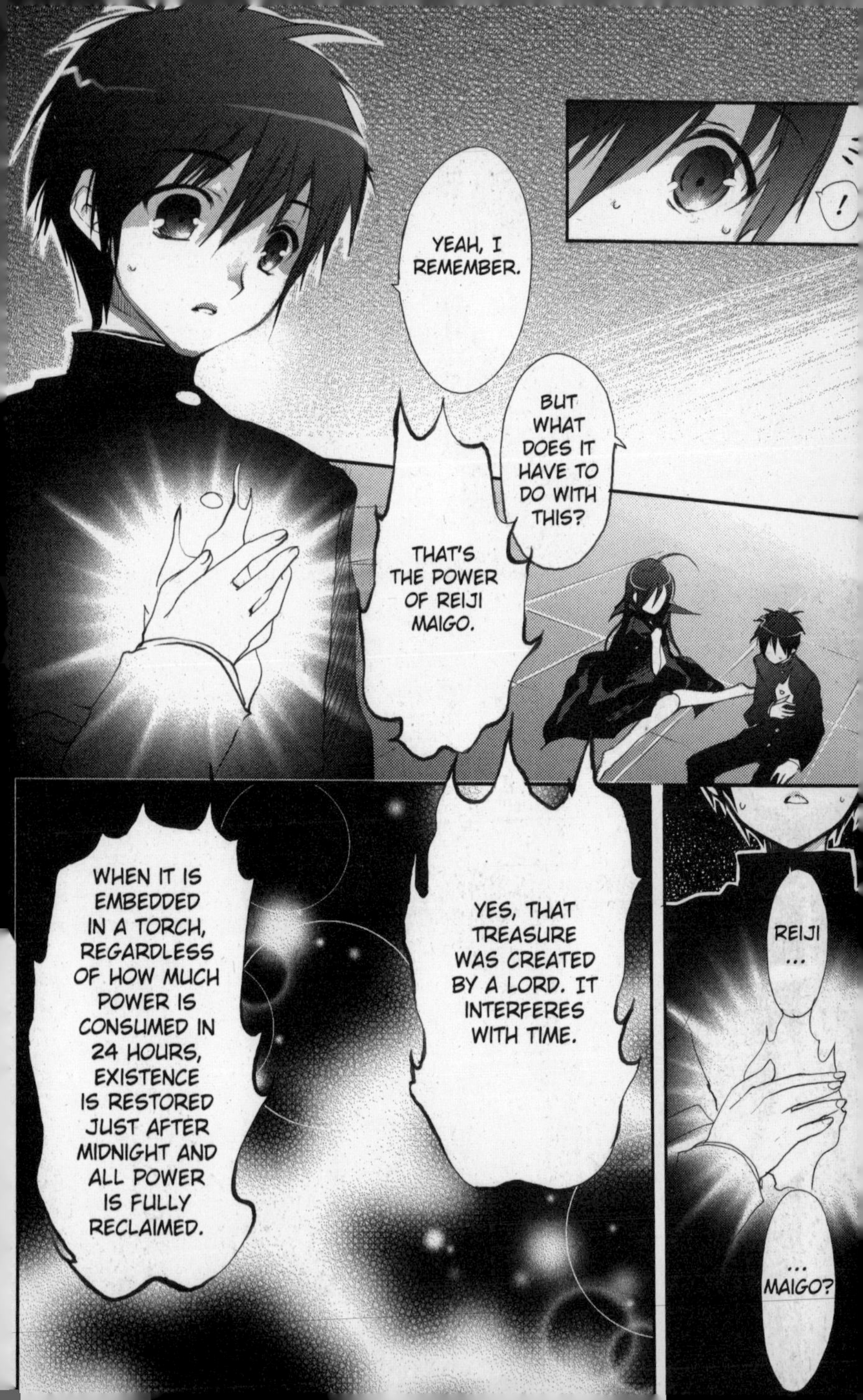
!
YEAH, I REMEMBER.
BUT WHAT DOES IT HAVE TO DO WITH THIS?
THAT'S THE POWER OF REIJI MAIGO.
REIJI ...
... MAIGO?
YES, THAT TREASURE WAS CREATED BY A LORD. IT INTERFERES WITH TIME.
WHEN IT IS EMBEDDED IN A TORCH, REGARDLESS OF HOW MUCH POWER IS CONSUMED IN 24 HOURS, EXISTENCE IS RESTORED JUST AFTER MIDNIGHT AND ALL POWER IS FULLY RECLAIMED.

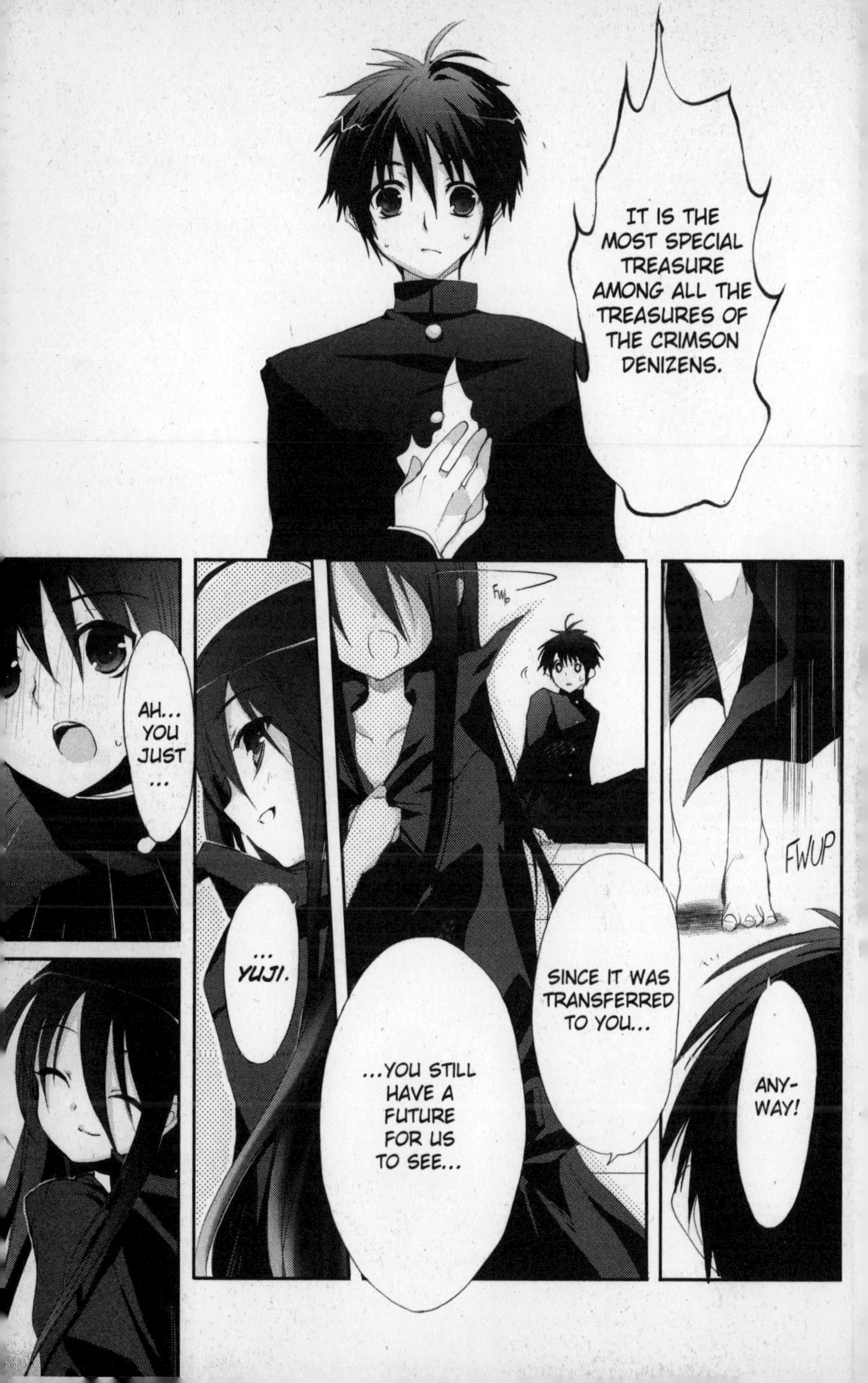
IT IS THE MOST SPECIAL TREASURE AMONG ALL THE TREASURES OF THE CRIMSON DENIZENS.
FWUP
ANY-WAY!
FWb
SINCE IT WAS TRANSFERRED TO YOU...
...YOU STILL HAVE A FUTURE FOR US TO SEE...
... YUJI.
AH... YOU JUST ...

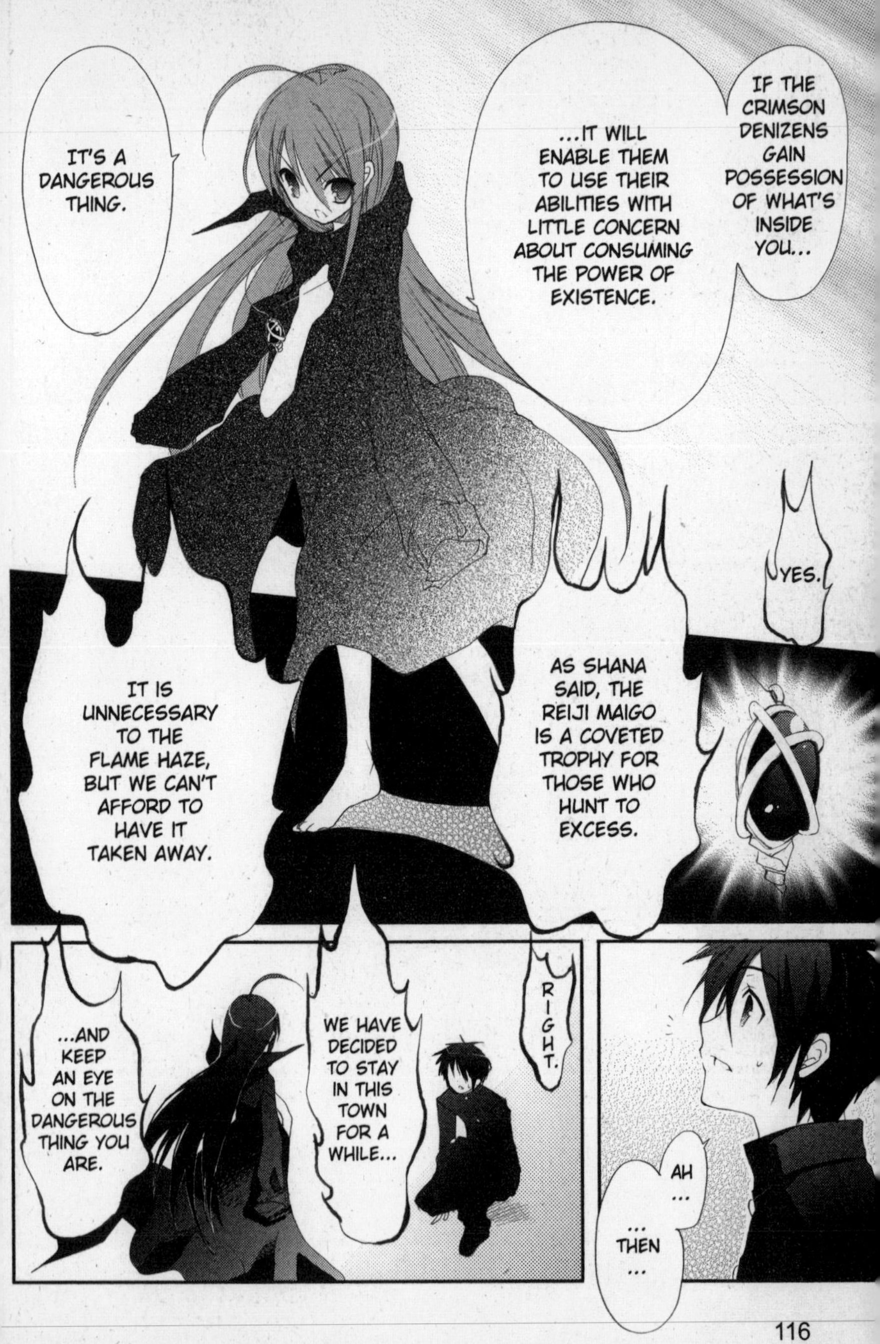
IF THE CRIMSON DENIZENS GAIN POSSESSION OF WHAT'S INSIDE YOU...
...IT WILL ENABLE THEM TO USE THEIR ABILITIES WITH LITTLE CONCERN ABOUT CONSUMING THE POWER OF EXISTENCE.
IT'S A DANGEROUS THING.
YES.
AS SHANA SAID, THE REIJI MAIGO IS A COVETED TROPHY FOR THOSE WHO HUNT TO EXCESS.
IT IS UNNECESSARY TO THE FLAME HAZE, BUT WE CAN'T AFFORD TO HAVE IT TAKEN AWAY.
AH ...
... THEN ...
RIGHT.
WE HAVE DECIDED TO STAY IN THIS TOWN FOR A WHILE...
...AND KEEP AN EYE ON THE DANGEROUS THING YOU ARE.

FWUP

...

ANY OBJEC-TIONS?

THAT'S IT.

GOOD.

NOPE.

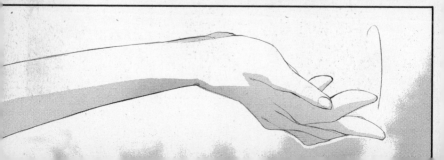

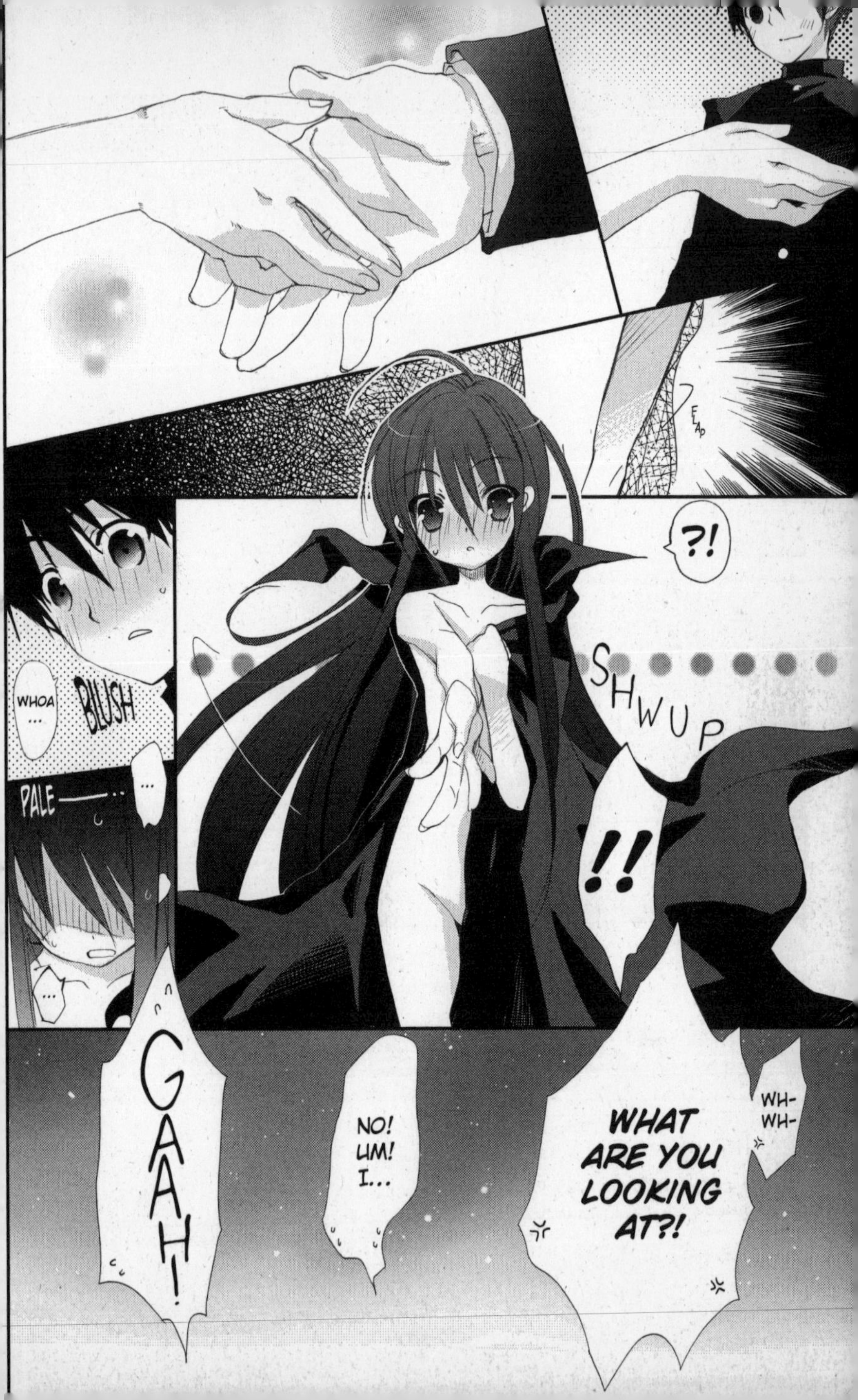
FLAP
?!
SHWUP
!!
WHOA ...
BLUSH
PALE
...
...
WH- WH-
WHAT ARE YOU LOOKING AT?!
NO! UM! I...
GAAH!

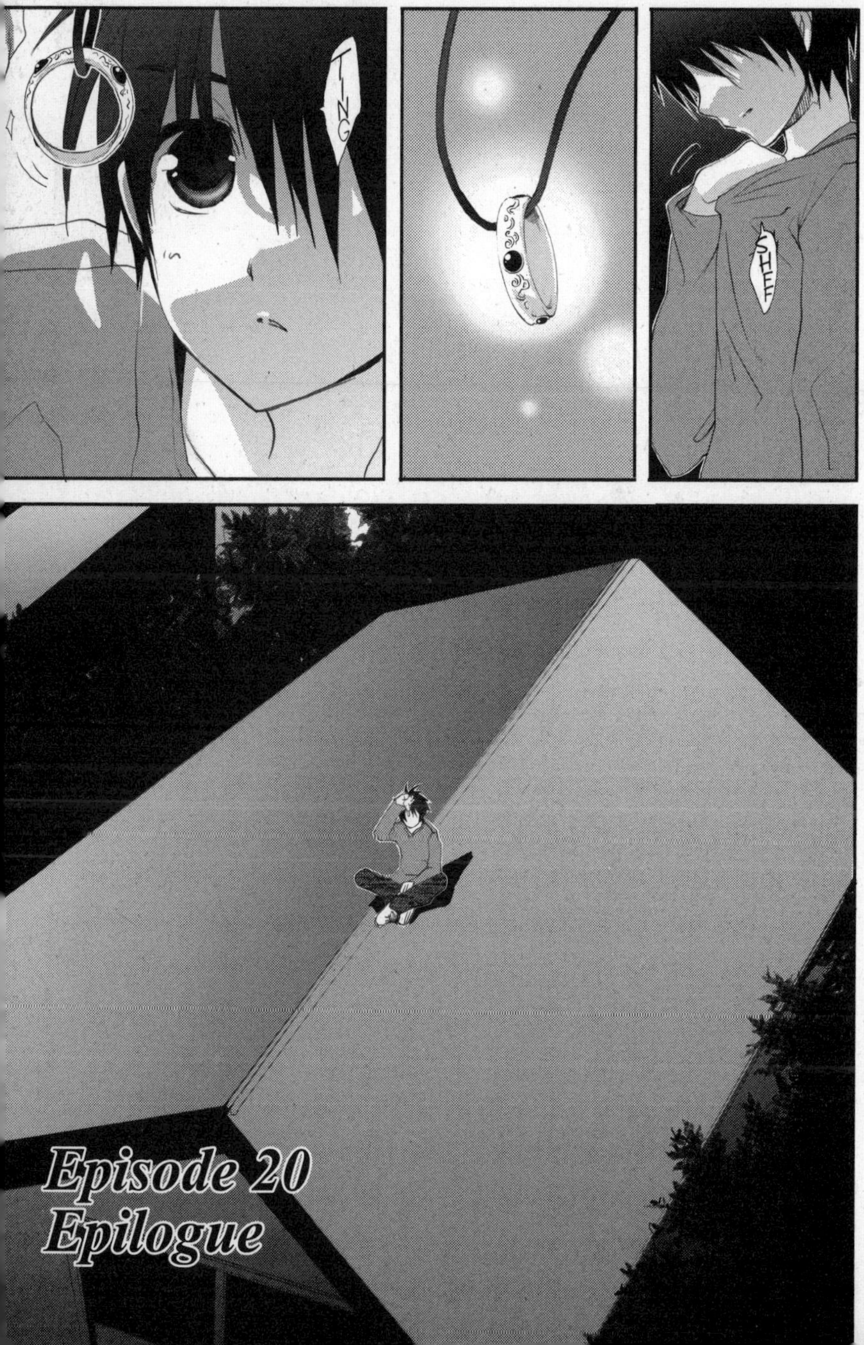
SHFF
TING
Episode 20
Epilogue

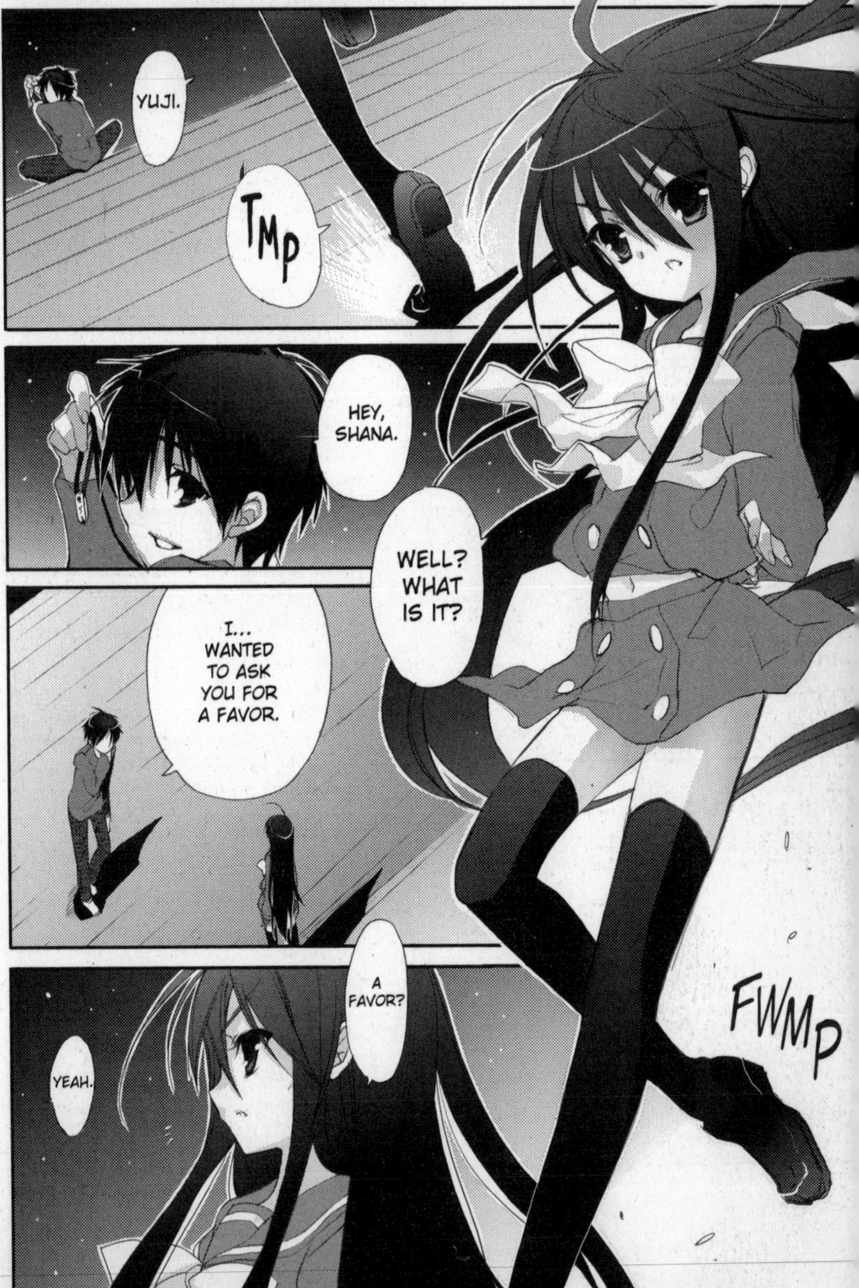
YUJI.
TMP
HEY, SHANA.
WELL? WHAT IS IT?
I... WANTED TO ASK YOU FOR A FAVOR.
A FAVOR?
YEAH.
FWMP

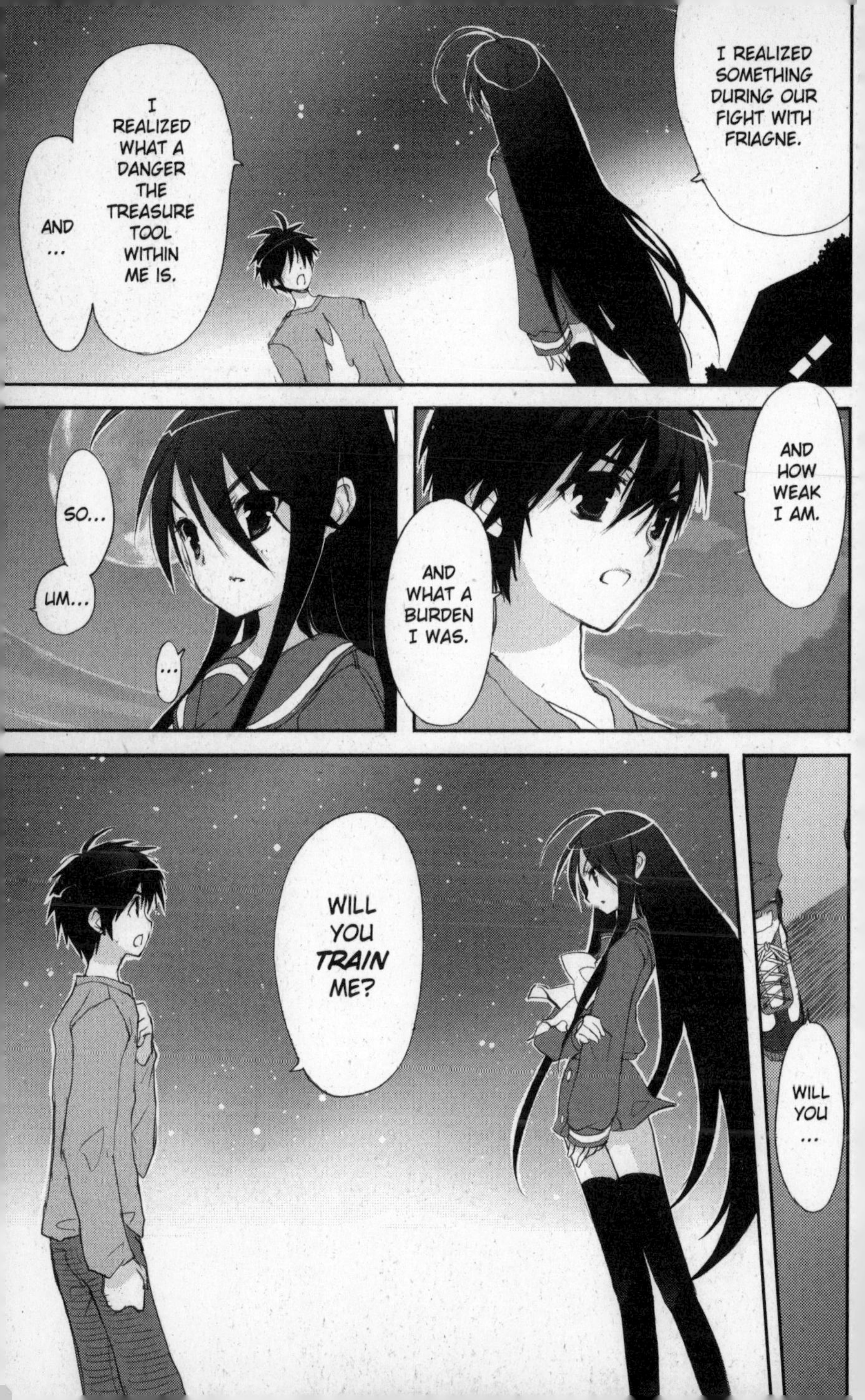
I REALIZED SOMETHING DURING OUR FIGHT WITH FRIAGNE.
I REALIZED WHAT A DANGER THE TREASURE TOOL WITHIN ME IS.
AND ...
AND HOW WEAK I AM.
AND WHAT A BURDEN I WAS.
SO...
UM...
...
WILL YOU ...
WILL YOU *TRAIN* ME?

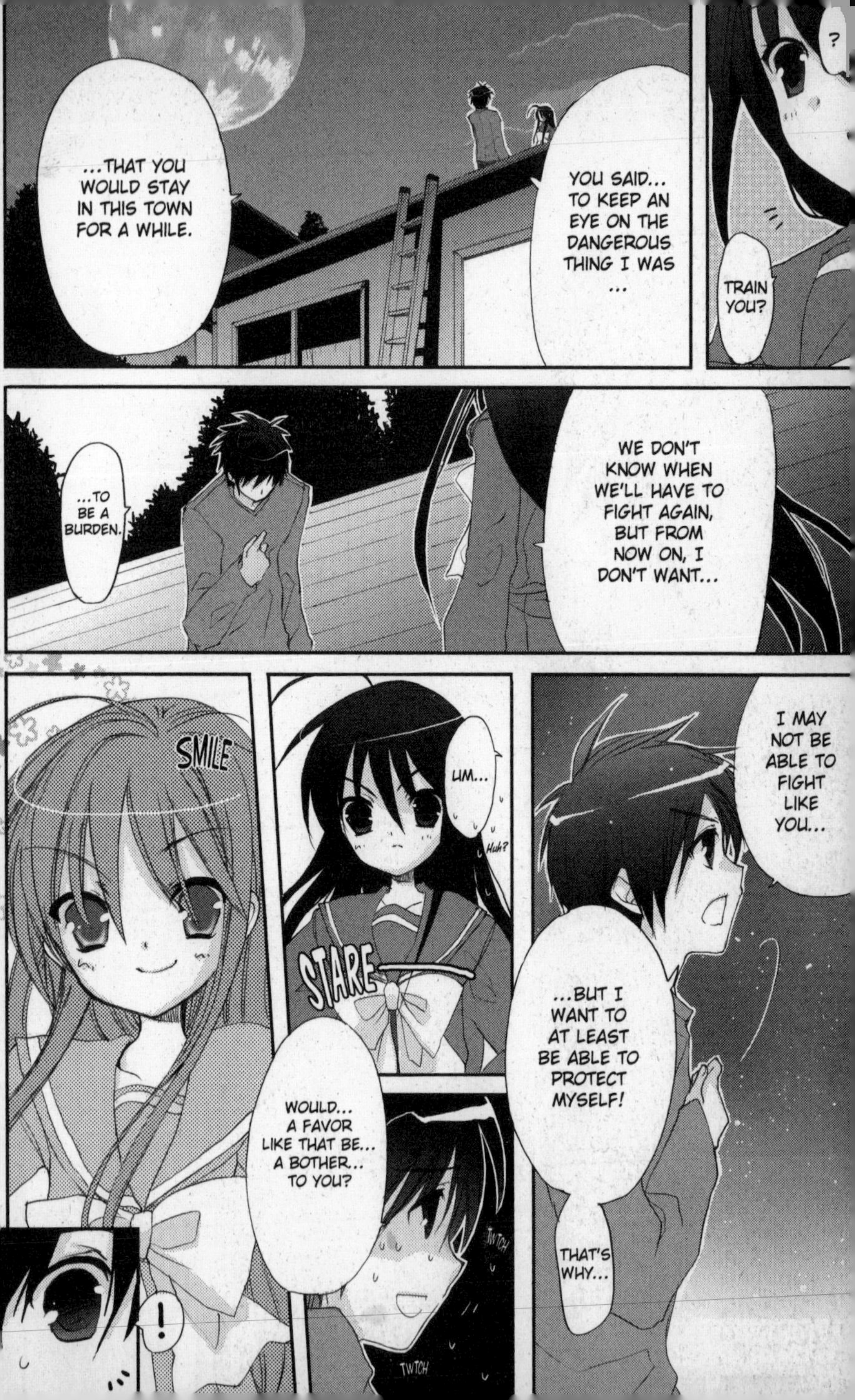
?
TRAIN YOU?
YOU SAID... TO KEEP AN EYE ON THE DANGEROUS THING I WAS ...
...THAT YOU WOULD STAY IN THIS TOWN FOR A WHILE.
WE DON'T KNOW WHEN WE'LL HAVE TO FIGHT AGAIN, BUT FROM NOW ON, I DON'T WANT...
...TO BE A BURDEN.
I MAY NOT BE ABLE TO FIGHT LIKE YOU...
...BUT I WANT TO AT LEAST BE ABLE TO PROTECT MYSELF!
THAT'S WHY...
UM...
Huh?
STARE
WOULD... A FAVOR LIKE THAT BE... A BOTHER... TO YOU?
TWITCH
TWITCH
SMILE
!

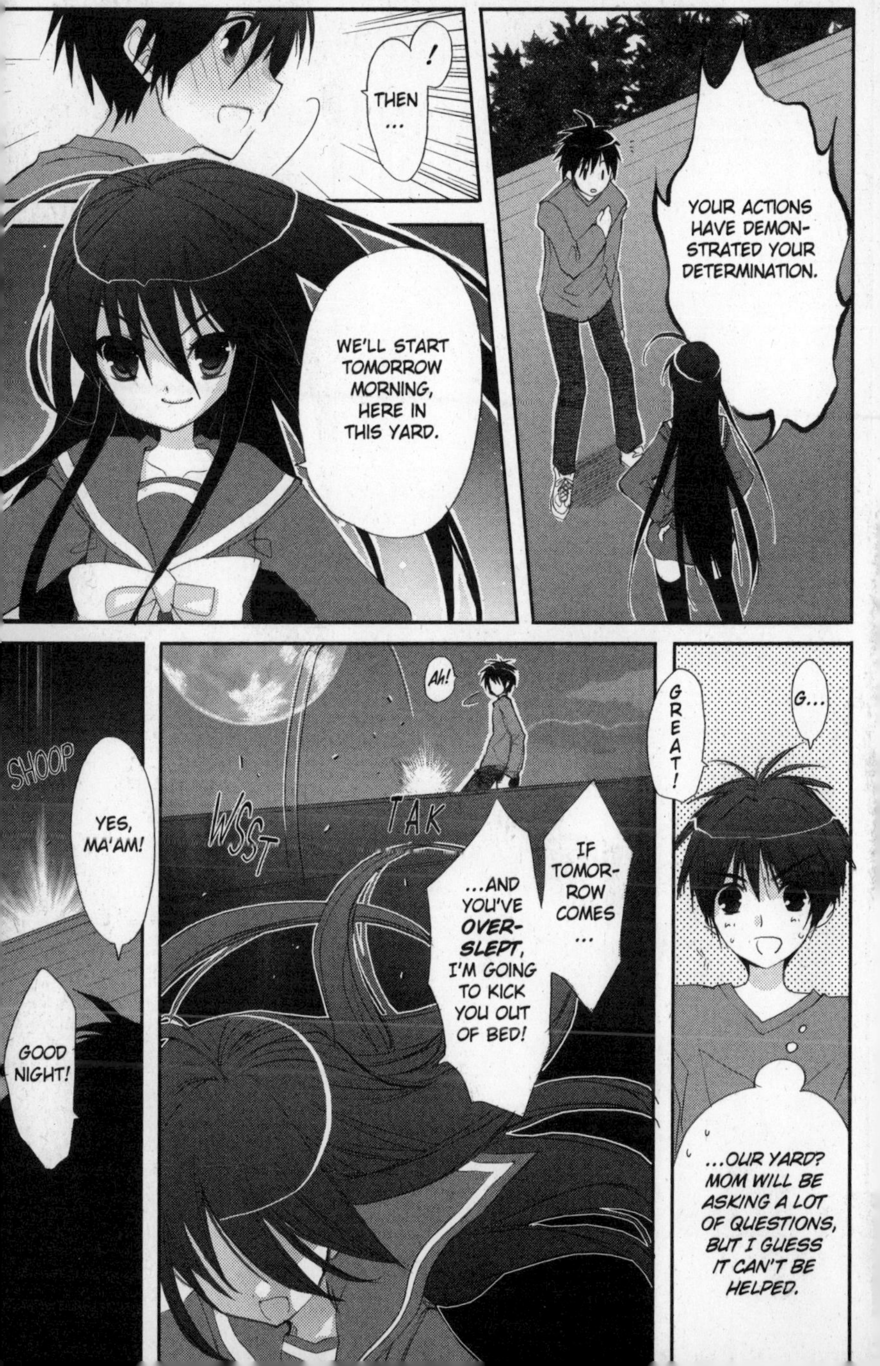
YOUR ACTIONS HAVE DEMON-STRATED YOUR DETERMINATION.
!
THEN ...
WE'LL START TOMORROW MORNING, HERE IN THIS YARD.
G...
GREAT!
...OUR YARD? MOM WILL BE ASKING A LOT OF QUESTIONS, BUT I GUESS IT CAN'T BE HELPED.
Ah!
TAK
WSST
IF TOMORROW COMES ...
...AND YOU'VE OVERSLEPT, I'M GOING TO KICK YOU OUT OF BED!
SHOOP
YES, MA'AM!
GOOD NIGHT!

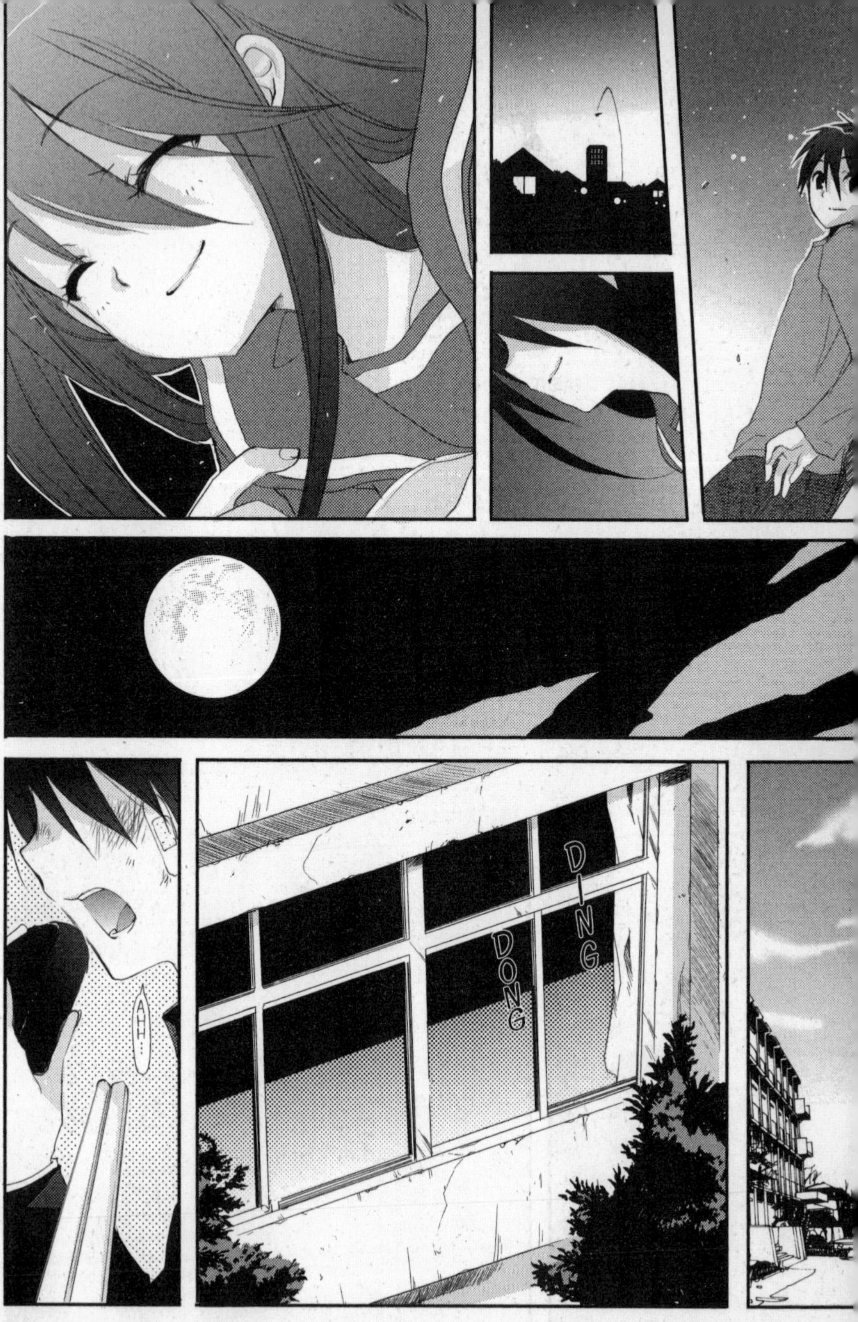
DING
DONG
AHH...

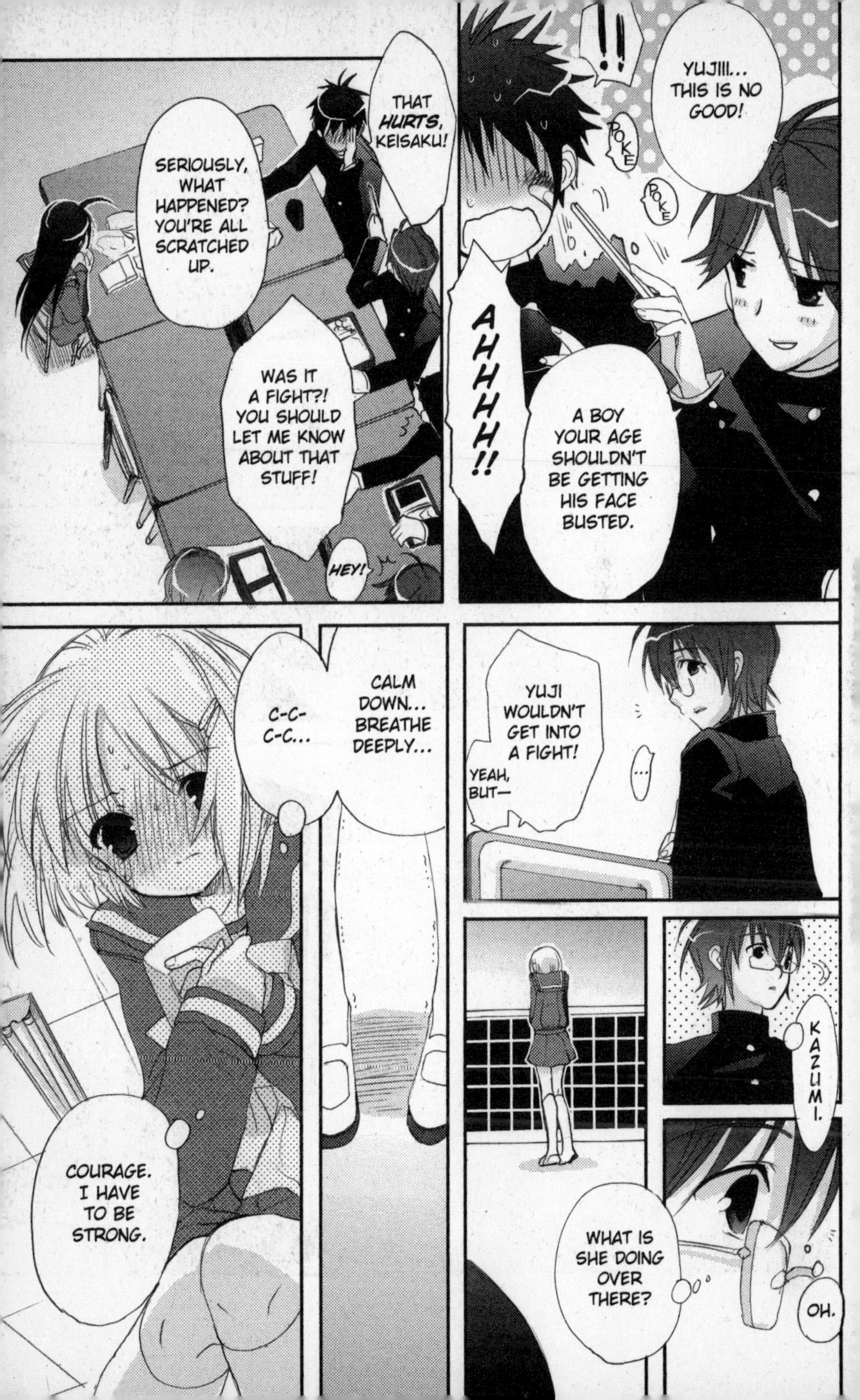
!!
YUJIII... THIS IS NO GOOD!
POKE
POKE
AHHHHH!!
A BOY YOUR AGE SHOULDN'T BE GETTING HIS FACE BUSTED.
THAT HURTS, KEISAKU!
SERIOUSLY, WHAT HAPPENED? YOU'RE ALL SCRATCHED UP.
WAS IT A FIGHT?! YOU SHOULD LET ME KNOW ABOUT THAT STUFF!
HEY!
YUJI WOULDN'T GET INTO A FIGHT!
YEAH, BUT—
...
KAZUMI.
OH.
WHAT IS SHE DOING OVER THERE?
CALM DOWN... BREATHE DEEPLY...
C-C-C-C...
COURAGE. I HAVE TO BE STRONG.

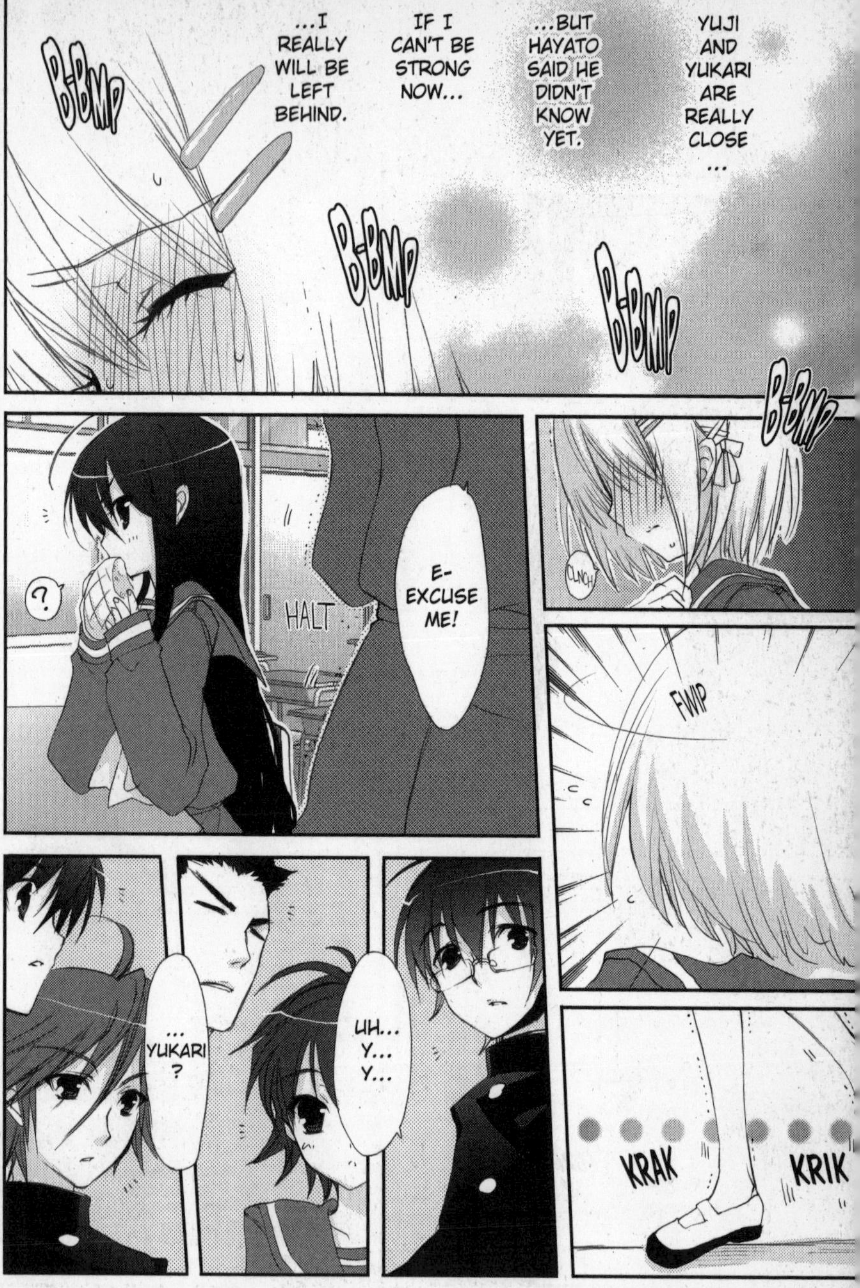
YUJI AND YUKARI ARE REALLY CLOSE...
...BUT HAYATO SAID HE DIDN'T KNOW YET.
IF I CAN'T BE STRONG NOW...
...I REALLY WILL BE LEFT BEHIND.
B-BMP
B-BMP
B-BMP
B-BMP
B-BMP
CLINCH
FWIP
KRIK
KRAK
E-EXCUSE ME!
HALT
?
UH... Y... Y...
...YUKARI?

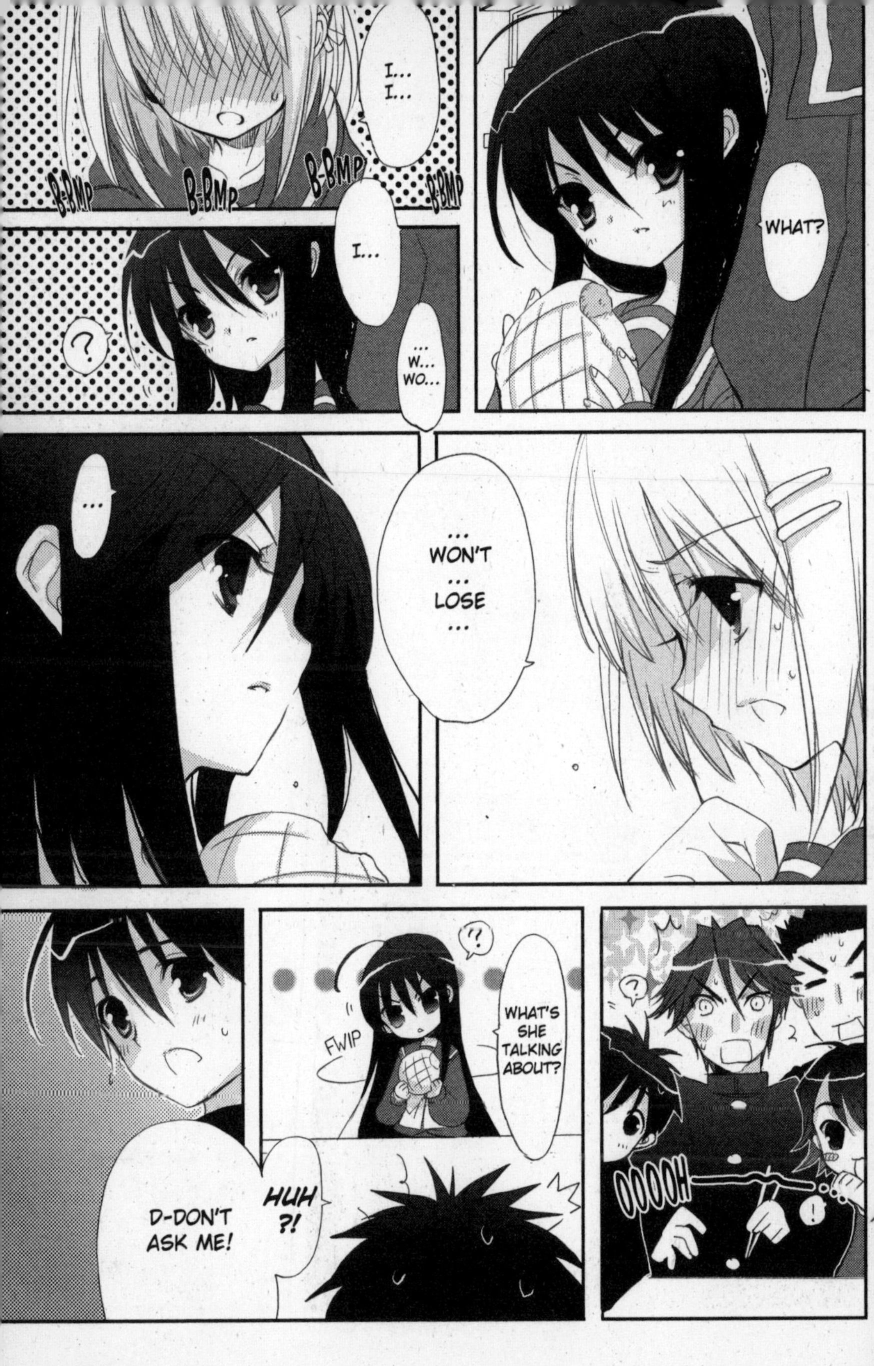
WHAT?
I... I...
B-BMP
B-BMP
B-BMP
B-BMP
I...
... W... WO...
?
... WON'T ... LOSE ...
...
?
!
OOOOH
?
WHAT'S SHE TALKING ABOUT?
FWIP
HUH ?!
D-DON'T ASK ME!

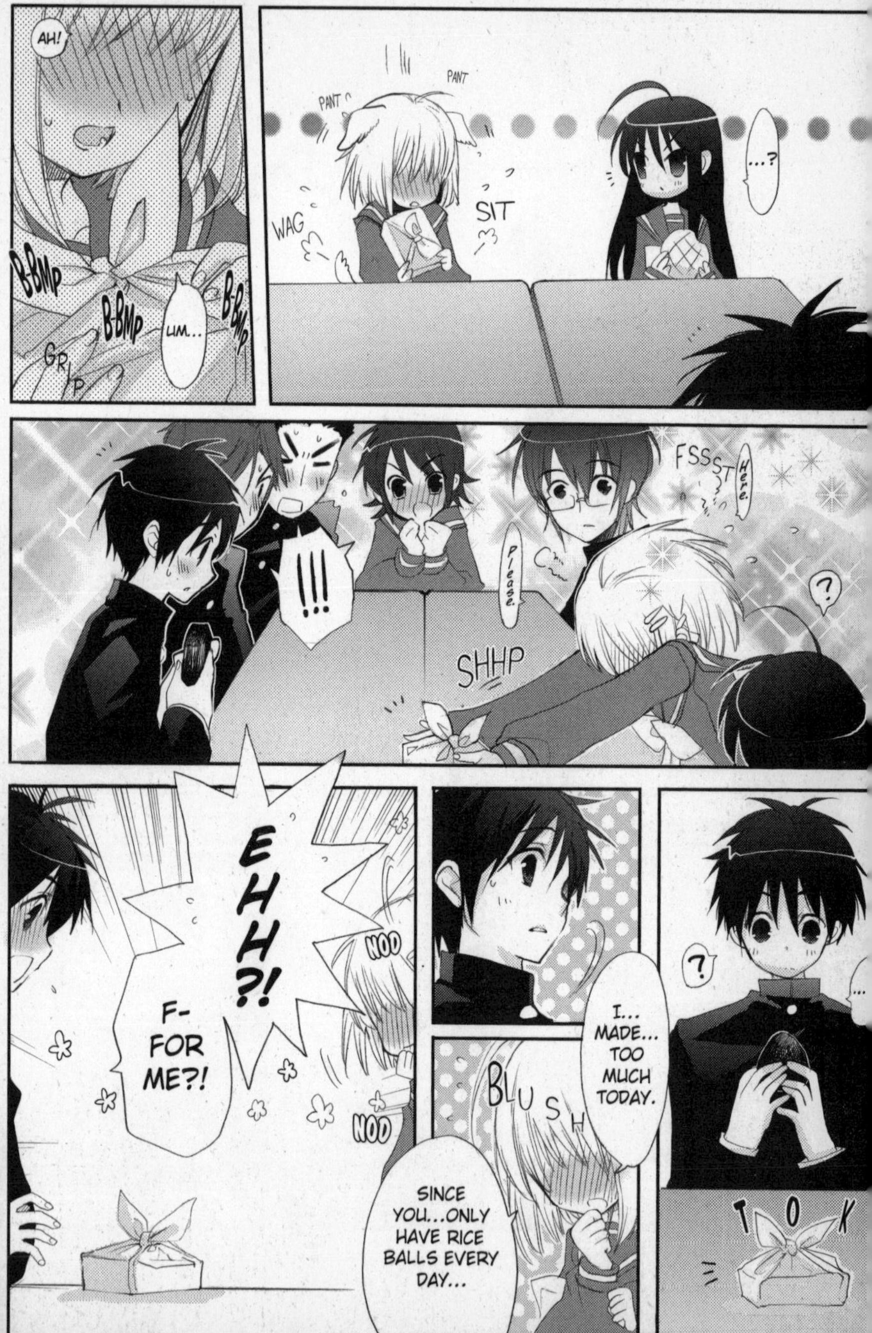

...?
PANT
PANT
SIT
WAG
AH!
B-BMP
UM...
B-BMP
B-BMP
GRIP
FSSST
Here.
?
Please.
!!!
SHHP
...
?
TOK
I... MADE... TOO MUCH TODAY.
BLUSH
SINCE YOU...ONLY HAVE RICE BALLS EVERY DAY...
NOD
NOD
EHH?!
F-FOR ME?!

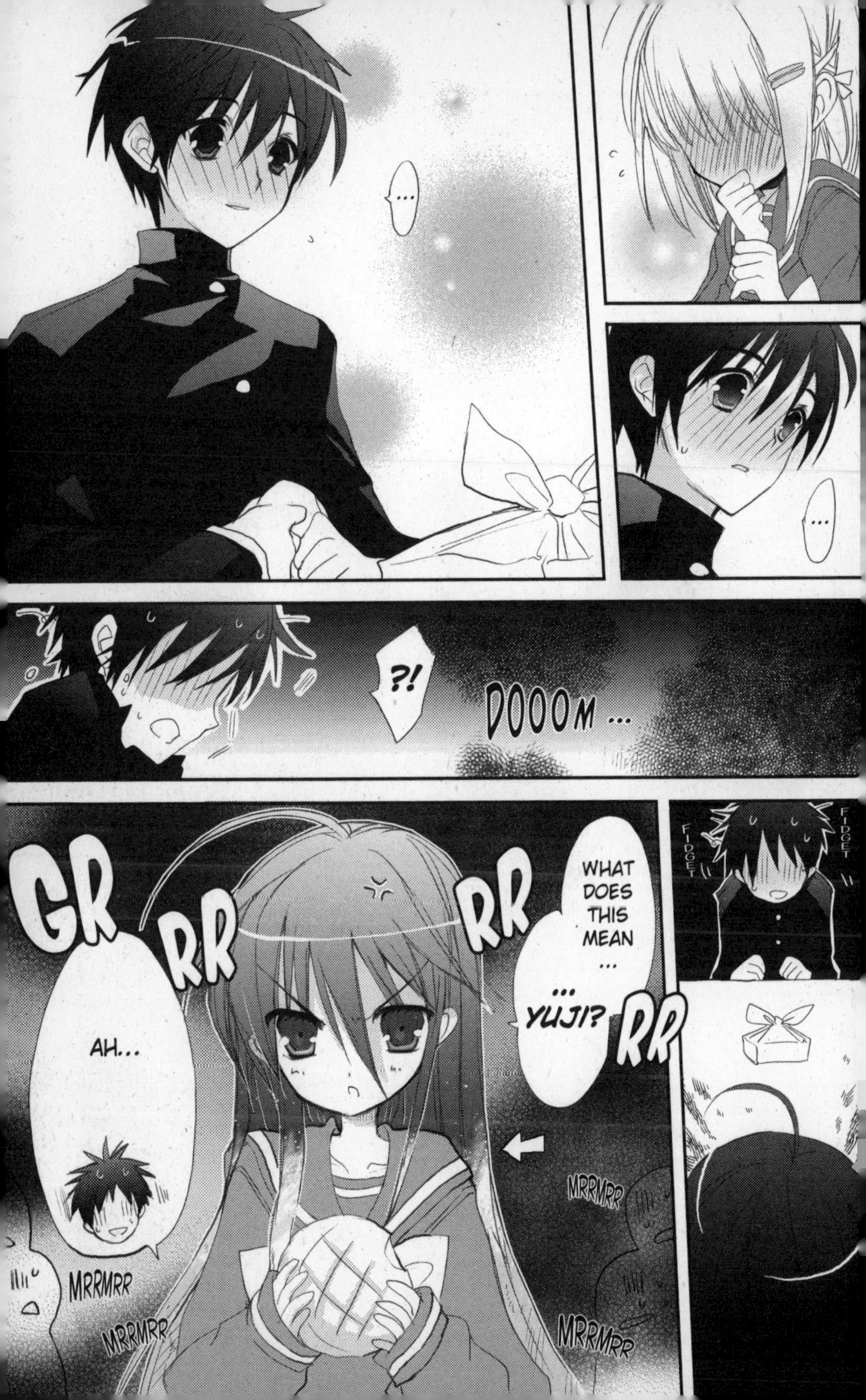
...
...
?!
DOOOM ...
FIDGET
FIDGET
GR RR RR
WHAT DOES THIS MEAN ...
... YUJI?
RR
AH...
MRRMRR
MRRMRR
MRRMRR
MRRMRR

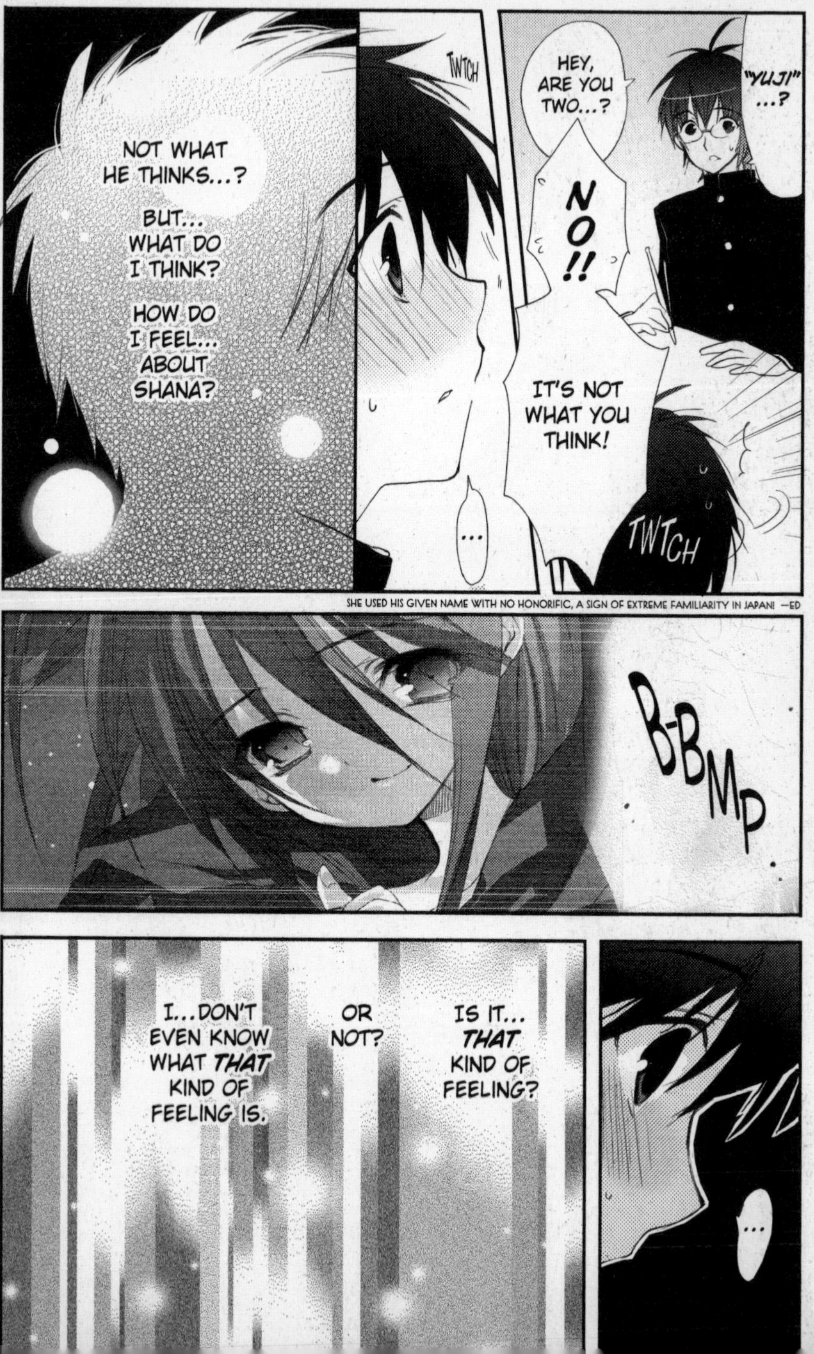
"YUJI" ...?
HEY, ARE YOU TWO...?
NO!!
IT'S NOT WHAT YOU THINK!
TWTCH
TWTCH
...
NOT WHAT HE THINKS...?
BUT... WHAT DO I THINK?
HOW DO I FEEL... ABOUT SHANA?
SHE USED HIS GIVEN NAME WITH NO HONORIFIC, A SIGN OF EXTREME FAMILIARITY IN JAPAN! —ED
B-BMP
...
IS IT... *THAT* KIND OF FEELING?
OR NOT?
I...DON'T EVEN KNOW WHAT *THAT* KIND OF FEELING IS.

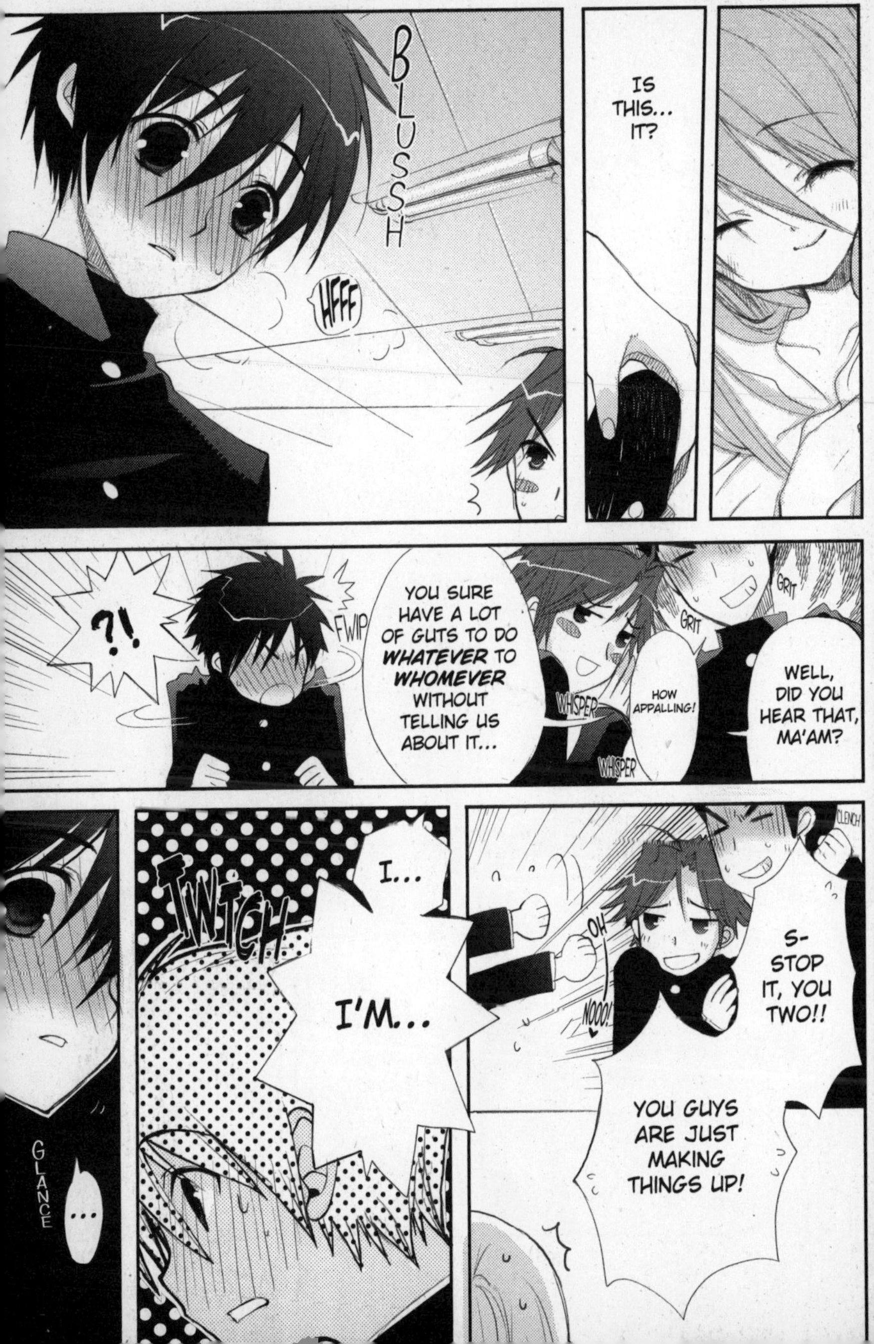
IS THIS... IT?
BLUSSH
HFFF
WELL, DID YOU HEAR THAT, MA'AM?
GRIT
GRIT
HOW APPALLING!
WHISPER
WHISPER
YOU SURE HAVE A LOT OF GUTS TO DO ***WHATEVER*** TO ***WHOMEVER*** WITHOUT TELLING US ABOUT IT...
FWIP
?!
CLENCH
S-STOP IT, YOU TWO!!
OH
NOOO!
YOU GUYS ARE JUST MAKING THINGS UP!
TWITCH
I...
I'M...
GLANCE
...

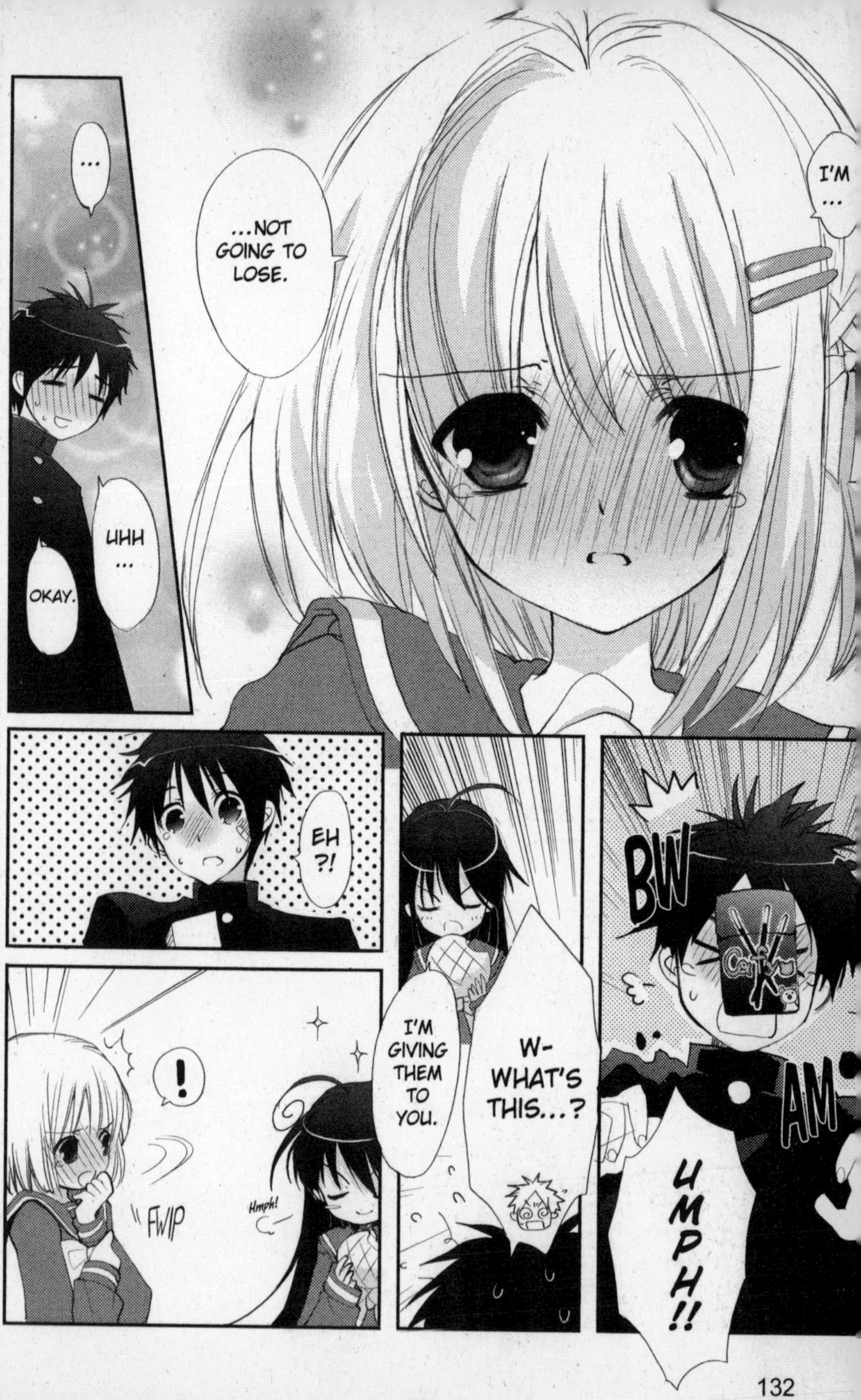
I'M ...
...NOT GOING TO LOSE.
...
UHH ...
OKAY.
BWAM
UMPH!!
W-WHAT'S THIS...?
I'M GIVING THEM TO YOU.
EH ?!
!
FWIP
Hmph!

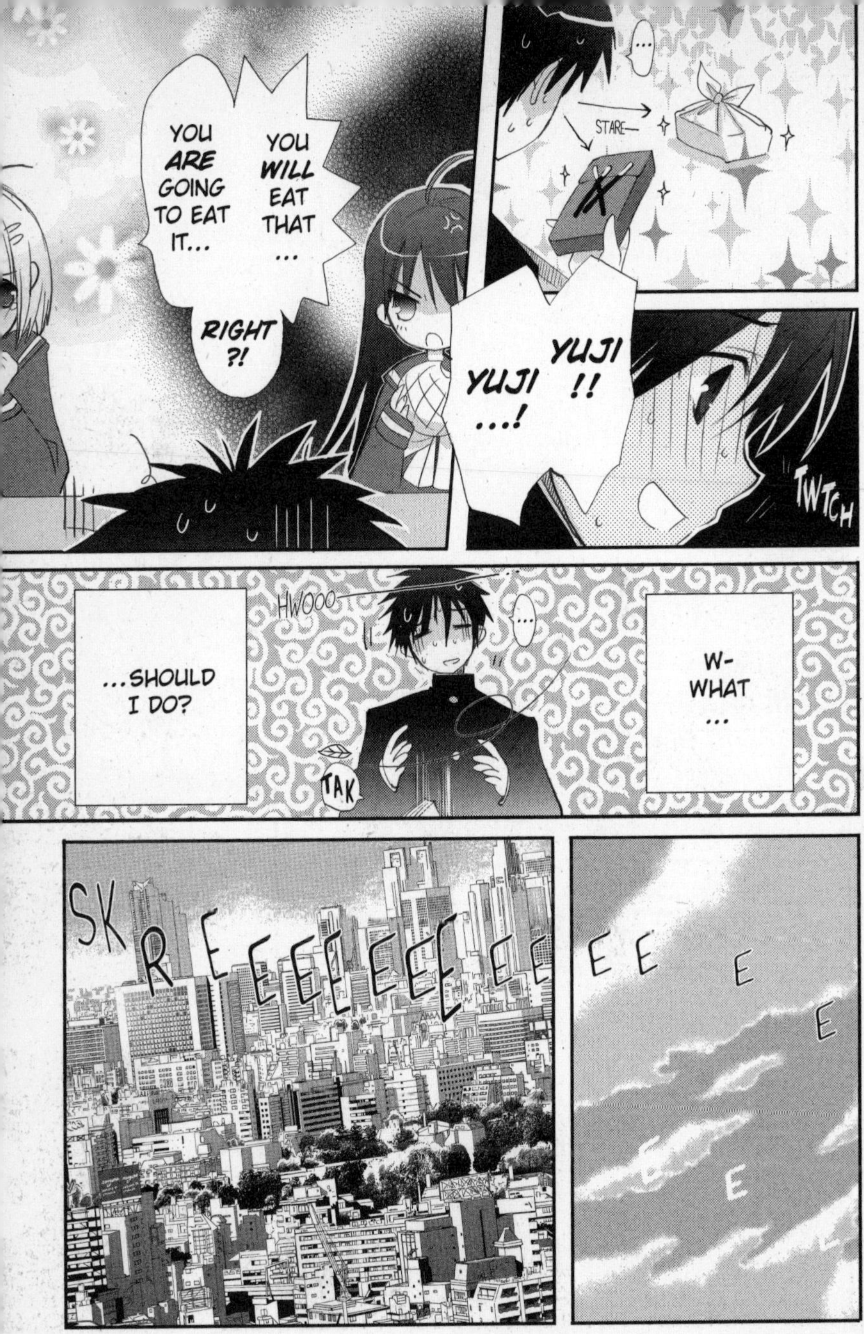
...
STARE—
YUJI !!
YUJI ...!
TWTCH
YOU WILL EAT THAT ...
YOU ARE GOING TO EAT IT...
RIGHT ?!
W-WHAT ...
...
HWOOO
TAK
...SHOULD I DO?
SKREEEEEEEEEEEEEEEEEE

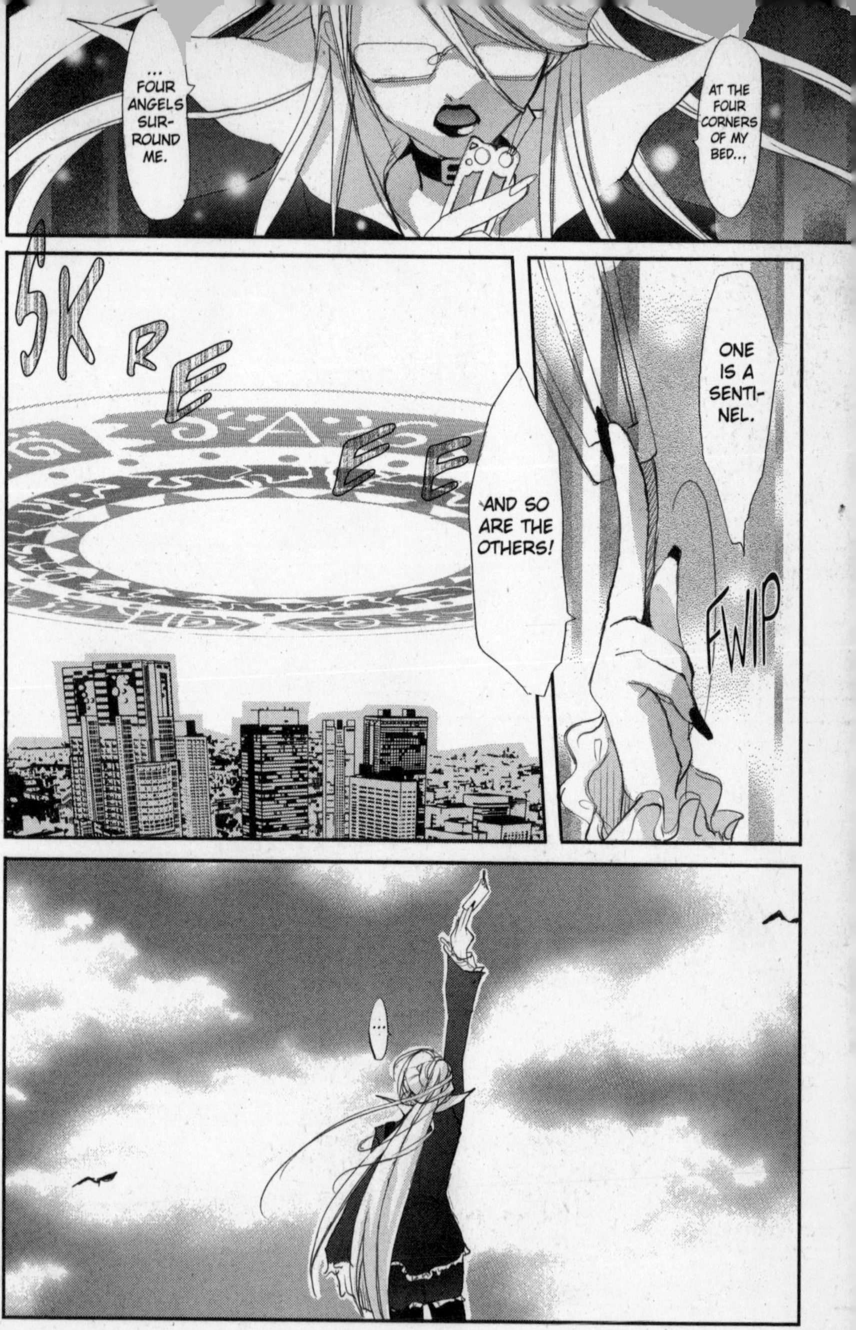
AT THE FOUR CORNERS OF MY BED...
... FOUR ANGELS SUR-ROUND ME.
ONE IS A SENTI-NEL.
FWIP
AND SO ARE THE OTHERS!
SKREEEE
...

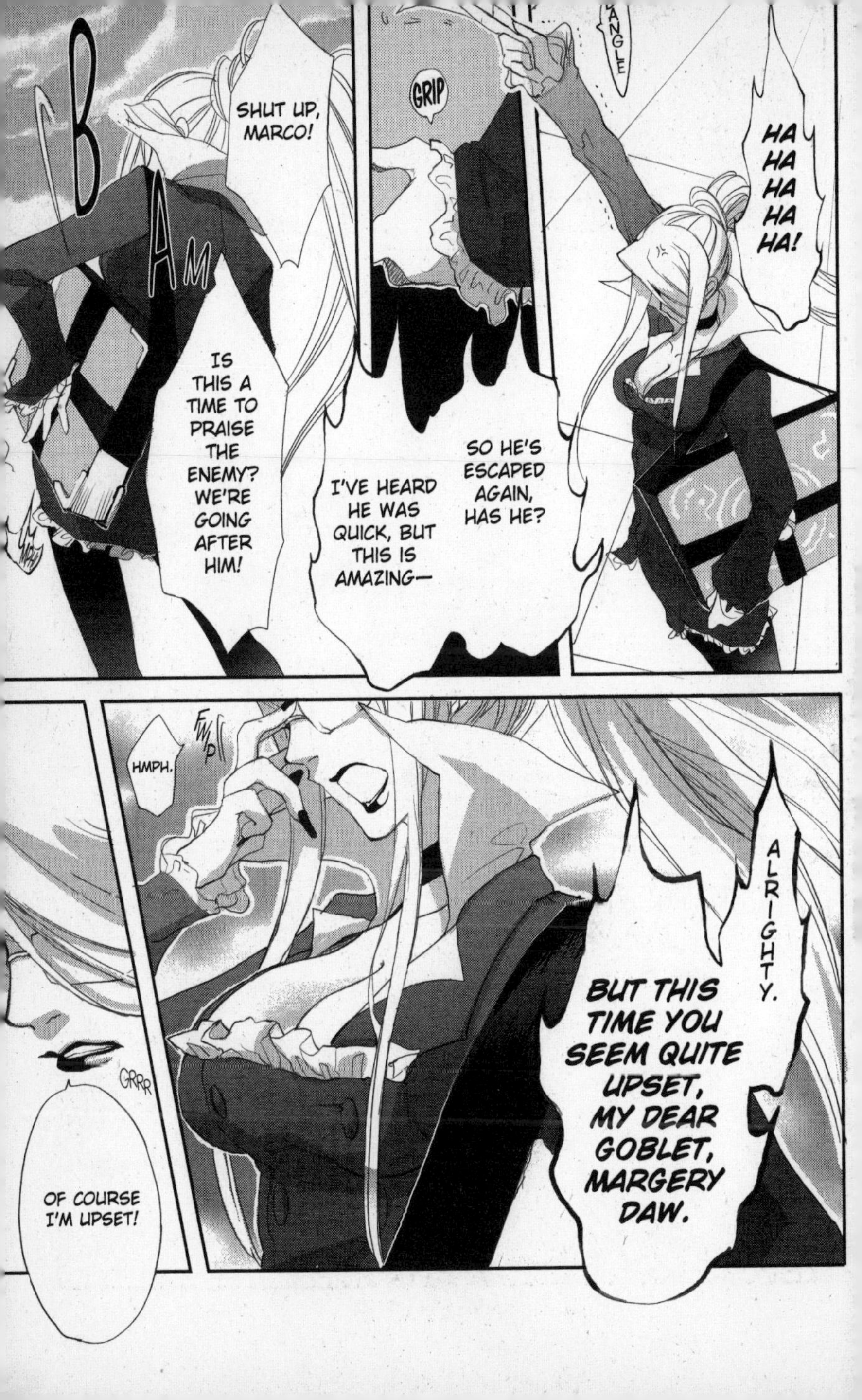
ANGLE
HA HA HA HA HA!
SO HE'S ESCAPED AGAIN, HAS HE?
I'VE HEARD HE WAS QUICK, BUT THIS IS AMAZING—
GRIP
SHUT UP, MARCO!
BAM
IS THIS A TIME TO PRAISE THE ENEMY? WE'RE GOING AFTER HIM!
ALRIGHTY.
BUT THIS TIME YOU SEEM QUITE UPSET, MY DEAR GOBLET, MARGERY DAW.
FWIP
HMPH.
GRRR
OF COURSE I'M UPSET!

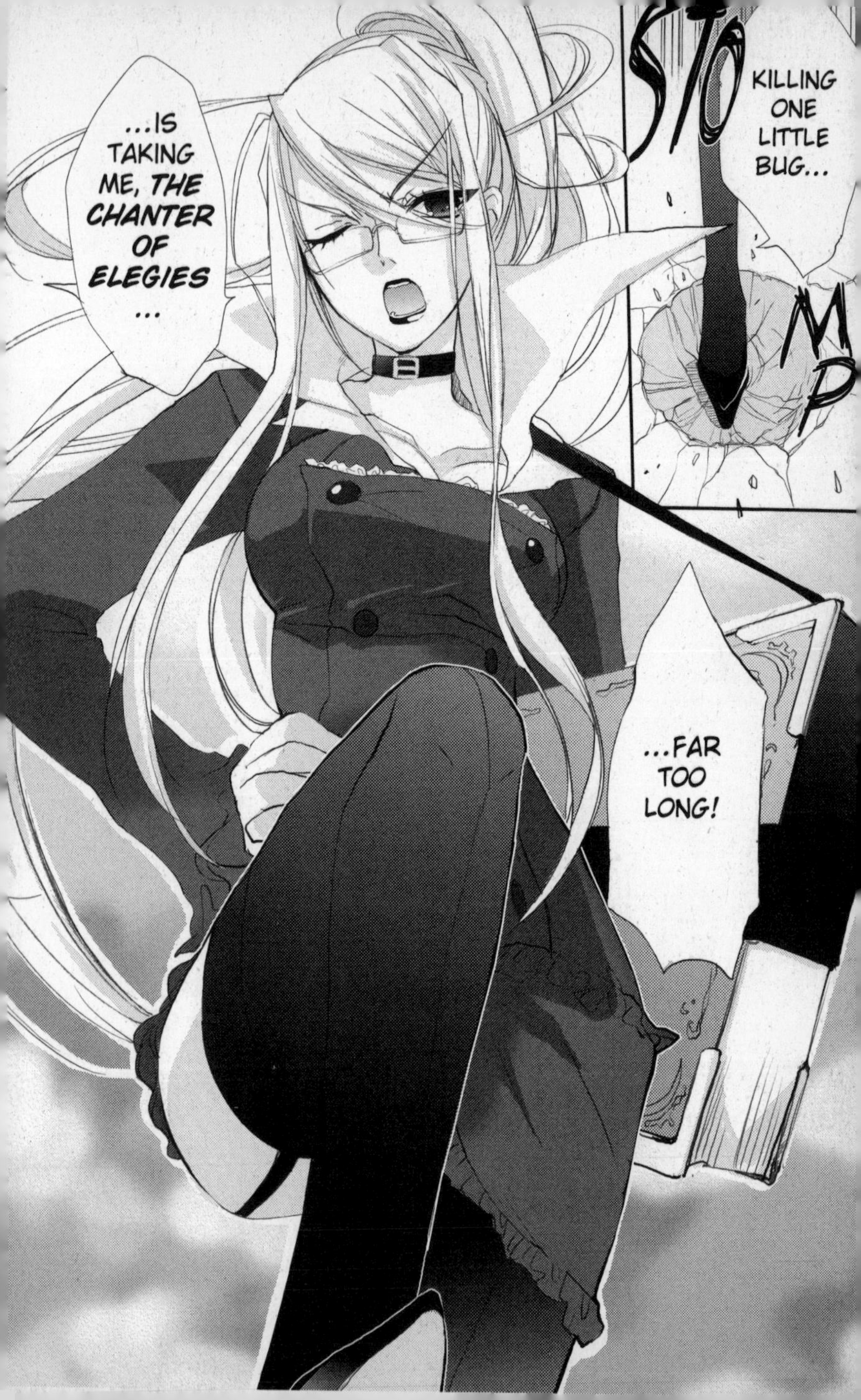
STOMP
KILLING ONE LITTLE BUG...
...IS TAKING ME, THE CHANTER OF ELEGIES...
...FAR TOO LONG!

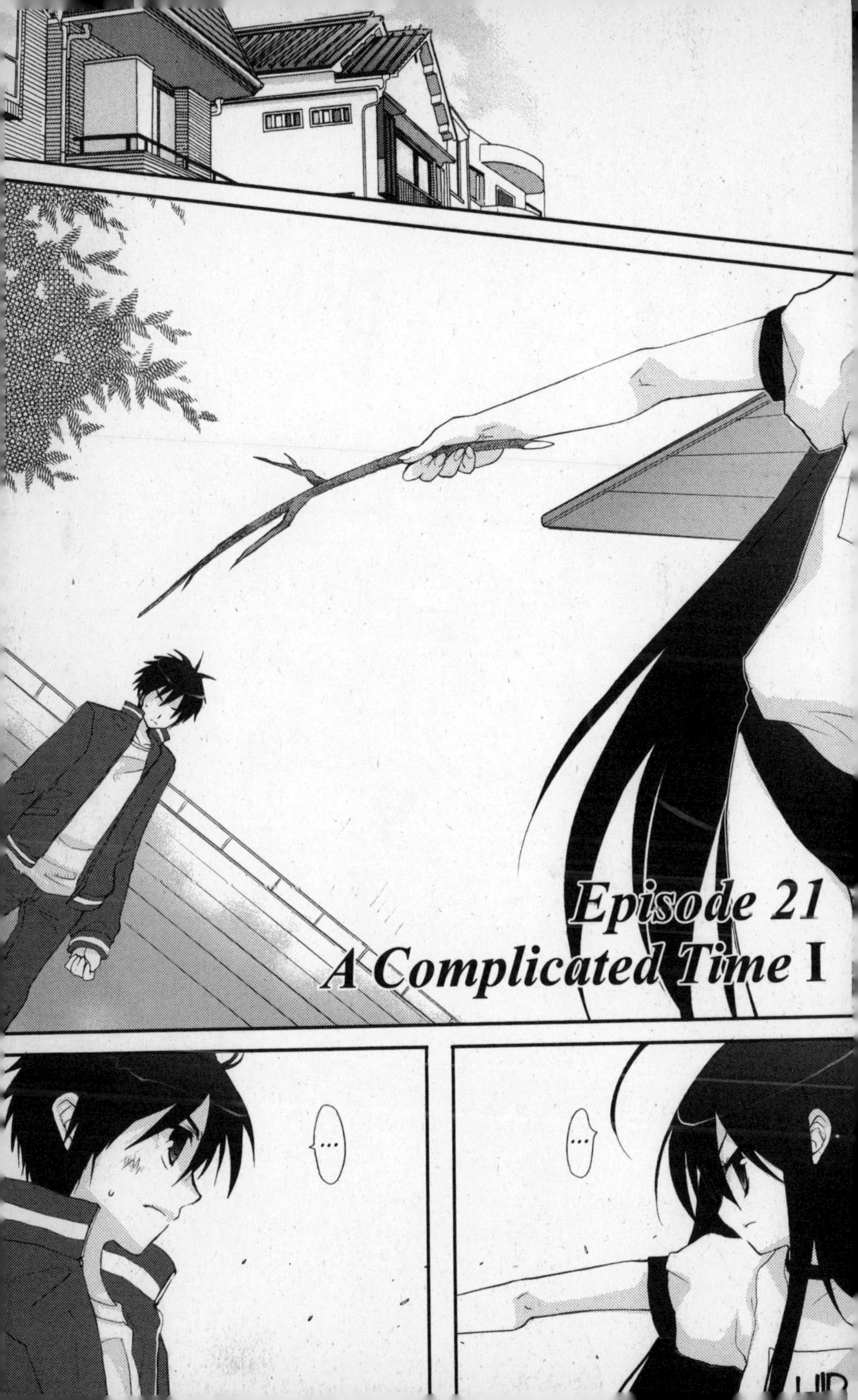
Episode 21
A Complicated Time I
…
…

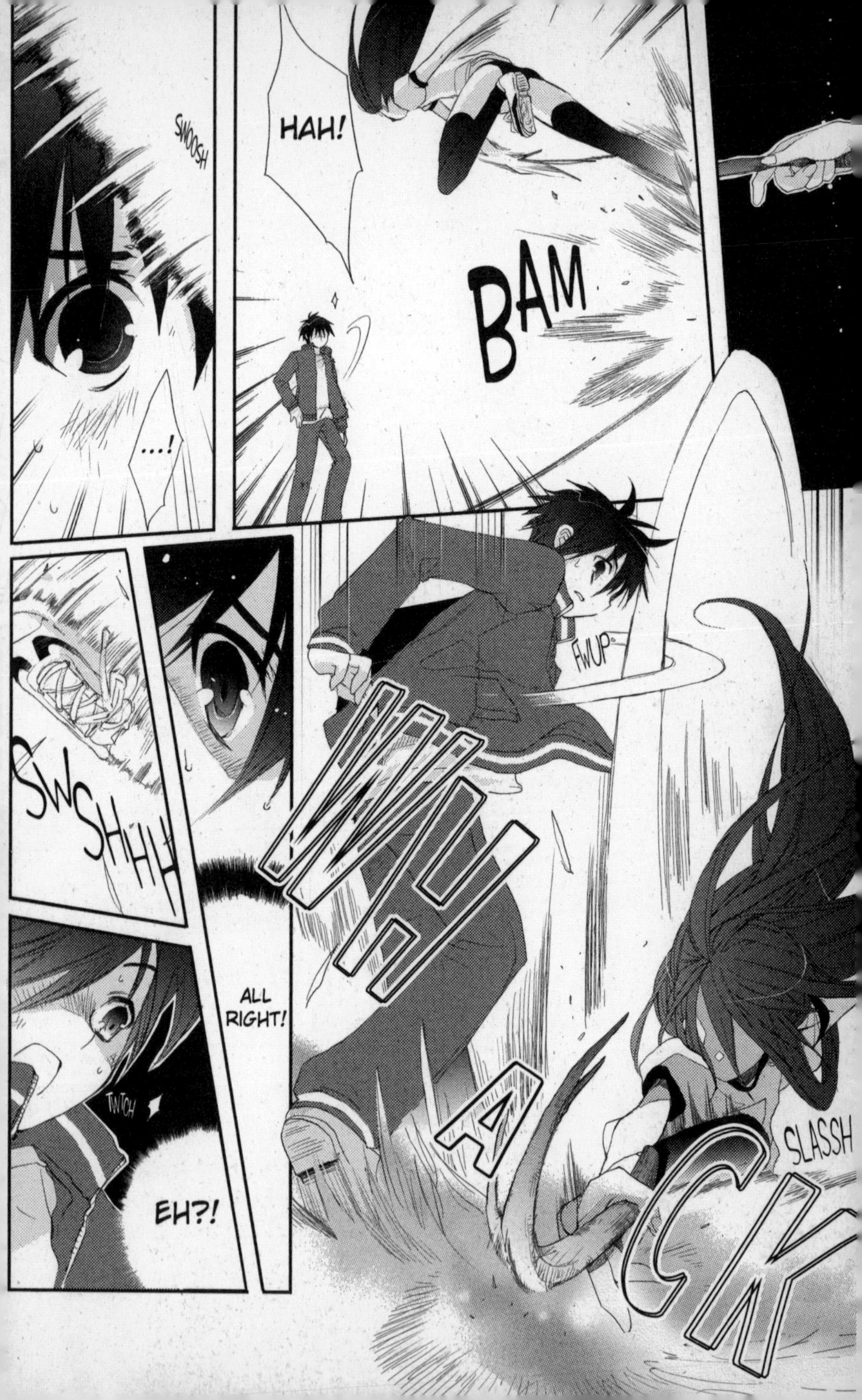
HAH!
BAM
SWOOSH
...!
FWUP
WHACK
SLASSH
SWSHHH
ALL RIGHT!
TWITCH
EH?!

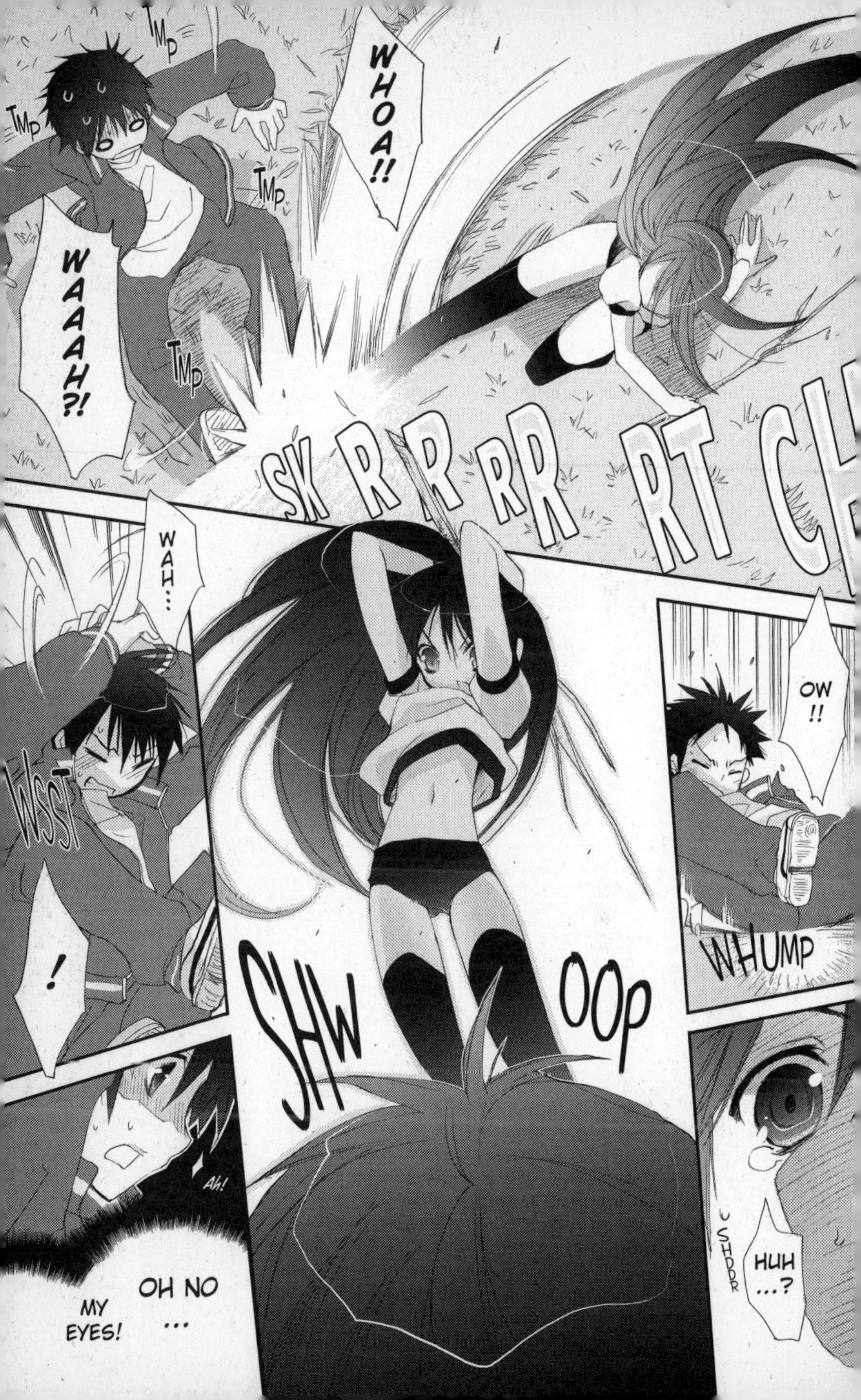
WHOA!!
TMP
TMP
TMP
TMP
WAAAAH?!
SKRRRRRT CH
OW!!
WHUMP
SHWOOP
WAH...
WSST
!
HUH...?
SHDDR
Ah!
OH NO...
MY EYES!

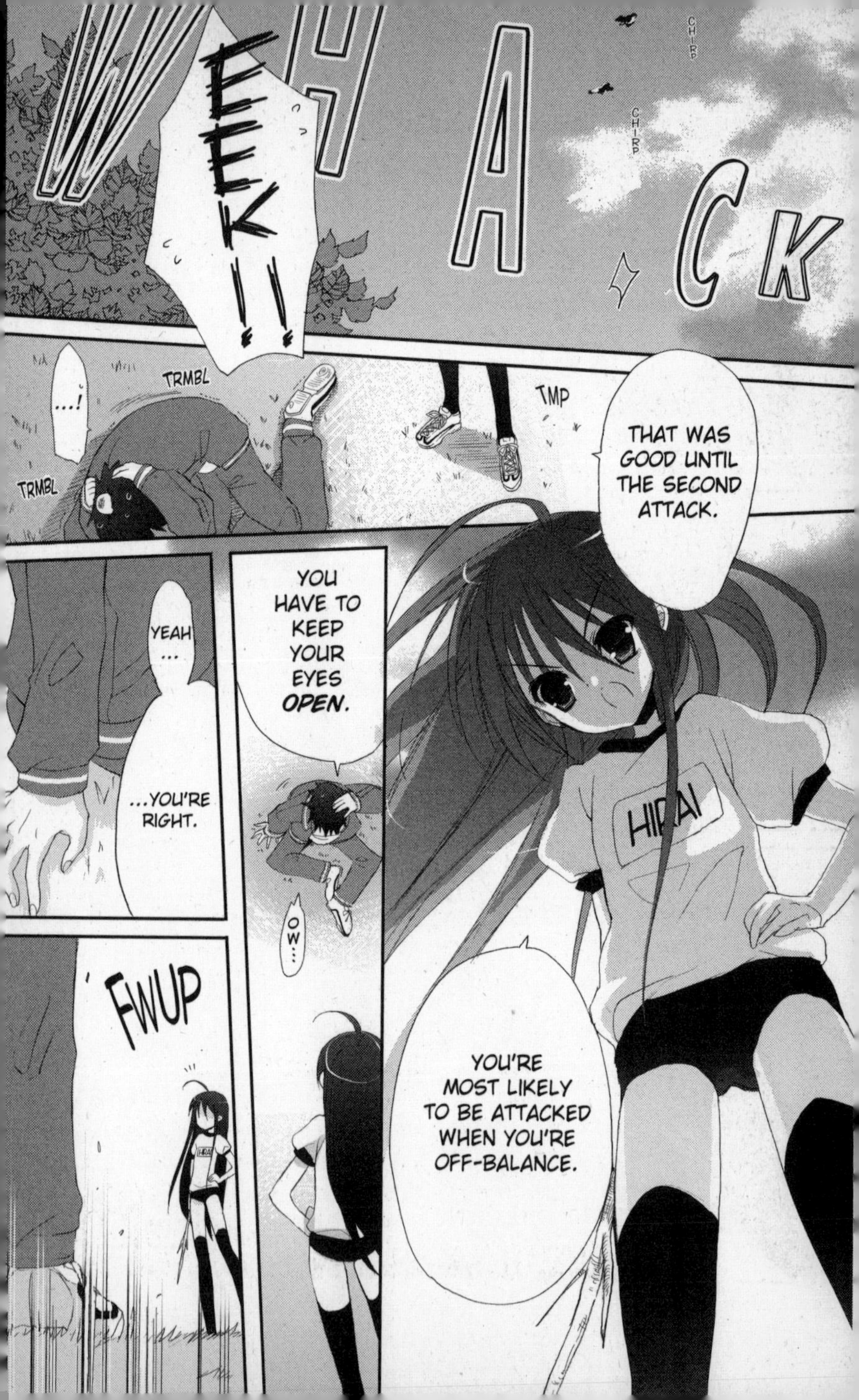

CHIRP
CHIRP
WHACK
WEEK!!
TMP
TRMBL
...!
TRMBL
THAT WAS GOOD UNTIL THE SECOND ATTACK.
YOU HAVE TO KEEP YOUR EYES ***OPEN***.
OW...
YEAH...
...YOU'RE RIGHT.
YOU'RE MOST LIKELY TO BE ATTACKED WHEN YOU'RE OFF-BALANCE.
FWUP

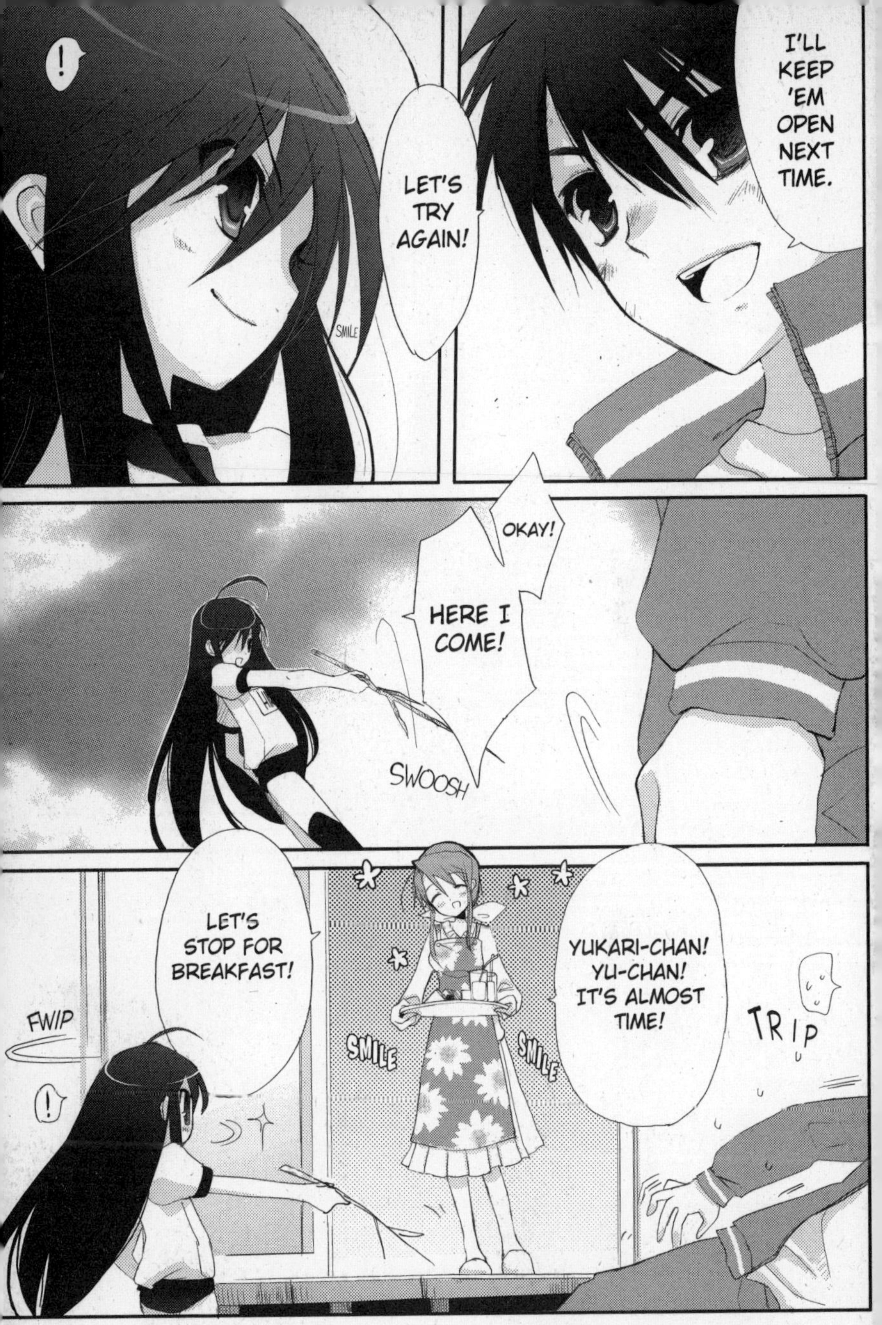
I'LL KEEP 'EM OPEN NEXT TIME.
!
LET'S TRY AGAIN!
SMILE
OKAY!
HERE I COME!
SWOOSH
TRIP
YUKARI-CHAN! YU-CHAN! IT'S ALMOST TIME!
SMILE
SMILE
LET'S STOP FOR BREAKFAST!
FWIP
!

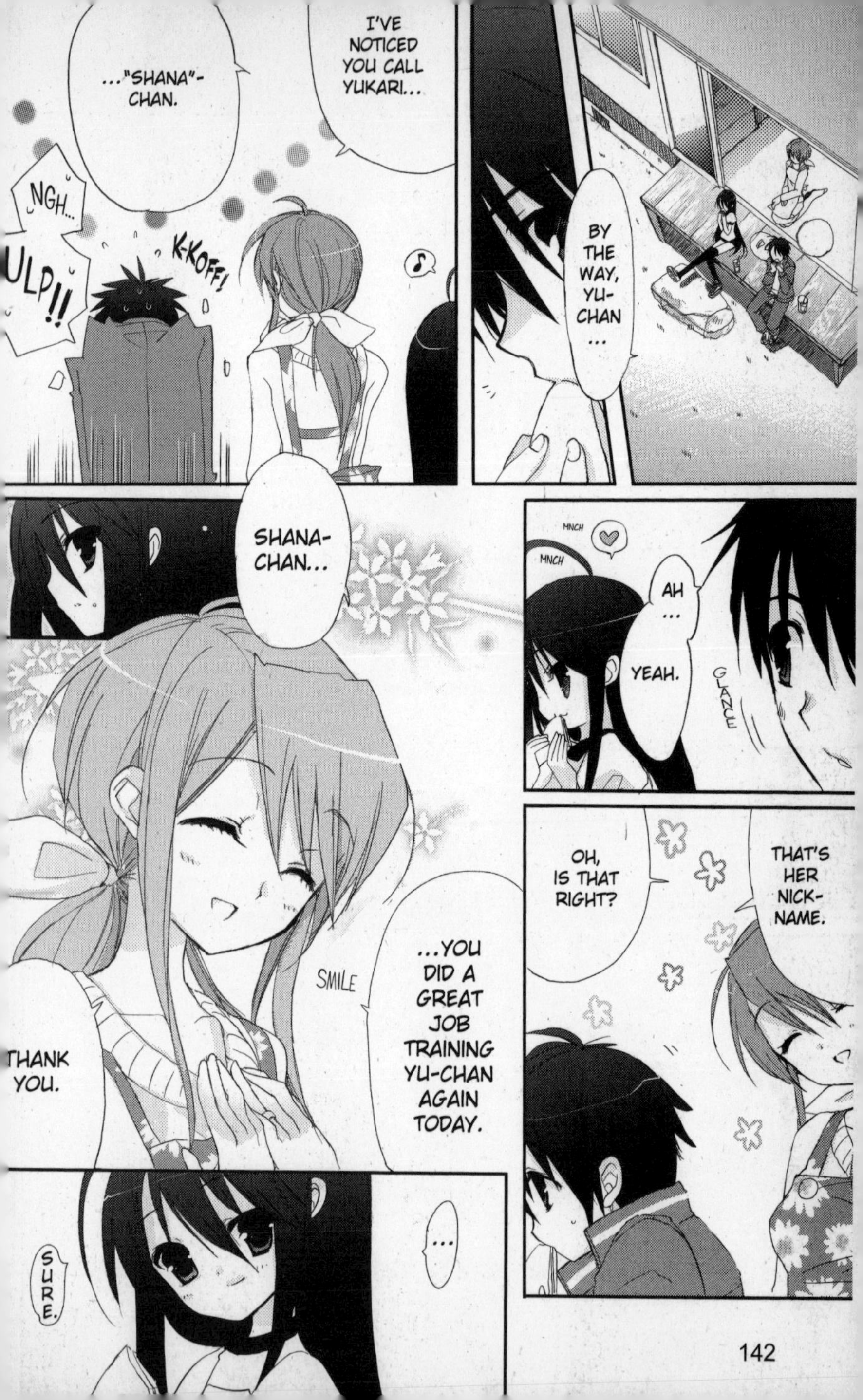
BY THE WAY, YU-CHAN...
I'VE NOTICED YOU CALL YUKARI...
..."SHANA"-CHAN.
K-KOFF!
NGH...
ULP!!
MNCH
MNCH
AH...
YEAH.
GLANCE
THAT'S HER NICK-NAME.
OH, IS THAT RIGHT?
SHANA-CHAN...
...YOU DID A GREAT JOB TRAINING YU-CHAN AGAIN TODAY.
SMILE
THANK YOU.
...
SURE.

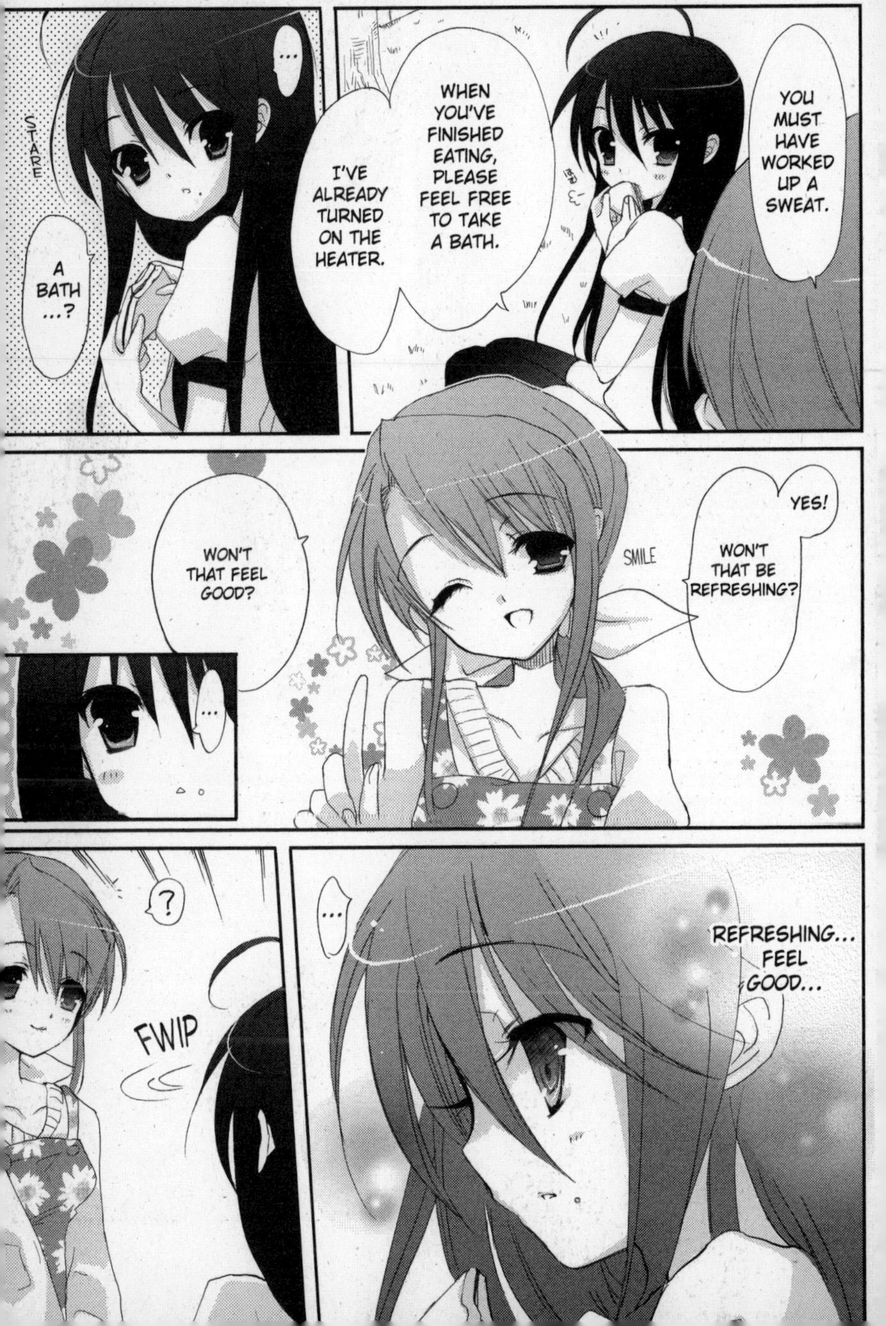
YOU MUST HAVE WORKED UP A SWEAT.
WHEN YOU'VE FINISHED EATING, PLEASE FEEL FREE TO TAKE A BATH.
I'VE ALREADY TURNED ON THE HEATER.
...
STARE
A BATH ...?
YES!
WON'T THAT BE REFRESHING?
SMILE
WON'T THAT FEEL GOOD?
...
...
REFRESHING... FEEL GOOD...
?
FWIP

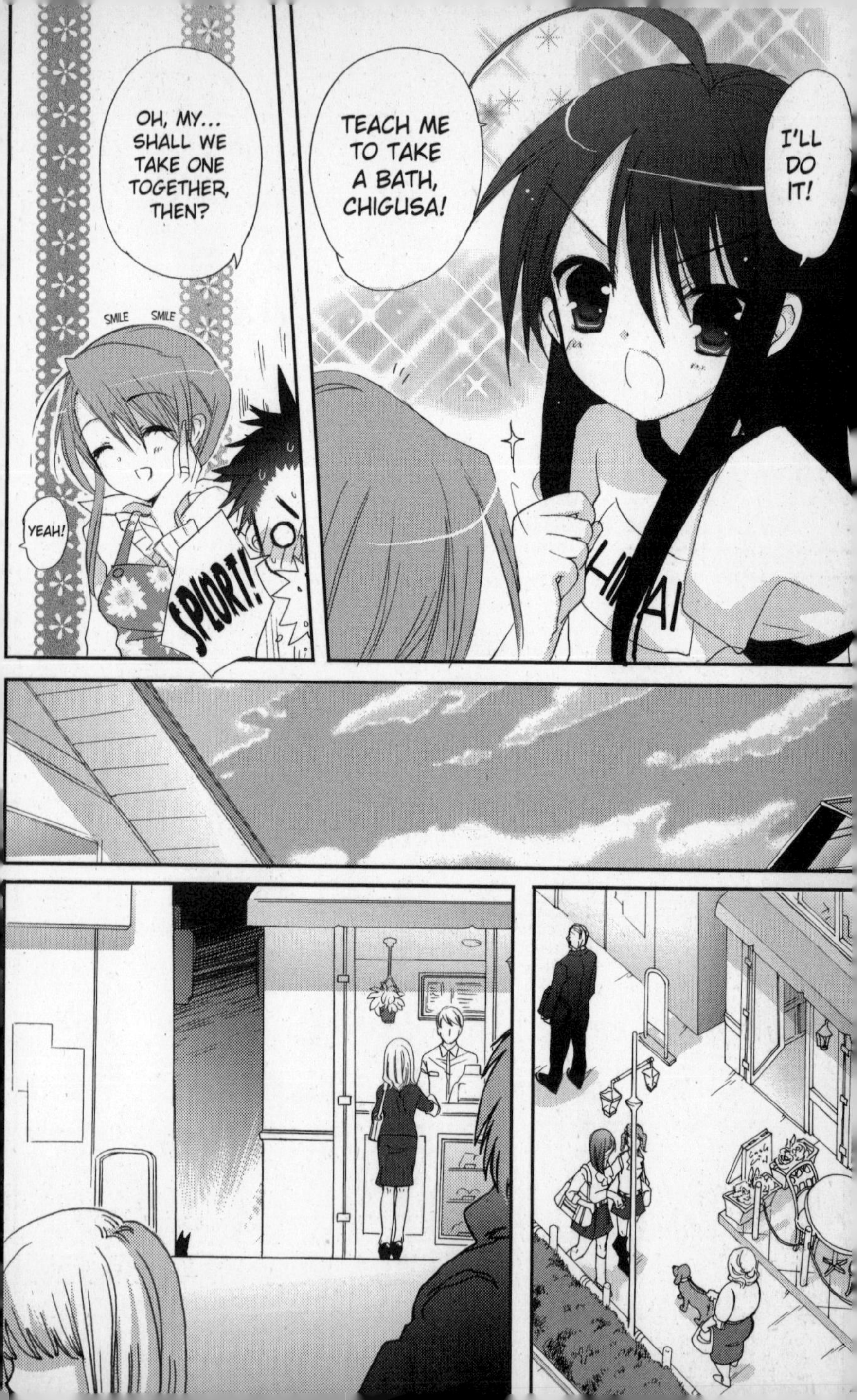
I'LL DO IT!
TEACH ME TO TAKE A BATH, CHIGUSA!
OH, MY... SHALL WE TAKE ONE TOGETHER, THEN?
SMILE SMILE
YEAH!
SPLORT!

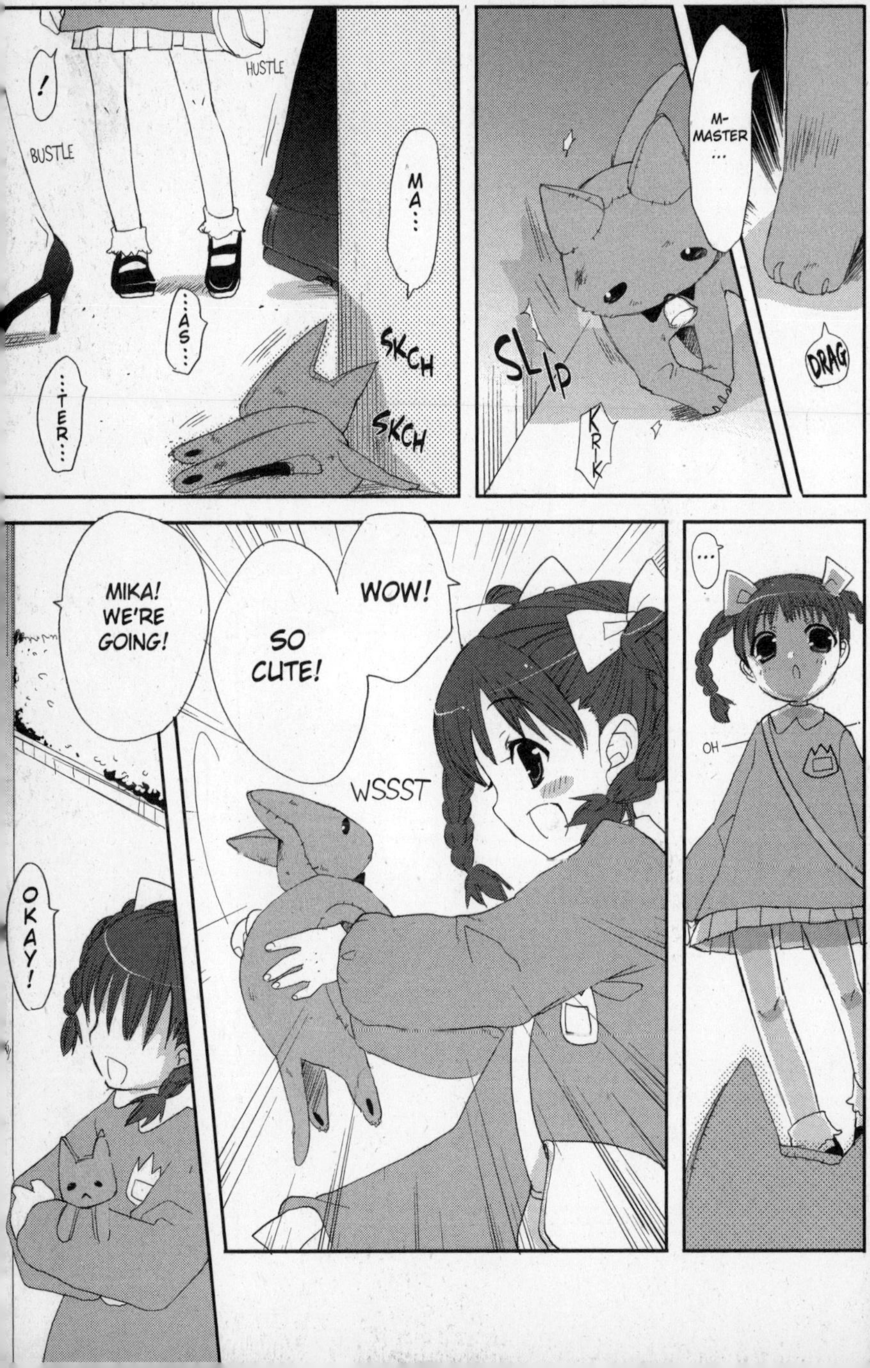
M-MASTER...
DRAG
SLIP
KRIK
HUSTLE
MA...
!
BUSTLE
SKCH
...AS...
SKCH
...TER...
...
OH
WOW! SO CUTE!
WSSST
MIKA! WE'RE GOING!
OKAY!

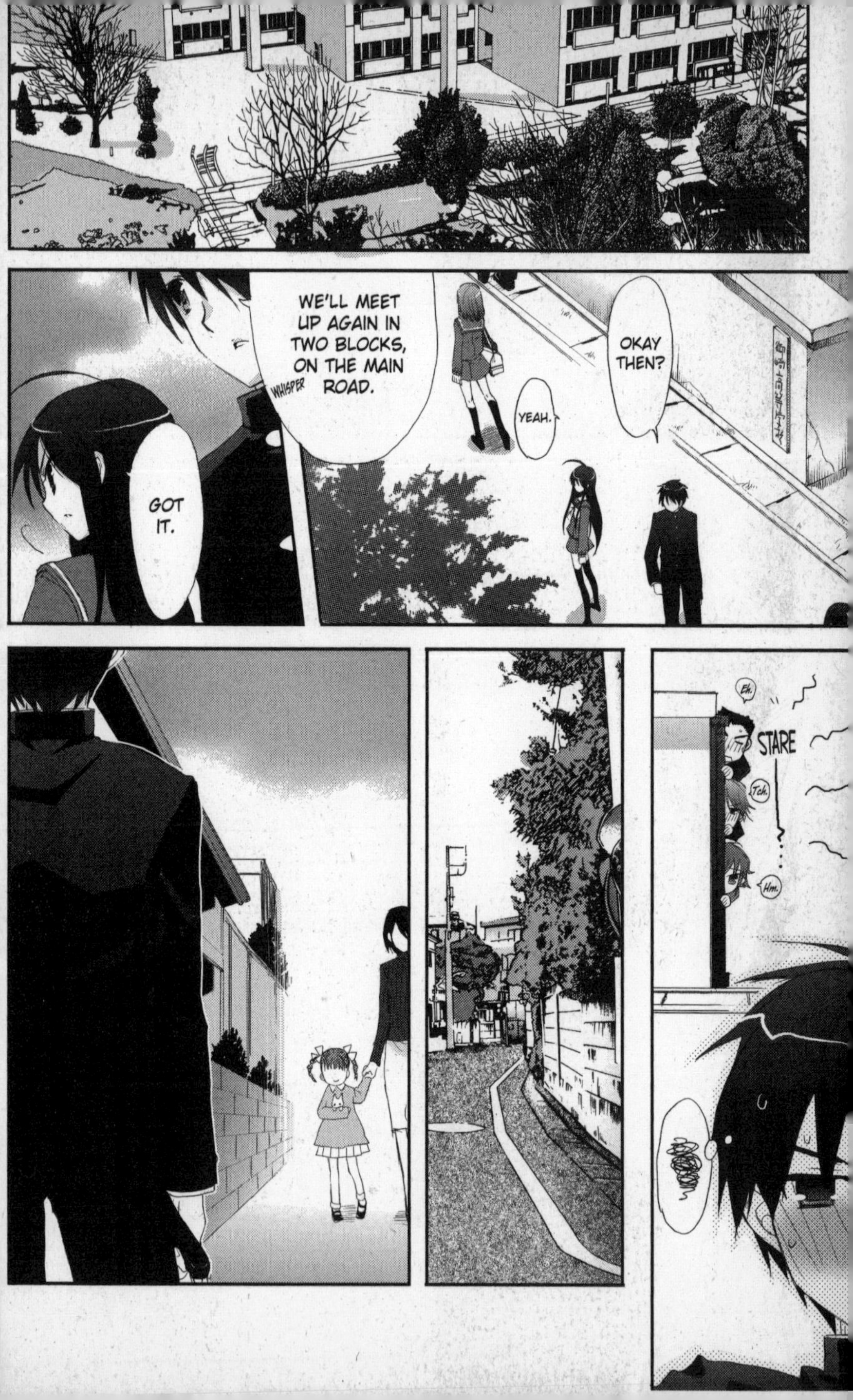
OKAY THEN?
YEAH.
WE'LL MEET UP AGAIN IN TWO BLOCKS, ON THE MAIN ROAD.
WHISPER
GOT IT.
Eh.
STARE
Tch.
Hm.

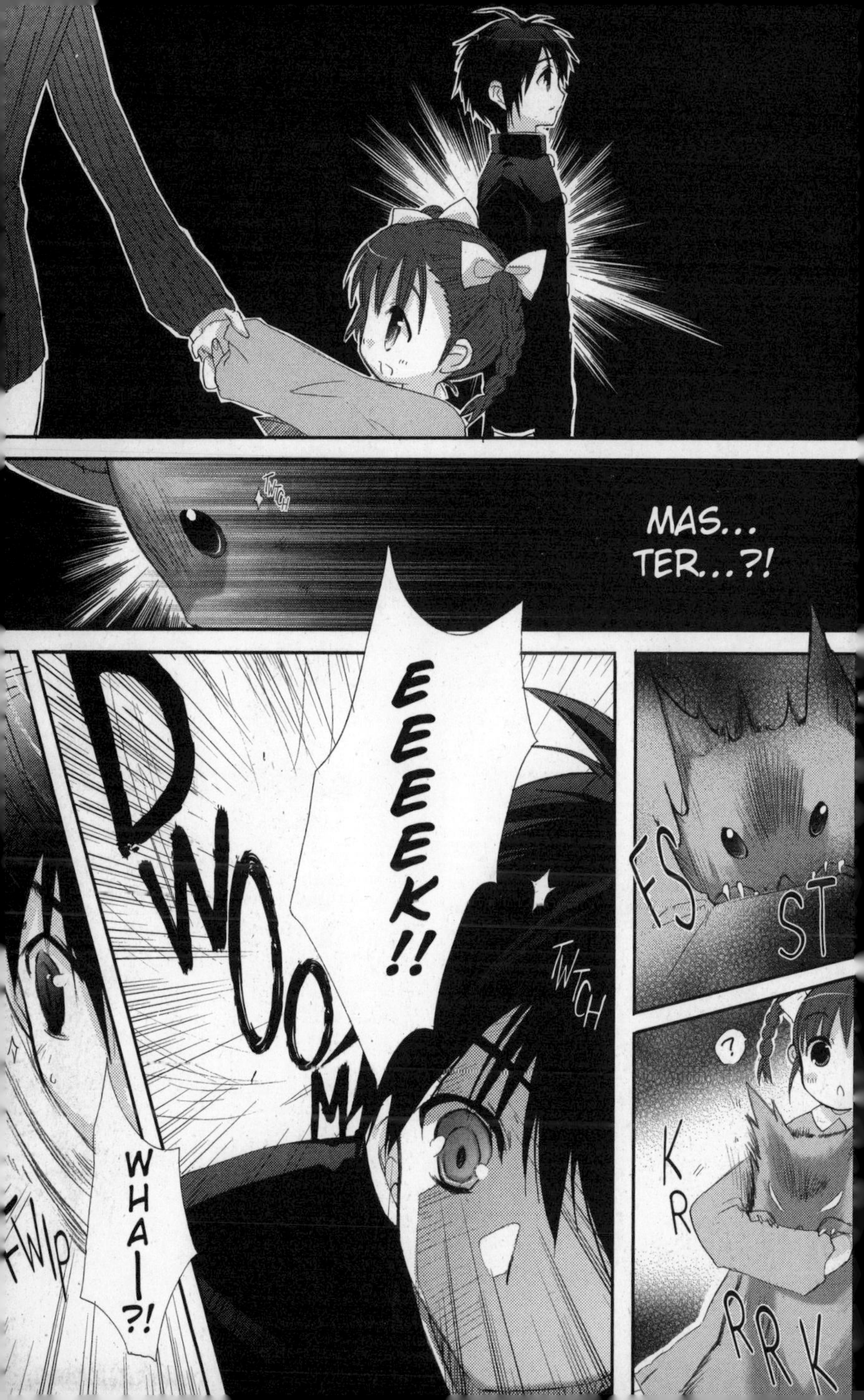
MAS... TER...?!
TWITCH
FSST
?
KRRRK
EEEEEK!!
TWITCH
DWOOOM
WHA!?!
FWIP

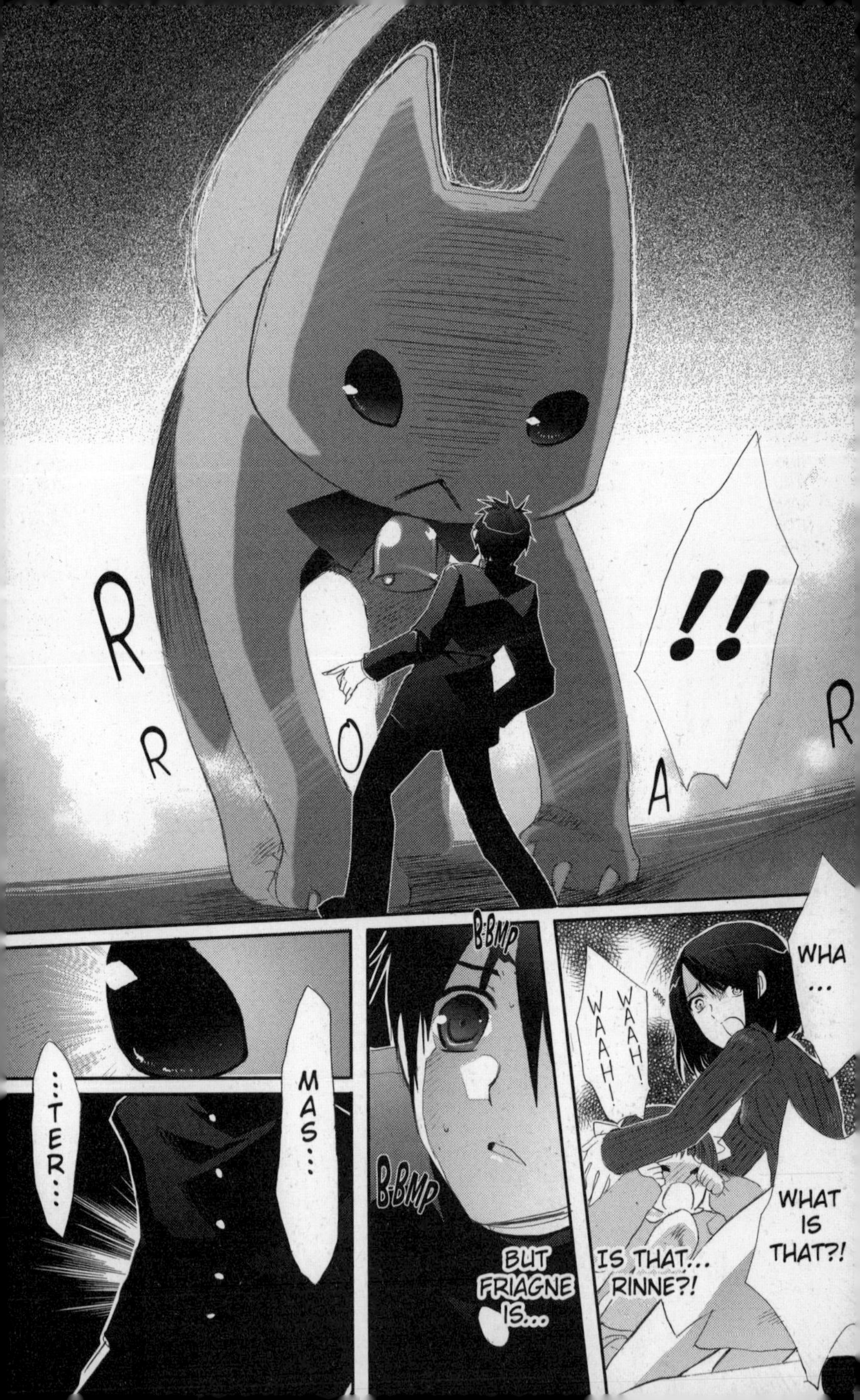
!!
R R O A R
WHA...
WAAH!
WAAH!
WHAT IS THAT?!
IS THAT... RINNE?!
B-BMP
B-BMP
BUT FRIAGNE IS...
MAS...
...TER...

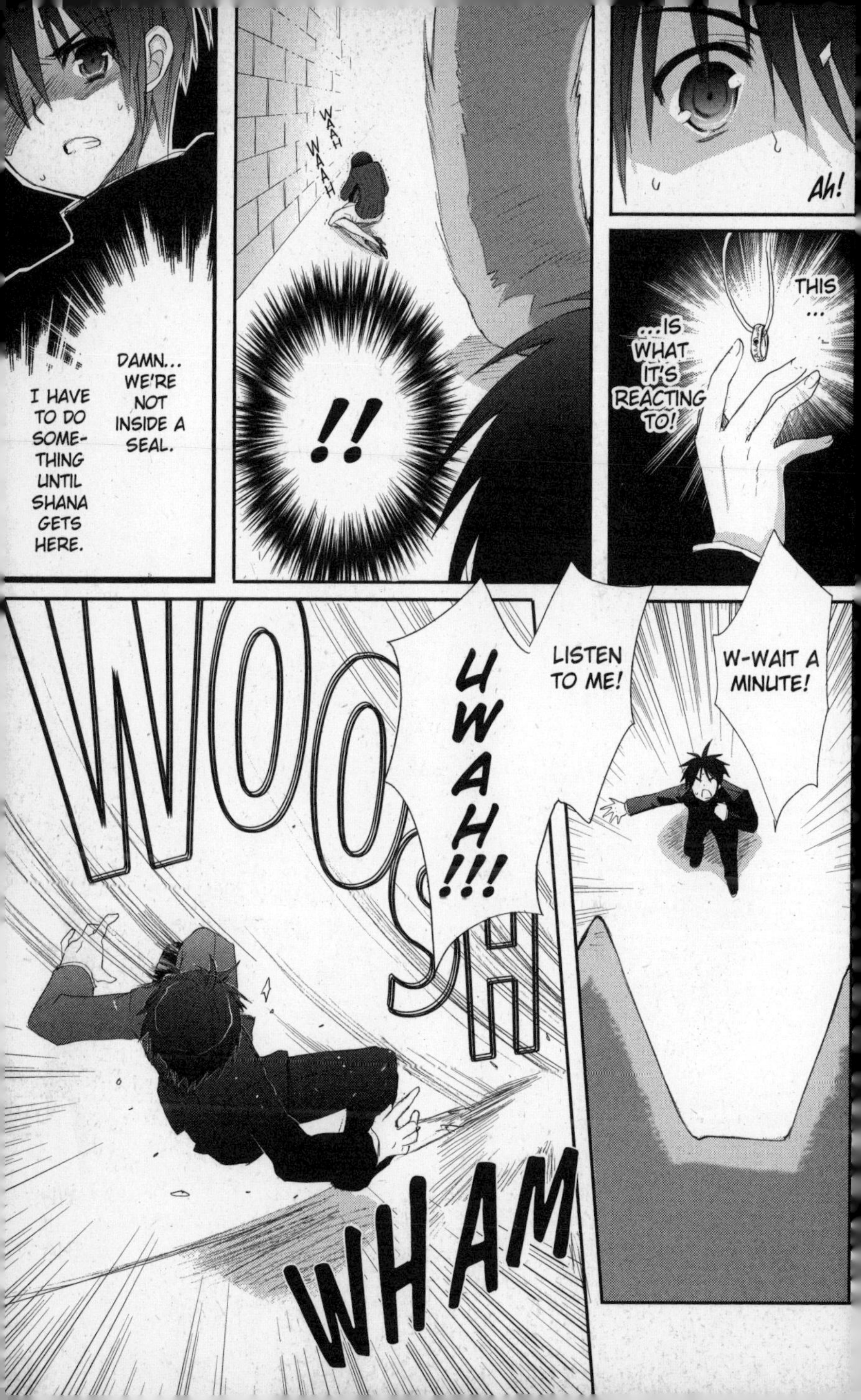
Ah!
THIS ...
...IS WHAT IT'S REACTING TO!
WAAH WAAH
!!
DAMN... WE'RE NOT INSIDE A SEAL.
I HAVE TO DO SOME-THING UNTIL SHANA GETS HERE.
W-WAIT A MINUTE!
LISTEN TO ME!
UWAH!!!
WOOOSH
WHAM

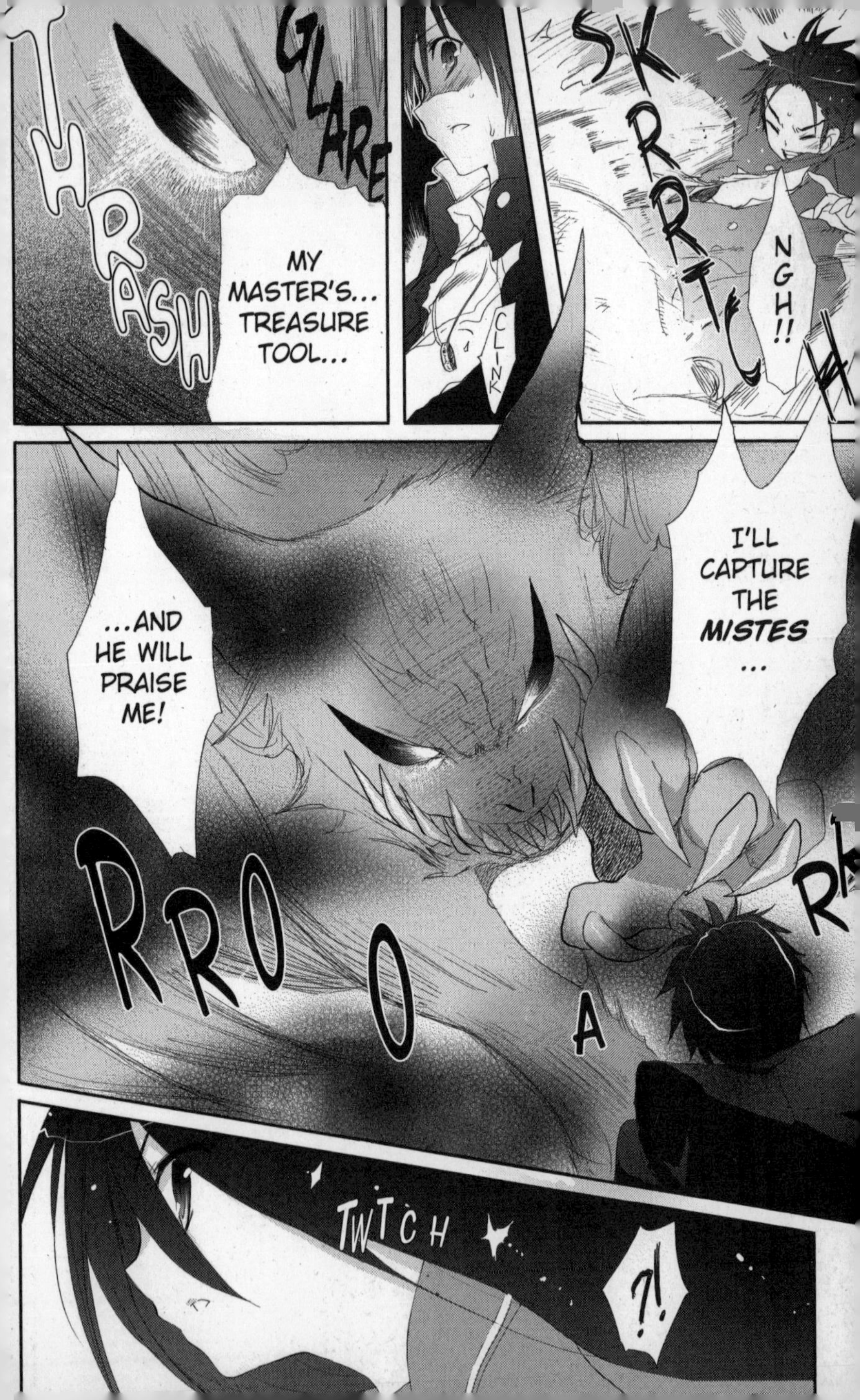

SKRRRTCH
NGH!!
CLINK
GLARE
MY MASTER'S... TREASURE TOOL...
THRASH
I'LL CAPTURE THE *MISTES* ...
...AND HE WILL PRAISE ME!
RROOAR
TWTCH
?!

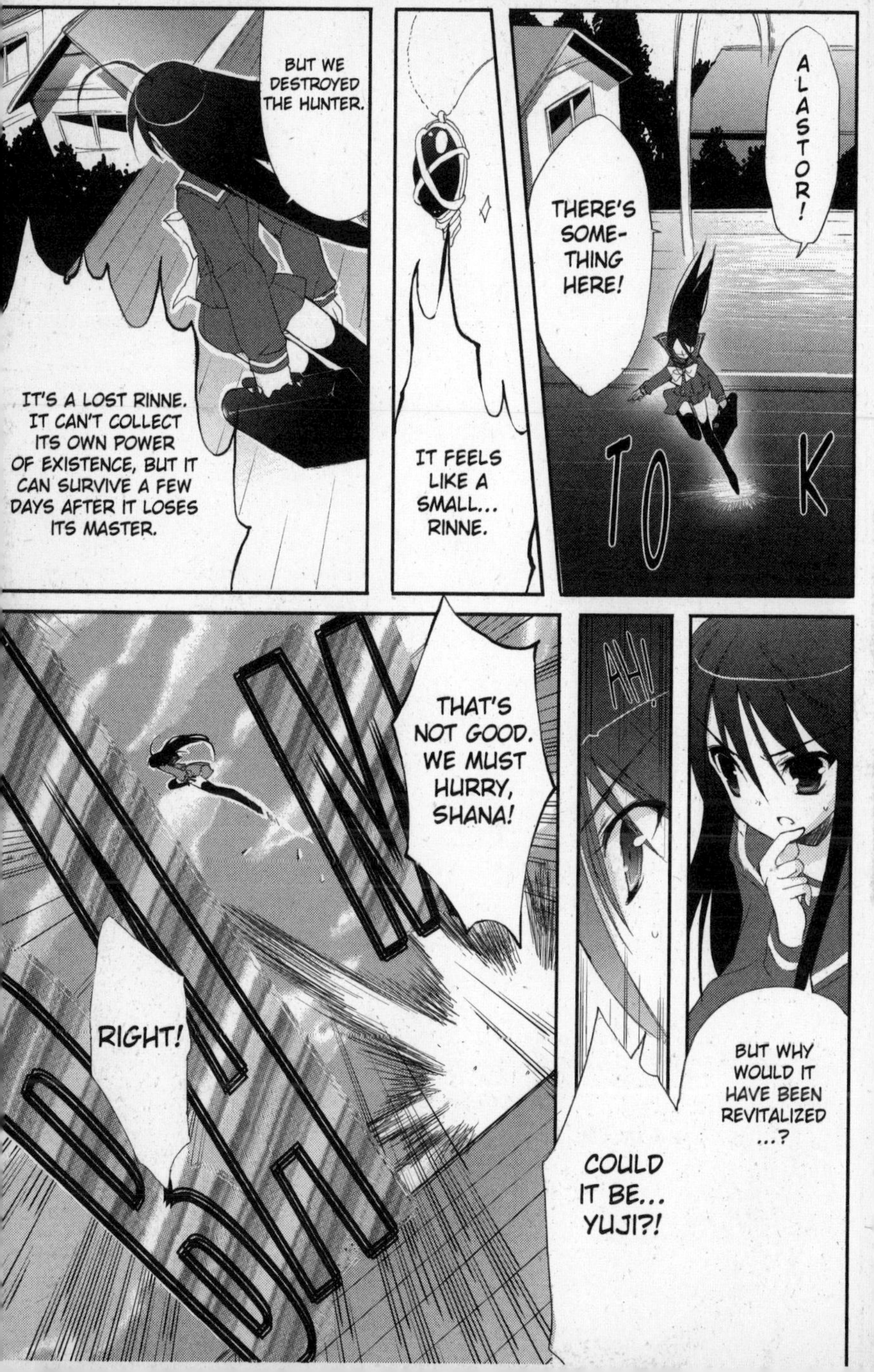
ALASTOR!
THERE'S SOME-THING HERE!
TOK
IT FEELS LIKE A SMALL... RINNE.
BUT WE DESTROYED THE HUNTER.
IT'S A LOST RINNE. IT CAN'T COLLECT ITS OWN POWER OF EXISTENCE, BUT IT CAN SURVIVE A FEW DAYS AFTER IT LOSES ITS MASTER.
BUT WHY WOULD IT HAVE BEEN REVITALIZED ...?
COULD IT BE... YUJI?!
AH!
THAT'S NOT GOOD. WE MUST HURRY, SHANA!
RIGHT!

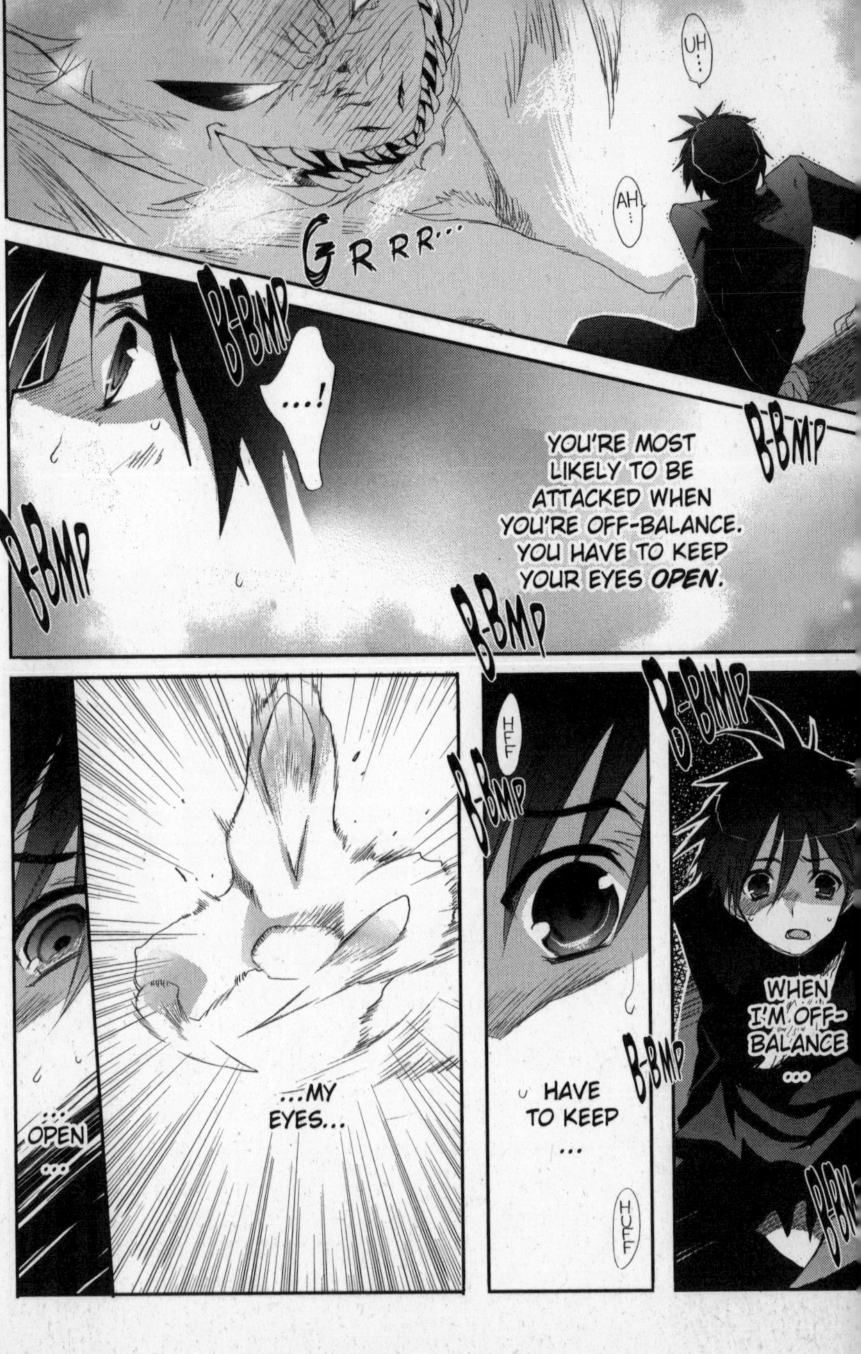
UH...
AH...
GRRR...
B-BMP
YOU'RE MOST LIKELY TO BE ATTACKED WHEN YOU'RE OFF-BALANCE. YOU HAVE TO KEEP YOUR EYES *OPEN*.
...!
B-BMP
B-BMP
B-BMP
B-BMP
WHEN I'M OFF-BALANCE...
B-BMP
HEFF
B-BMP
HAVE TO KEEP...
HUFF
...MY EYES...
...OPEN...

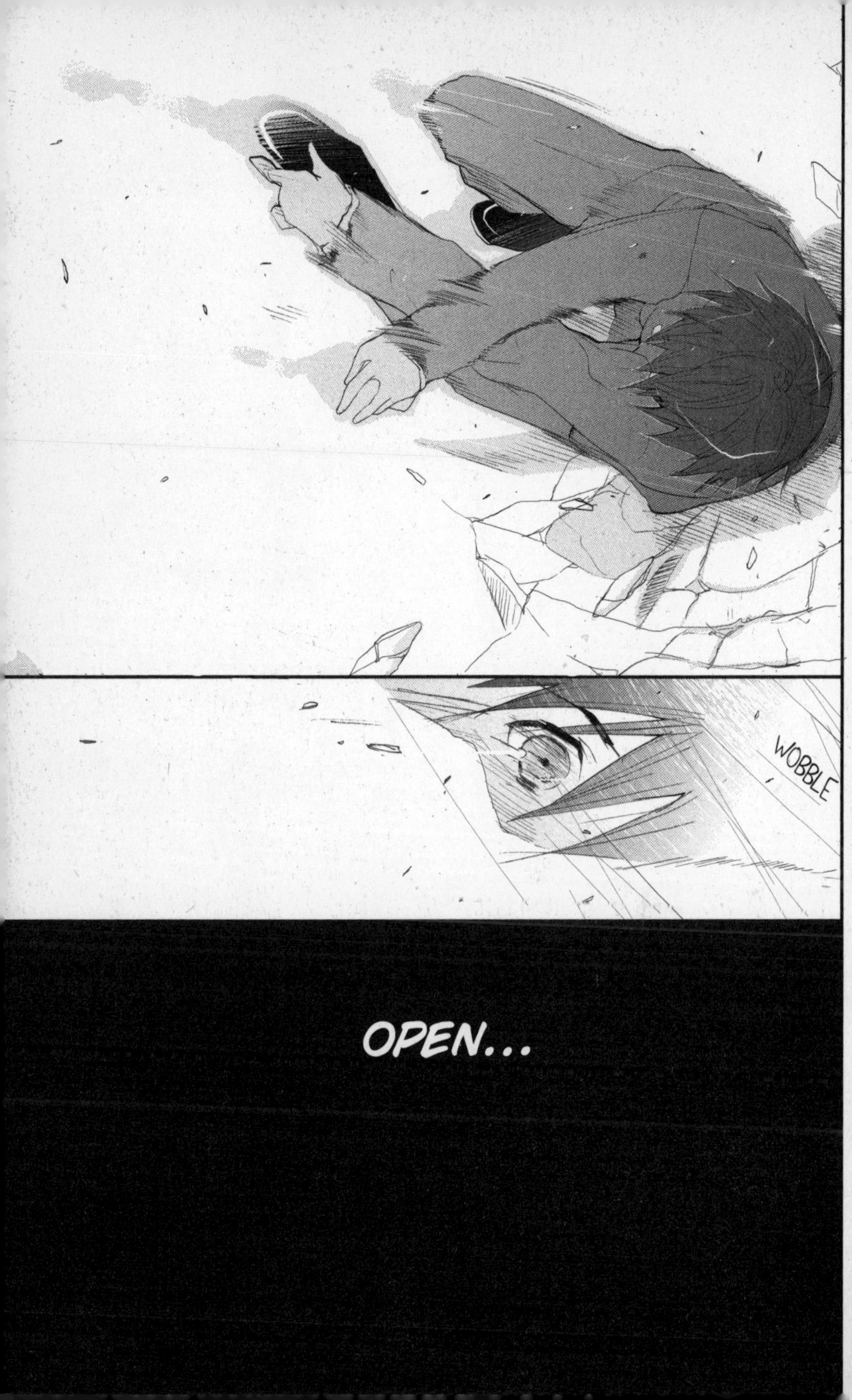
WOBBLE
OPEN...

Manga version of Shana Volume 3

I've finally finished the story covered in Volume 1 of the novel! It was a long haul, very long. I appreciate everyone who patiently saw this through and didn't give up. I'm also grateful that, as inexperienced as I am, I was able to translate into art what I saw and felt in this story arc. It's far from perfect, but I hope I was able to express in the manga version what I felt when I read about Shana's world. Farewell and thank you, Friagne & Marianne (tears!) and hello to "big sis" Margery!

Once again, many thanks to all of you who helped me!

Shiro-sensei, Alastor was terrific! Az, O-sempai, H-sempai and station staff, thanks for your help too! (°w°*)

Finally, thank you to my editor, Hagino-san, for dragging me along this far as if we were in a three-legged race.

Let's continue on together!~♪

2007.4 笹倉綾人

Ayato Sasakura
April 2007

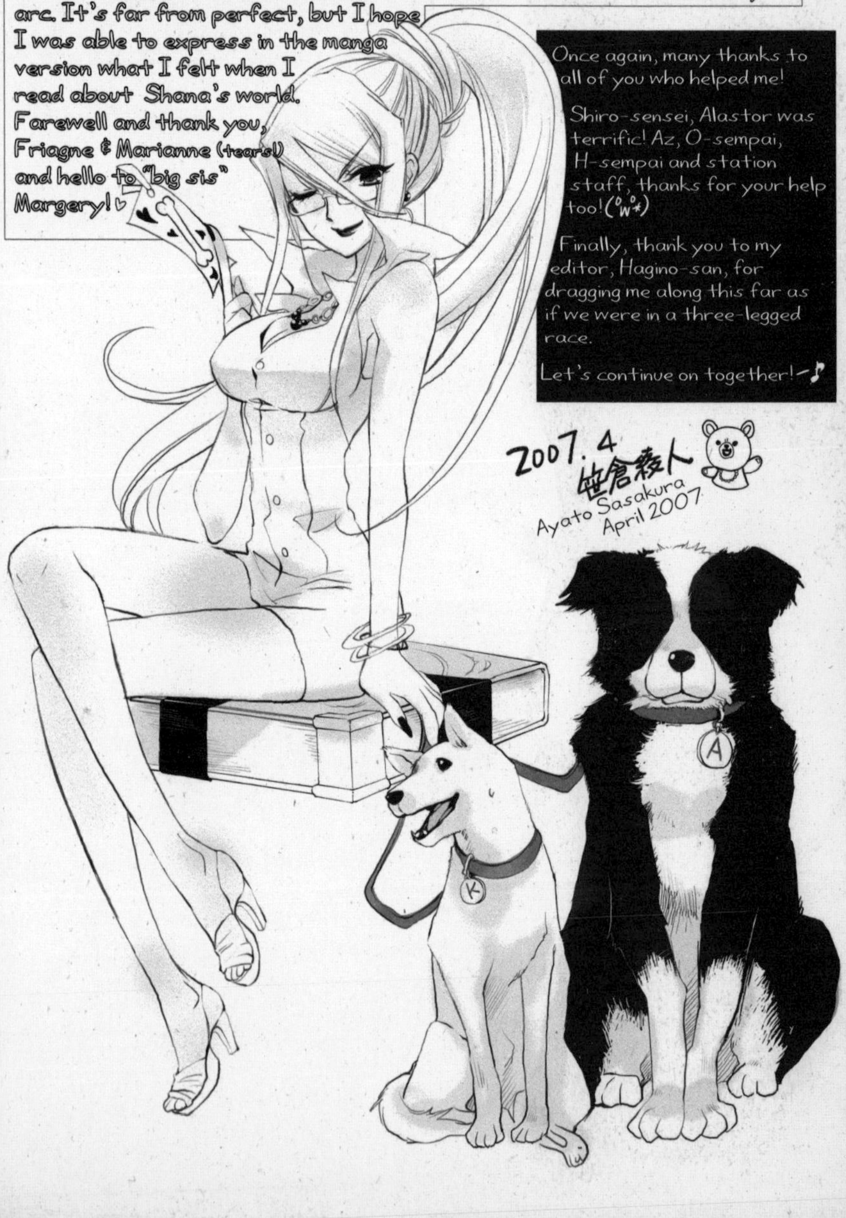
A
K

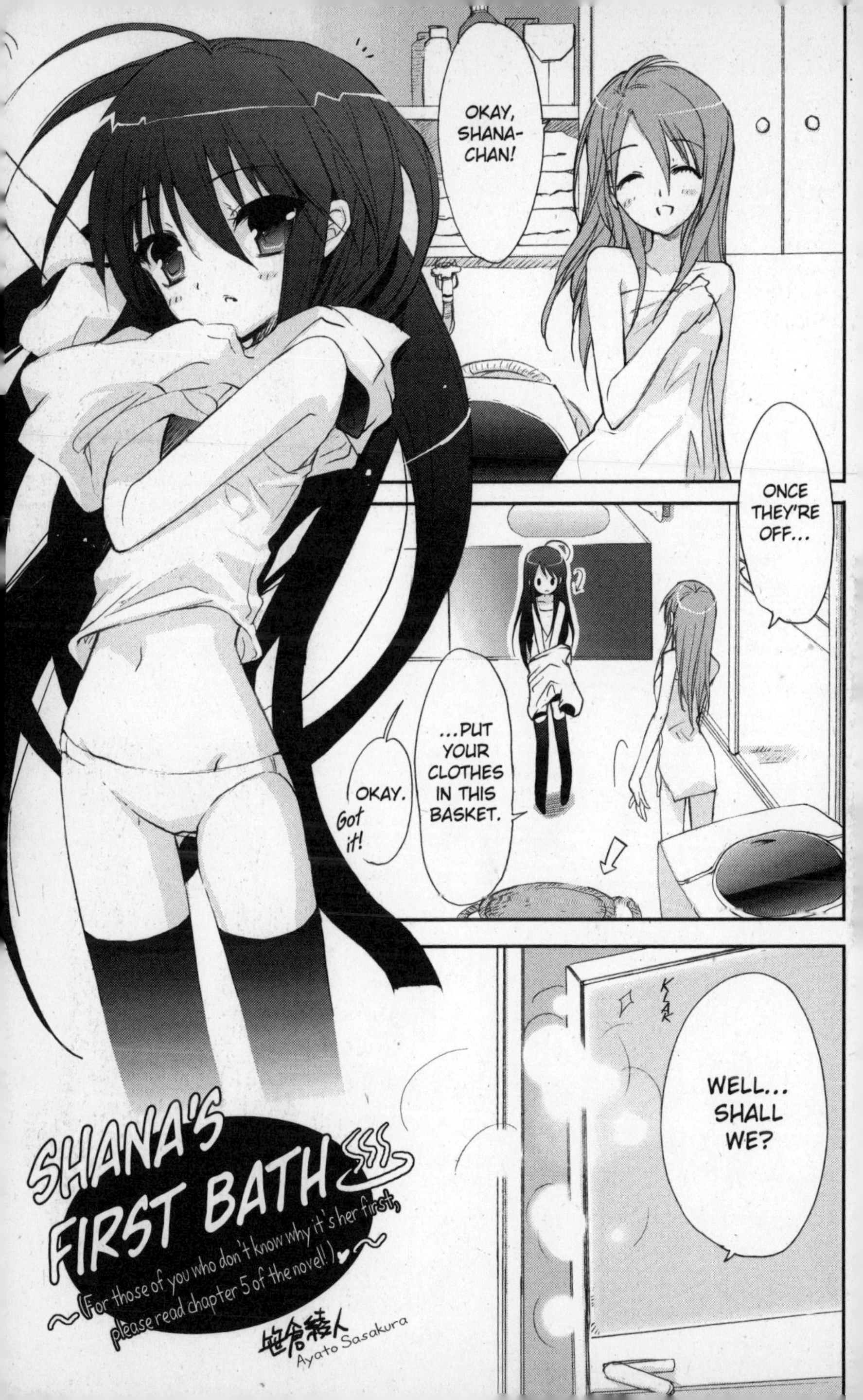
OKAY, SHANA-CHAN!
ONCE THEY'RE OFF...
...PUT YOUR CLOTHES IN THIS BASKET.
OKAY. Got it!
KLAK
WELL... SHALL WE?
SHANA'S FIRST BATH
~(For those of you who don't know why it's her first, please read chapter 5 of the novel!)~
笹倉綾人
Ayato Sasakura

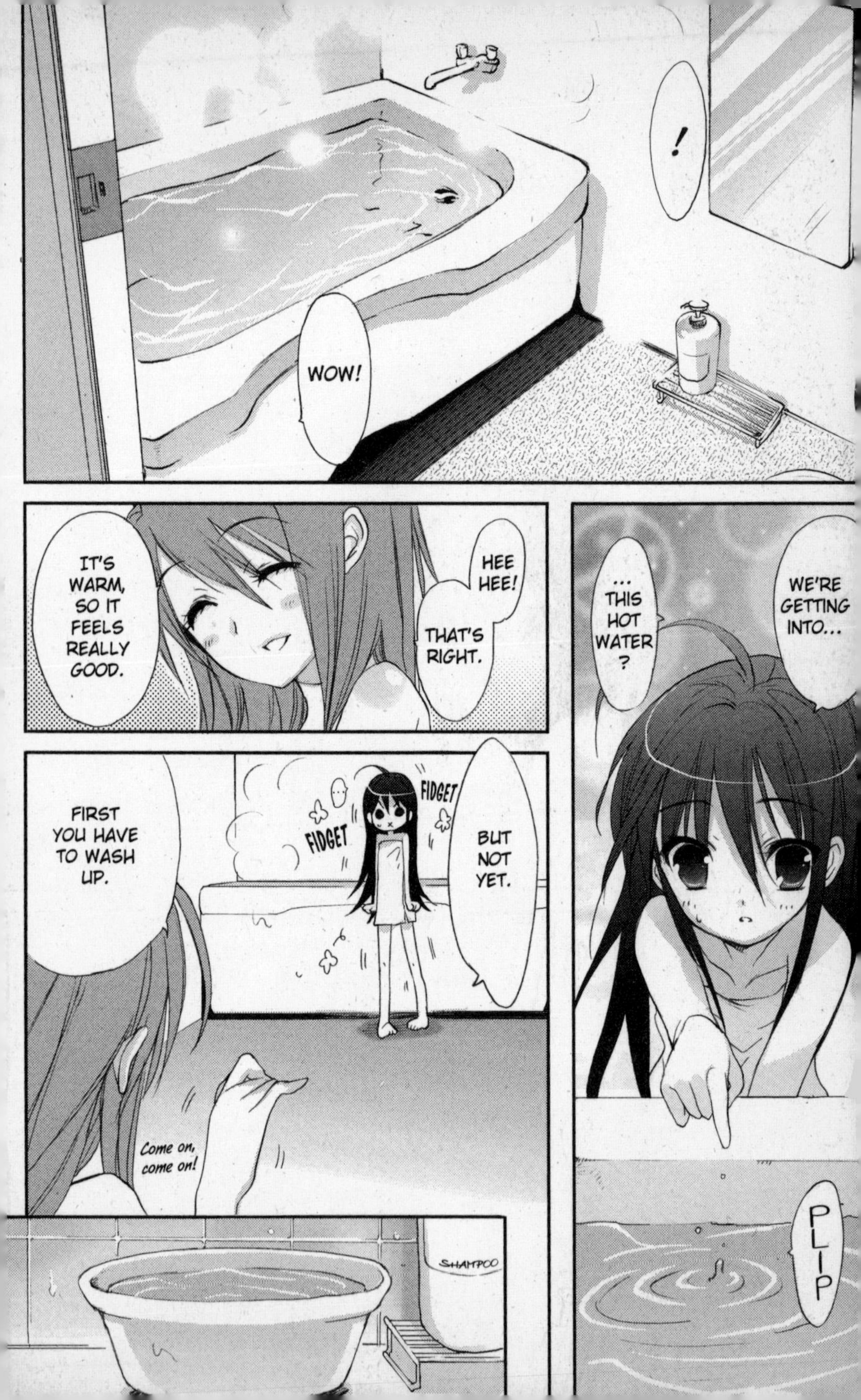
!
WOW!
WE'RE GETTING INTO...
...THIS HOT WATER?
HEE HEE! THAT'S RIGHT.
IT'S WARM, SO IT FEELS REALLY GOOD.
BUT NOT YET.
FIDGET
FIDGET
FIRST YOU HAVE TO WASH UP.
Come on, come on!
PLIP
SHAMPOO

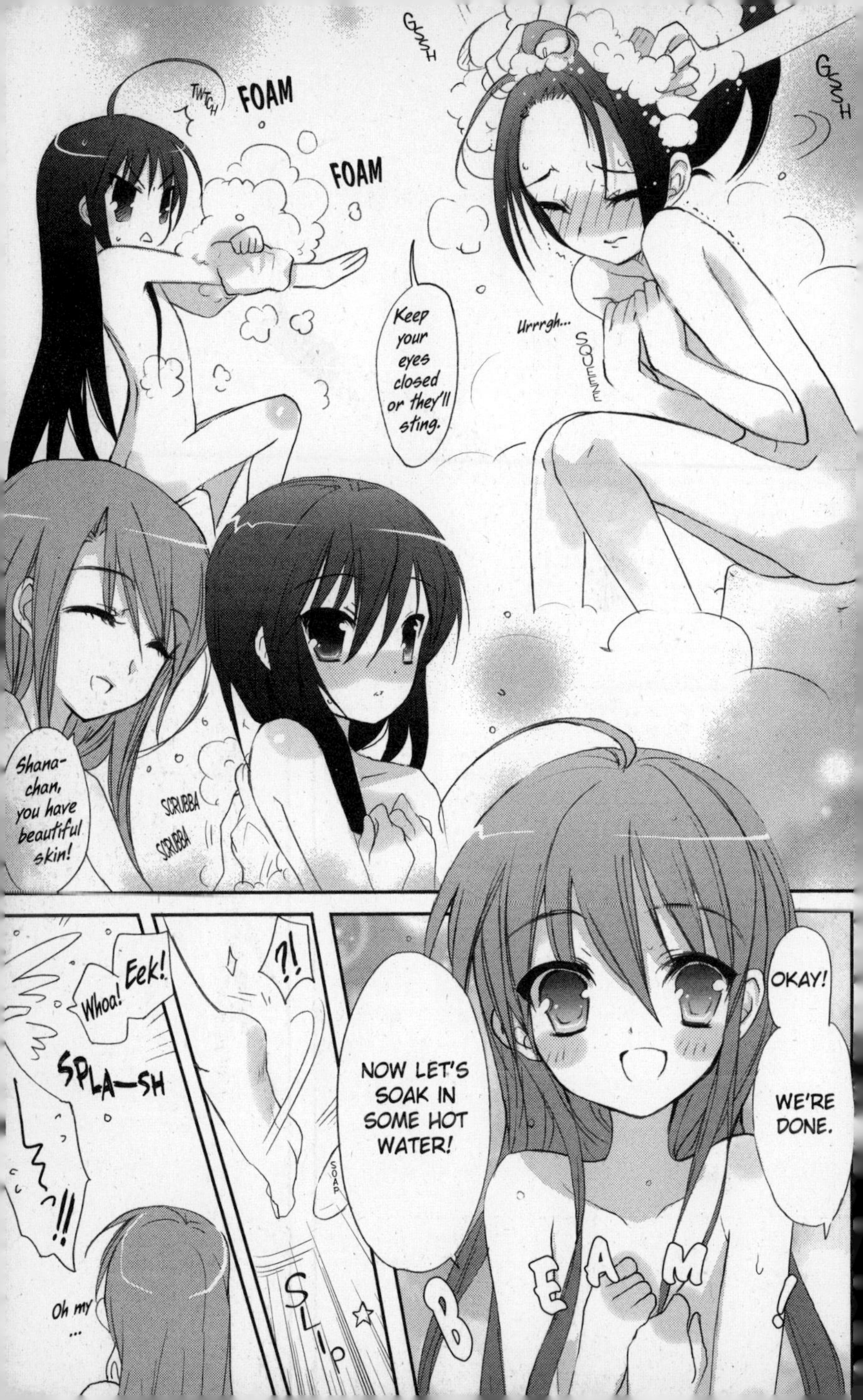
GSSSH
GSSSH
Keep your eyes closed or they'll sting.
Urrrgh...
SQUEEZE
TWITCH
FOAM
FOAM
Shana-chan, you have beautiful skin!
SCRUBBA
SCRUBBA
OKAY!
WE'RE DONE.
NOW LET'S SOAK IN SOME HOT WATER!
BEAM!
?!
SOAP
SLIP
Eek!
Whoa!
SPLA—SH
Oh my ...

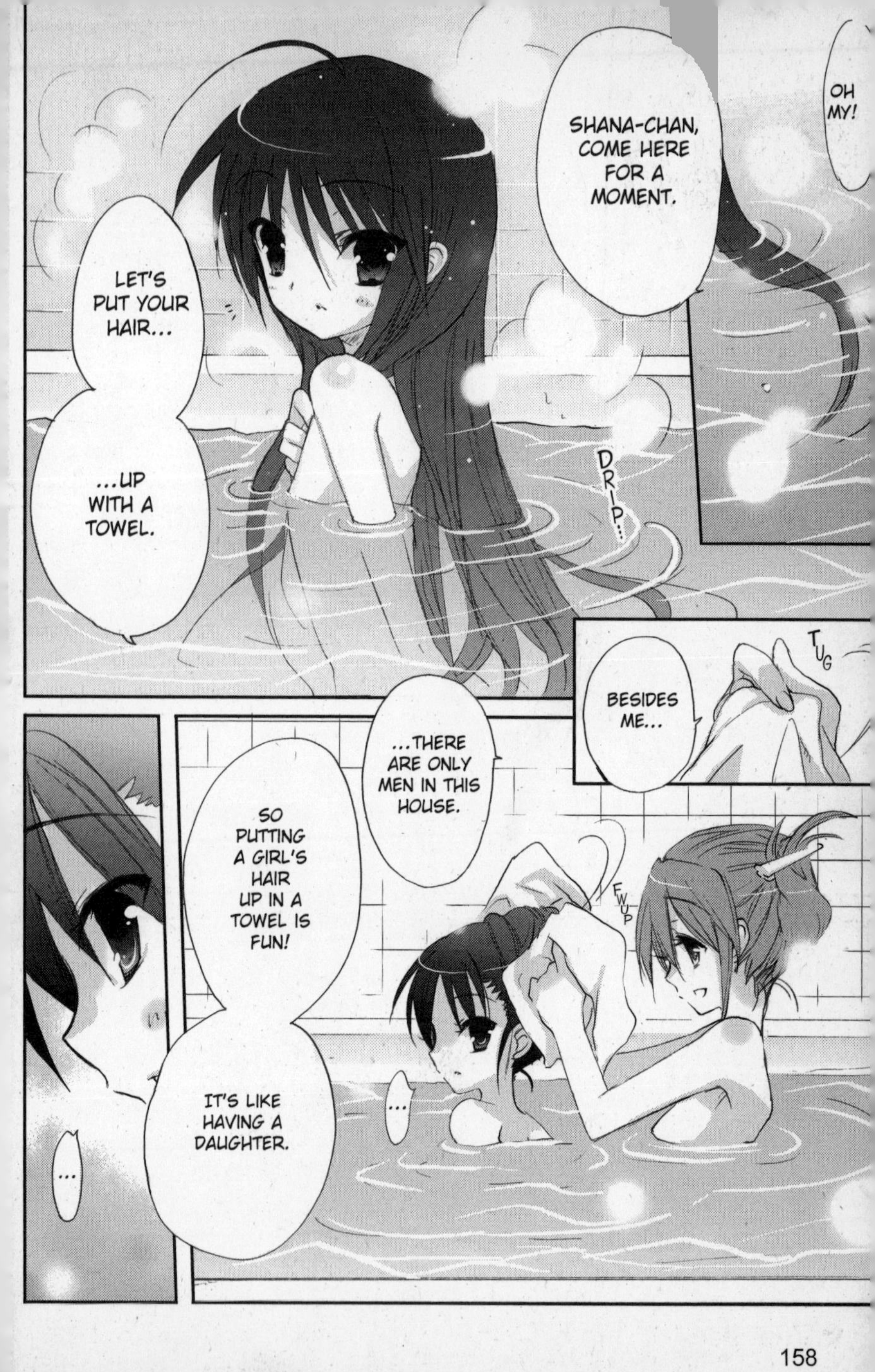
OH MY!
SHANA-CHAN, COME HERE FOR A MOMENT.
DRIP...
LET'S PUT YOUR HAIR...
...UP WITH A TOWEL.
TUG
BESIDES ME...
...THERE ARE ONLY MEN IN THIS HOUSE.
FWUP
SO PUTTING A GIRL'S HAIR UP IN A TOWEL IS FUN!
...
IT'S LIKE HAVING A DAUGHTER.
...

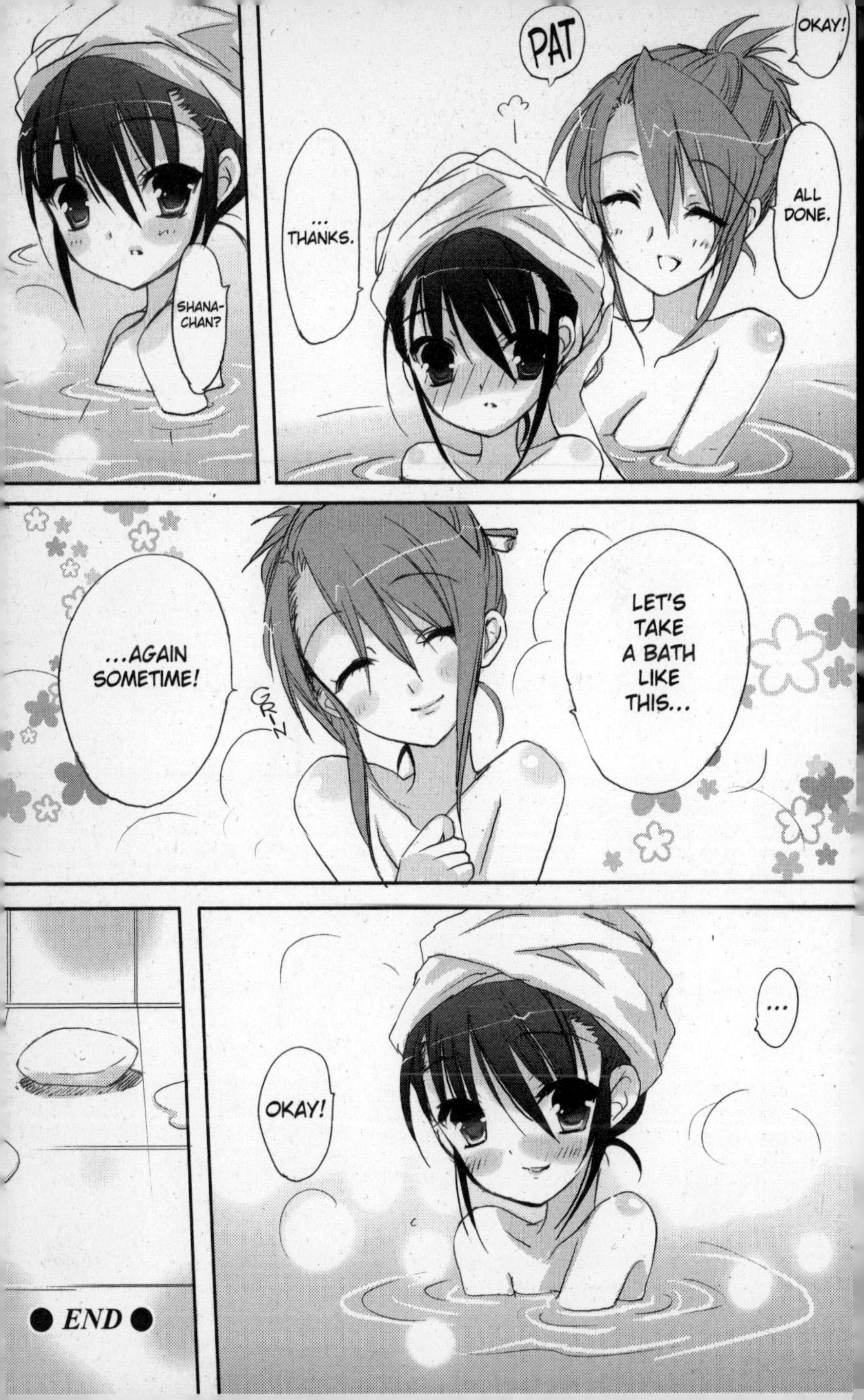
OKAY!
PAT
ALL DONE.
...THANKS.
SHANA-CHAN?
LET'S TAKE A BATH LIKE THIS...
GRIN
...AGAIN SOMETIME!
...
OKAY!
● END ●

SHAKUGAN SHANA

SHAKUGAN NO SHANA
Vol. 3
VIZ Media Edition

Story by
YASHICHIRO TAKAHASHI

Art by
AYATO SASAKURA

Character design by
NOIZI ITO

English Adaptation/Mark Giambruno
Translation/Yumi Okamoto
Touch-up Art & Lettering/James Gaubatz
Design/Matt Hinrichs
Editor/Carol Fox

Editor in Chief, Books/Alvin Lu
Editor in Chief, Magazines/Marc Weidenbaum
Sr. Director of Acquisitions/Rika Inouye
VP of Sales/Gonzalo Ferreyra
Sr. VP of Marketing/Liza Coppola
Publisher/Hyoe Narita

Printed in the U.S.A.

Published by VIZ Media, LLC
P.O. Box 77010
San Francisco, CA 94107

10 9 8 7 6 5 4 3 2 1
First printing, June 2008

INUYASHA

Read the action from the start with the original manga series

Full color adaptation of the popular TV series

Art book with cel art, paintings, character profiles and more

TV SERIES & MOVIES ON DVD!

See more of the action in *Inuyasha* full-length movies

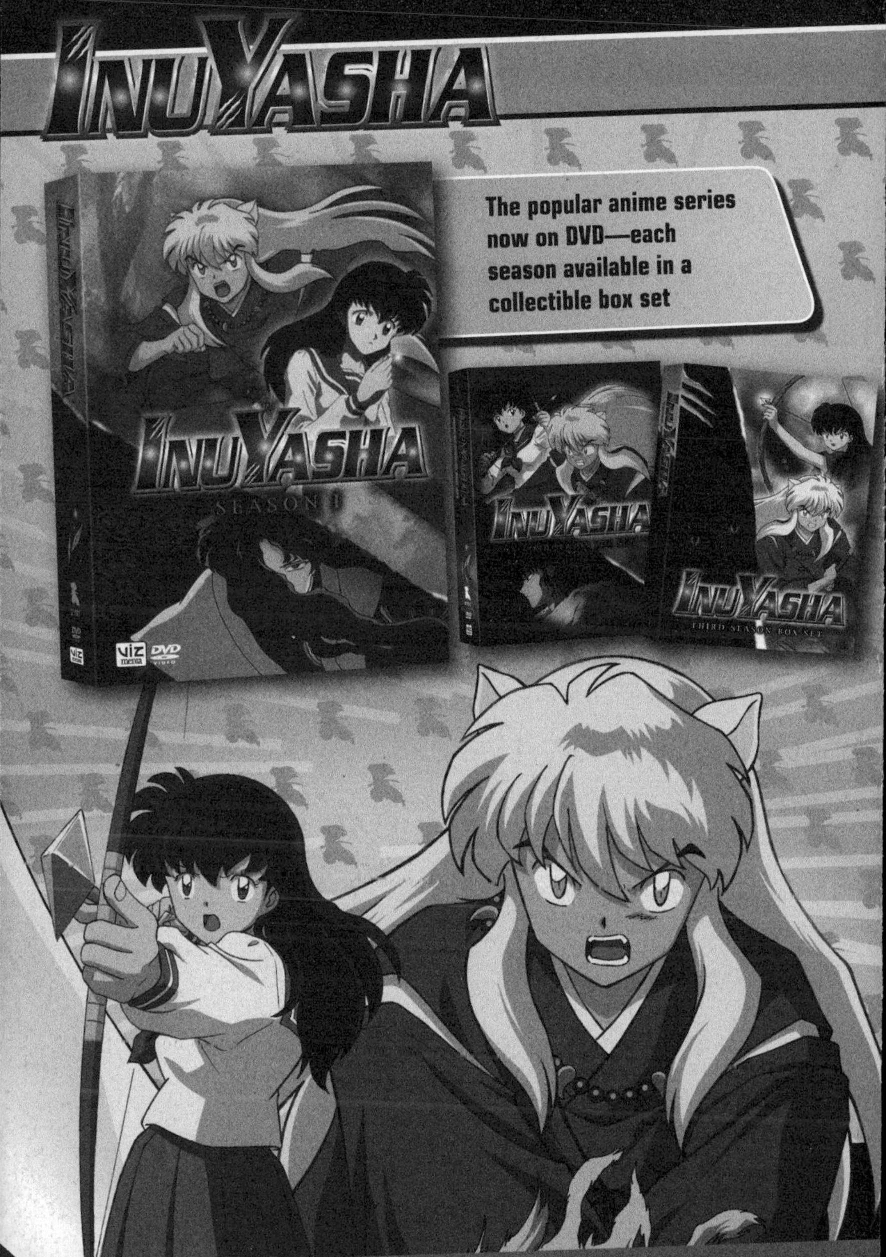
INUYASHA
The popular anime series now on DVD—each season available in a collectible box set
INUYASHA
SEASON 1
INUYASHA
INUYASHA
THIRD SEASON BOX SET

GA?
YOU THINK!

OUR MANGA SURVEY IS NOW
AVAILABLE ONLINE. PLEASE VISIT:
VIZ.COM/MANGASURVEY

HELP US MAKE THE MANGA YOU LOVE BETTER!